Judith Wright
COLLECTED POEMS

Judith Wright was born in Armidale, New South Wales in 1915. Her collections of poetry include *The Moving Image* (1946), *Woman to Man* (1949), *The Gateway* (1953), *The Two Fires* (1955), *Birds* (1962), *Five Senses (The Forest)* (1963), *City Sunrise* (1964), *The Other Half* (1966), *Shadow* (1970), *Alive* (1973), *Fourth Quarter* (1976) and *Phantom Dwelling* (1985), as well as other selected and collected volumes. Over a long and distinguished literary career, she has also published literary essays, biographies, histories, children's books, and other non-fiction including *We Call For A Treaty*, on the work of the Aboriginal Treaty Committee, and *The Coral Battleground*, on the conservation of the Great Barrier Reef.

Judith Wright's writing has won many honours, including the Grace Leven Award (twice), the New South Wales Premier's Prize, the Encyclopedia Britannica Prize for Literature, and the Asan World Prize for Poetry. She has received honorary degrees (D. Litt.) from the Universities of New England, Sydney, Monash and New South Wales, and the Australian National University. In 1994 Judith Wright received the Human Rights Commission Award for this volume, *Collected Poems*.

To My Dear Friend,
Shelia
in Memory of an Australian
Journey Hugs.

Judith Wright

COLLECTED POEMS

Fri 9. avril '99

1942–1985

Angus&Robertson
An imprint of HarperCollins*Publishers*

Angus&Robertson

An imprint of HarperCollins*Publishers,* Australia

This collection first published in Australia in 1994
Reprinted in 1996, 1998 (twice)
by HarperCollins*Publishers* Pty Limited
ACN 009 913 517
A member of the HarperCollins*Publishers* (Australia) Pty Limited Group
http://www.harpercollins.com.au

HarperCollins*Publishers*
25 Ryde Road, Pymble, Sydney, NSW 2073, Australia
31 View Road, Glenfield, Auckland 10, New Zealand
77-85 Fulham Palace Road, London W6 8JB, United Kingdom
Hazelton Lanes, 55 Avenue Road, Suite 2900, Toronto, Ontario M5R 3L2
and 1995 Markham Road, Scarborough, Ontario M1B 5M8, Canada
10 East 53rd Street, New York NY 10032, USA

National Library of Australia Cataloguing-in-Publication data:

Wright, Judith, 1915 – .
Collected poems.
Includes index.
ISBN 0 207 18135 7.
I. Title.
A821.3

Cover illustration by Vanessa Forbes
Printed in Australia by Griffin Press Pty Ltd on 80gsm Econoprint

9 8 7 6 5 4   98 99 00 01

FOREWORD

The earliest poems republished here date from 1942, a year now almost unimaginable to most of today's readers and critics. In the years since then, not only the conditions of life and of feeling have changed immensely, but even the methods of literary criticism have altered. It seems worthwhile, then, to include a brief foreword to this collection of poems written over forty-five years—from the early years of World War II to the end of my seventieth year.

The poems have been written out of the events, the thinking and feeling, the whole emotional climate and my own involvements of that time. Because of that tide of change, their background and therefore part of their significance will be unfamiliar to many people. Today's shifts in critical practice have begun to tear texts from their contexts. Indeed, the need to know something of the context, historical or personal, of poems has almost disappeared from critical practice.

So a reader of a poem like "The Company of Lovers" may know little of the great displacements of people during World War II, their snatching into armies and other defence forces, the desperation of lovers faced with the prospect of a separation which might last forever, and the urgency of need which drove the young into each others' arms. Readers of "The Two Fires" also may not be able to imagine the feelings of people suddenly confronted with the news of whole cities wiped out in an instant by the first uses of the new atomic bombs.

But I doubt whether literary critics and teachers take it on themselves to explain the context of poems; and no historian is likely to provide the necessary emotional background of the times during which the poems were written. Much has to be left to the reader's own response in imaginative terms—and that is not a bad thing, provided that the reader has been encouraged to use her or his imagination. But imagination and feeling are now devalued in favour of the harder values of so-called rationalism.

From the rational viewpoint, what one produces must be in some way useful. What use is poetry? It certainly does not provide a living for the poet, though it may help the book-producing trade a little. What it does, for the poet, is to express and exemplify the feeling which brought the poem into existence; that is, to help with the process of understanding one's life and its meaning. For the reader, it can help in the same way. That is what art is for.

Judith Wright
Braidwood
1993

Contents

Foreword

From THE MOVING IMAGE *1946*

From WOMAN TO MAN *1949*

From THE GATEWAY *1953*

From THE TWO FIRES *1955*

From BIRDS *1962*

From THE OTHER HALF *1966*

From SHADOW *1970*

From ALIVE *1973*

From FOURTH QUARTER *1976*

From PHANTOM DWELLING *1985*

FROM

The Moving Image

1946

Time is a moving image of eternity

PLATO

THE MOVING IMAGE

I

Here is the same clock that walked quietly
through those enormous years I half recall,
when between one blue summer and another
time seemed as many miles as round the world,
and world a day, a moment or a mile,
or a sweet slope of grass edged with the sea,
or a new song to sing, or a tree dressed in gold—
time and the world that faster spin until
mind cannot grasp them now or heart take hold.

Only the sound of the clock is still the same.
Each of us followed it to a different hour
that like a bushranger held its guns on us
and forced our choice. And the clock begins to race.
We are caught in the endless circle of time and star
that never chime with the blood; we weary, we grow lame,
stumbling after their incessant pace
that slackens for us only when we are
caught deep in sleep, or music, or a lover's face.

Here where I walk was the green world of a child;
the infinity of day that closed in day,
the widening spiral turning and returning,
the same and not the same, that had no end.
Does the heart know no better than to pray
that time unwind its coil, the bone unbuild
till that lost world sit like a fruit in the hand—
till the felled trees rise upright where they lay
and leaves and birds spring on them as they stand?

And yet the lovelier distance is ahead.
I would go farther with you, clock and star,
though the earth break under my feet and storm
snatch at my breath and night ride over me.
I am the maker. I have made both time and fear,
knowing that to yield to either is to be dead.
All that is real is to live, to desire, to be,
till I say to the child I was, "It is this; it is here.
In the doomed cell I have found love's whole eternity."

II

Dust blows harsh from the airfield; dust in the mouth.
This is the field that once was the world's end
(nothing beyond but hills water-hyacinth-coloured,
nothing in the field but supplejack and black-sally).
Dust blows back from the airfield; dust on the hand,
dust in the eyes that watch the plane turn north;
and to the plane the hills, the mysterious valley,
are bald and meagre as a map made out of sand—
hills of the wild horses, gullies of the rock-lily.

Looking from so high the world is evil and small
like a dried head from the islands with a grin of shell,
brittle and easy to break. But there is no end to the
    breaking—
one smashed, another mocks from your enemy's eye—
put that out, there's a world in every skull.
Nothing left but to pray, God save us all;
nothing but the tick of the clock and a world sucked dry;
nothing; till the tide of time come back to the full
and drown a man too sane, who climbed too high.

Till the tide of life come back, till time's great tide
roar from our depths and send us mad again
with a singing madness, like poor Tom of Bedlam—
poor Tom, through whose feverish blood life poured like
  thunder
till the frail floodgates burst within his brain,
and sleepless in his cell he sang and cried;
till the straw of his prison broke into flowers of wonder;
till the universe was the limit of his chain
and galaxies glowed through the low roof he lay under.

All the lives that met in him and made
the tiny world of his life, his passion, his skill
shone from his eyes each as a separate star.
Age upon age of effort and terror and thought
stretched from his birth back to a single cell;
life upon life leapt from the fountaining seed,
lusted and took, hated, delighted and fought,
built from the thread of its dream a heaven and hell,
took up the search of man and died as it sought.

The first birth and the first cry and the first death,
the world of the first cell and the first man,
every sound and motion forgotten, remembered,
left their trace in his body, their voice in his speech.
One word in his mouth spread open like a fan,
the sound of it dwarfed the stars and stole his breath
as a million voices shouted it to each;
and through the web of all their lives he ran
to grasp the glory never in one man's reach.

Poor Tom, in whose blood's intricate channelled track,
in the unsailed sea of his heart, in his witchball eyes,
in his senses that spoke and mind that shaped a world
passionate terrible love never ceased burning;
who played with comets and stars like golden flies;
whose nights and days were whipmarks on his back,
whose birth and death were the sun and moon returning.
Whose songs shall a madman sing before he dies,
who makes one word of the song all life is learning?

Over the airfield looms the idol of night.
In its shadow the earth is spun by a stellar wind
in an eddy of spiralled stars. We are dwarfed by the dark.
We inherit a handful of dust and a fragment of stone.
Yet listen, the music grows around us, before us, behind,
there is sound in the silence; the dark is a tremor of light.
It is the corn rising when winter is done.
It is the madmen singing, the lovers, the blind;
the cry of Tom of Bedlam, naked under the sun.

NORTHERN RIVER

When summer days grow harsh
     my thoughts return to my river,
fed by white mountain springs,
beloved of the shy bird, the bellbird,
whose cry is like falling water.
O nighted with the green vine,
lit with the rock-lilies,
the river speaks in the silence,
and my heart will also be quiet.

Where your valley grows wide in the plains
they have felled the trees, wild river.
Your course they have checked, and altered
your sweet Alcaic metre.
Not the grey kangaroo, deer-eyed, timorous,
will come to your pools at dawn;
but their tamed and humbled herds
will muddy the watering places.
Passing their roads and cities
you will not escape unsoiled.

But where, grown old and weary,
stagnant among the mangroves,
you hope no longer—there on a sudden
with a shock like joy, beats up
the cold clean pulse of the tide,
the touch of the sea in greeting;
the sea that encompasses
all sorrow and delight
and holds the memories
of every stream and river.

THE COMPANY OF LOVERS

We meet and part now over all the world.
   We, the lost company,
take hands together in the night, forget
the night in our brief happiness, silently.
We who sought many things, throw all away
for this one thing, one only,
remembering that in the narrow grave
we shall be lonely.

Death marshals up his armies round us now.
Their footsteps crowd too near.
Lock your warm hand above the chilling heart
and for a time I live without my fear.
Grope in the night to find me and embrace,
for the dark preludes of the drums begin,
and round us, round the company of lovers,
Death draws his cordons in.

BLUE ARAB

The small blue Arab stallion dances on the hill
like a glancing breaker, like a storm rearing in the sky.
In his prick-ears the wind, that wanderer and spy,
sings of the dunes of Arabia, lioncoloured, still.

The small blue stallion poses like a centaur-god,
netting the sun in his sea-spray mane, forgetting
his stalwart mares for a phantom galloping unshod;
changing for a heat-mirage his tall and velvet hill.

BORA RING

The song is gone; the dance
is secret with the dancers in the earth,
the ritual useless, and the tribal story
lost in an alien tale.

Only the grass stands up
to mark the dancing-ring: the apple-gums
posture and mime a past corroboree,
murmur a broken chant.

The hunter is gone: the spear
is splintered underground; the painted bodies
a dream the world breathed sleeping and forgot.
The nomad feet are still.

Only the rider's heart
halts at a sightless shadow, an unsaid word
that fastens in the blood the ancient curse,
the fear as old as Cain.

TRAPPED DINGO

So here, twisted in steel, and spoiled with red
your sunlight hide, smelling of death and fear,
they crushed out of your throat the terrible song
you sang in the dark ranges. With what crying
you mourned him, the drinker of blood, the swift death-
    bringer
who ran with you many a night; and the night was long.
I heard you, desperate poet. Did you hear
my silent voice take up the cry?—replying
Achilles is overcome, and Hector dead,
and clay stops many a warrior's mouth, wild singer.

Voice from the hills and the river drunken with rain,
for your lament the long night was too brief.
Hurling your woes at the moon, that old cleaned bone,
till the white shorn mobs of stars on the hill of the sky
huddled and trembled, you tolled him, the rebel one.
Insane Andromache, pacing your towers alone,
death ends the verse you chanted; here you lie.
The lover, the maker of elegies is slain,
and veiled with blood her body's stealthy sun.

WAITING

Day's crystal hemisphere travels the land.
From starfrost to starfrost the folded hills lie bare
and the sheep move grazing or stand.
How can the sirens of danger pierce this air?
Only the parrots exploding in green and scarlet
shatter its glass for their shrill moment's flight.
From the houses on the hill the small smoke rises
in patterns of vague peace from dawn to night.

But the circling days weave tighter, and the spider
Time binds us helpless till his sting go in.
Moving in a dazed routine, we hardly wonder
what hour ahead waits with a basilisk grin.
Only the radio, like a seashell held to the ear,
gives back the echo of our own blood's fever;
its confused voices like the body's urgent warning
of a disease that it may not recover.

Oh, let time be only the monster of a dream,
the sick distortion of minds anaesthetised;
let time be only the calm surgeon, deciding
our cancer is not mortal, can be excised.
But past our prayers we know only ourselves
have choice or power to make us whole again;
time lifts no knives to heal or to destroy,
and did not cause, and cannot cure, our pain.

All that time gives is the crystal hour of waiting
through which we travel, listening to the radio
turn back ourselves upon us; our own Iscariots,
we know the agony we do not know.
The witchball hour returns the twisted face
of what we are; oh, let our weeping be
amendment for these lives, and make us whole
in man and time, who build eternity.

REMITTANCE MAN

The spendthrift, disinherited and graceless,
accepted his pittance with an easy air,
only surprised he could escape so simply
from the pheasant-shooting and the aunts in the close;
took to the life, dropped easily out of knowledge,
and tramping the backtracks in the summer haze
let everything but life slip through his fingers.

Blue blowing smoke of twigs from the noon fire,
red blowing dust of roads where the teams go slow,
sparse swinging shadow of trees no longer foreign
silted the memory of a greener climate.
The crazy tales, the hatters' crazy secrets,
the blind-drunk sprees indifferently forgiven,
and past them all, the track to escape and nowhere
suited his book, the freak who could never settle.
That pale stalk of a wench at the county ball
sank back forgotten in black Mary's eyes,
and past the sallow circle of the plains' horizon
faded the rainy elms seen through the nursery window.

That harsh biblical country of the scapegoat
closed its magnificence finally around his bones
polished by diligent ants. The squire his brother,
presuming death, sighed over the documents,
and lifting his eyes across the inherited garden
let a vague pity blur the formal roses.

SOLDIER'S FARM

This ploughland vapoured with the dust of dreams;
these delicate gatherings of dancing trees,
answered the question of his searching eyes
as his wife's body answered to his arms.

He let the whole gold day pass in a stare
walking the turning furrow. The horses drew
his line straight where the shakesword corn should grow.
He, lurching mooncalf, let his eyes stride far.

They stooped across the swell and sink of hill;
made record of the leaves that played with light.
The mist was early and the moon was late,
and in between he stared his whole day full.

He asked for nothing but the luck to live,
so now his willing blood moves in these trees
that hold his heart up sunwards with their arms.
The mists dissolve at morning like his dreams
and the creek answers light as once his eyes;
and yet he left here nothing but his love.

THE TRAINS

Tunnelling through the night, the trains pass
in a splendour of power, with a sound like thunder
shaking the orchards, waking
the young from a dream, scattering like glass
the old men's sleep; laying
a black trail over the still bloom of the orchards.
The trains go north with guns.

Strange primitive piece of flesh, the heart laid quiet
hearing their cry pierce through its thin-walled cave
recalls the forgotten tiger
and leaps awake in its old panic riot;
and how shall mind be sober,
since blood's red thread still binds us fast in history?
Tiger, you walk through all our past and future,
troubling the children's sleep; laying
a reeking trail across our dream of orchards.

Racing on iron errands, the trains go by,
and over the white acres of our orchards
hurl their wild summoning cry, their animal cry ...
the trains go north with guns.

THE IDLER

The treasure islands were his desired landfall:
        past the grey discipline of streets and past
the minatory towers with their clocks
the sails rose bannering on the saltwhite mast.
The islands ran like emeralds through his fingers
(Oparo, Manahiki, Tubuai)
till he turned truant, cleared the heads at dawn
and half-forgot the seasons, under that sky.

But time sprang from its coil and struck his heart,
and all the world shrank small as a grenade.
Over the sun of an idle afternoon
a doom of planes drew darkness like a shade.
Now trapped in a mad traffic, he stands and sees
the map ruled off in squares of black and white,
and all his islands vanished with their palms
under the hostile despotism of night.

COUNTRY TOWN

This is no longer the landscape that they knew,
        the sad green enemy country of their exile,
those branded men whose songs were of rebellion.
The nights were cold, shepherding; and the dingoes
bawling like banshees in the hills, the mist coming over
from eastward chilled them. Beside the fire in the hut
their pannikin of rum filled them with songs
that were their tears for Devonshire and Ireland
and chains and whips and soldiers. Or by day
a slope of grass with small sheep moving on it,
the sound of the creek talking, a glimpse of mountains,
looked like another country and wrenched the heart.
They are dead, the bearded men who sang of women
in another world (sweet Alice) and another world.

This is a landscape that the town creeps over;
a landscape safe with bitumen and banks.
The hostile hills are netted in with fences
and the roads lead to houses and the pictures.
Thunderbolt was killed by Constable Walker
long ago; the bones are buried, the story printed.

And yet in the night of the sleeping town, the voices:
This is not ours, not ours the flowering tree.
What is it we have lost and left behind?
Where do the roads lead? It is not where we expected.
The gold is mined and safe, and where is the profit?
The church is built, the bishop is ordained,
and this is where we live: where do we live?
And how should we rebel? The chains are stronger.

Remember Thunderbolt, buried under the air-raid trenches.
Remember the bearded men singing of exile.
Remember the shepherds under their strange stars.

THE HAWTHORN HEDGE

How long ago she planted the hawthorn hedge—
she forgets how long ago—
that barrier thorn across the hungry ridge;
thorn and snow.

It is twice as tall as the rider on the tall mare
who draws his reins to peer
in through the bee-hung blossom. Let him stare.
No one is here.

Only the mad old girl from the hut on the hill,
unkempt as an old tree.
She will hide away if you wave your hand or call;
she will not see.

Year-long, wind turns her grindstone heart and whets
a thornbranch like a knife,
shouting in winter "Death"; and when the white bud sets,
more loudly, "Life".

She has forgotten when she planted the hawthorn hedge;
that thorn, that green, that snow;
birdsong and sun dazzled across the ridge—
it was long ago.

Her hands were strong in the earth, her glance on the sky,
her song was sweet on the wind.
The hawthorn hedge took root, grew wild and high
to hide behind.

NIGGER'S LEAP, NEW ENGLAND

The eastward spurs tip backward from the sun.
Night runs an obscure tide round cape and bay
and beats with boats of cloud up from the sea
against this sheer and limelit granite head.
Swallow the spine of range; be dark, O lonely air.
Make a cold quilt across the bone and skull
that screamed falling in flesh from the lipped cliff
and then were silent, waiting for the flies.

Here is the symbol, and the climbing dark
a time for synthesis. Night buoys no warning
over the rocks that wait our keels; no bells
sound for her mariners. Now must we measure
our days by nights, our tropics by their poles,
love by its end and all our speech by silence.
See in these gulfs, how small the light of home.

Did we not know their blood channelled our rivers,
and the black dust our crops ate was their dust?
O all men are one man at last. We should have known
the night that tided up the cliffs and hid them
had the same question on its tongue for us.
And there they lie that were ourselves writ strange.

Never from earth again the coolamon
or thin black children dancing like the shadows
of saplings in the wind. Night lips the harsh
scarp of the tableland and cools its granite.
Night floods us suddenly as history
that has sunk many islands in its good time.

SONNET

Now let the draughtsman of my eyes be done
marking the line of petal and of hill.
Let the long commentary of the brain
be silent. Evening and the earth are one,
and bird and tree are simple and stand still.
Now, fragile heart swung in your webs of vein,
and perilous self won hardly out of clay,
gather the harvest of last light, and reap
the luminous fields of sunset for your bread.
Blurs the laborious focus of the day
and shadow brims the hillside slow as sleep.
Here is the word that, when all words are said,
shall compass more than speech. The sun is gone;
draws on the night at last; the dream draws on.

BULLOCKY

B eside his heavy-shouldered team,
thirsty with drought and chilled with rain,
he weathered all the striding years
till they ran widdershins in his brain:

Till the long solitary tracks
etched deeper with each lurching load
were populous before his eyes,
and fiends and angels used his road.

All the long straining journey grew
a mad apocalyptic dream,
and he old Moses, and the slaves
his suffering and stubborn team.

Then in his evening camp beneath
the half-light pillars of the trees
he filled the steepled cone of night
with shouted prayers and prophecies.

While past the campfire's crimson ring
the star-struck darkness cupped him round,
and centuries of cattlebells
rang with their sweet uneasy sound.

Grass is across the waggon-tracks,
and plough strikes bone beneath the grass,
and vineyards cover all the slopes
where the dead teams were used to pass.

O vine, grow close upon that bone
and hold it with your rooted hand.
The prophet Moses feeds the grape,
and fruitful is the Promised Land.

BROTHER AND SISTERS

The road turned out to be a cul-de-sac;
    stopped like a lost intention at the gate
and never crossed the mountains to the coast.
But they stayed on. Years grew like grass and leaves
across the half-erased and dubious track
until one day they knew the plans were lost,
the blue-print for the bridge was out of date,
and now their orchards never would be planted.
The saplings sprouted slyly; day by day
the bush moved one step nearer, wondering when.
The polished parlour grew distrait and haunted
where Millie, Lucy, John each night at ten
wound the gilt clock that leaked the year away.

The pianola—oh, listen to the mocking-bird—
wavers on Sundays and has lost a note.
The wrinkled ewes snatch pansies through the fence
and stare with shallow eyes into the garden
where Lucy shrivels waiting for a word,
and Millie's cameos loosen round her throat.
The bush comes near, the ranges grow immense.

Feeding the lambs deserted in early spring
Lucy looked up and saw the stockman's eye
telling her she was cracked and old.
                                    The wall
groans in the night and settles more awry.
O how they lie awake. Their thoughts go fluttering
from room to room like moths: "Millie, are you awake?"
"Oh John, I have been dreaming." "Lucy, do you cry?"
—meet tentative as moths. Antennae stroke a wing.
"There is nothing to be afraid of. Nothing at all."

HALF-CASTE GIRL

Little Josie buried under the bright moon
is tired of being dead, death lasts too long.
She would like to push death aside, and stand on the hill
and beat with a waddy on the bright moon like a gong.

Across the hills, the hills that belong to no people
and so to none are foreign,
once she climbed high to find the native cherry;
the lithe darkhearted lubra
who in her beads like blood
dressed delicately for love
moves her long hands among the strings of the wind,
singing the songs of women,
the songs of love and dying.

Against the world's stone walls she thrust her heart—
endless the strength of its beating—
atom of flesh that cannot move a stone.
She used her love for lever;
but the wall is cunningly made.
Not even the strong break jail.
So she is restless still under her rootwarm cover,
hearing the noise of living,
forgetting the pain of dying.

Little Josie buried under the bright sun
would like to open her eyes and dance in the light.
Who is it has covered the sun and the beautiful moon
with a wallaby skin, and left her alone in the night?

SOUTH OF MY DAYS

South of my days' circle, part of my blood's country,
rises that tableland, high delicate outline
of bony slopes wincing under the winter,
low trees blue-leaved and olive, outcropping granite—
clean, lean, hungry country. The creek's leaf-silenced,
willow-choked, the slope a tangle of medlar and crabapple
branching over and under, blotched with a green lichen;
and the old cottage lurches in for shelter.

O cold the black-frost night. The walls draw in to the
   warmth
and the old roof cracks its joints; the slung kettle
hisses a leak on the fire. Hardly to be believed that summer
will turn up again some day in a wave of rambler roses,
thrust its hot face in here to tell another yarn—
a story old Dan can spin into a blanket against the winter.
Seventy years of stories he clutches round his bones.
Seventy summers are hived in him like old honey.

Droving that year, Charleville to the Hunter,
nineteen-one it was, and the drought beginning;
sixty head left at the McIntyre, the mud round them
hardened like iron; and the yellow boy died
in the sulky ahead with the gear, but the horse went on,
stopped at the Sandy Camp and waited in the evening.
It was the flies we seen first, swarming like bees.
Came to the Hunter, three hundred head of a thousand—
cruel to keep them alive—and the river was dust.

Or mustering up in the Bogongs in the autumn
when the blizzards came early. Brought them down; we
   brought them
down, what aren't there yet. Or driving for Cobb's on the
   run
up from Tamworth—Thunderbolt at the top of Hungry
   Hill,
and I give him a wink. I wouldn't wait long, Fred,
not if I was you; the troopers are just behind,
coming for that job at the Hillgrove. He went like a luny,
him on his big black horse.

                              Oh, they slide and they vanish
as he shuffles the years like a pack of conjuror's cards.
True or not, it's all the same; and the frost on the roof
cracks like a whip, and the back-log breaks into ash.
Wake, old man. This is winter, and the yarns are over.
No one is listening.

                    South of my days' circle
I know it dark against the stars, the high lean country
full of old stories that still go walking in my sleep.

THE SURFER

He thrust his joy against the weight of the sea;
climbed through, slid under those long banks of
   foam—
(hawthorn hedges in spring, thorns in the face stinging).
How his brown strength drove through the hollow and coil
of green-through weirs of water!
Muscle of arm thrust down long muscle of water;
and swimming so, went out of sight
where mortal, masterful, frail, the gulls went wheeling
in air as he in water, with delight.

Turn home, the sun goes down; swimmer, turn home.
Last leaf of gold vanishes from the sea-curve.
Take the big roller's shoulder, speed and swerve;
come to the long beach home like a gull diving.

For on the sand the grey-wolf sea lies snarling,
cold twilight wind splits the waves' hair and shows
the bones they worry in their wolf-teeth. O, wind blows
and sea crouches on sand, fawning and mouthing;
drops there and snatches again, drops and again snatches
its broken toys, its whitened pebbles and shells.

FOR NEW ENGLAND

Your trees, the homesick and the swarthy native,
blow all one way to me, this southern weather
that smells of early snow:
                              And I remember
The house closed in with sycamore and chestnut
fighting the foreign wind.
Here I will stay, she said; be done with the black north,
the harsh horizon rimmed with drought.—
Planted the island there and drew it round her.
Therefore I find in me the double tree.

And therefore I, deserted on the wharves,
have watched the ships fan out their web of streamers
(thinking of how the lookout at the heads
leaned out towards the dubious rims of sea
to find a sail blown over like a message
you are not forgotten),
or followed through the taproot of the poplar ...
But look, oh look, the Gothic tree's on fire
with blown galahs, and fuming with wild wings.

The hard inquiring wind strikes to the bone
and whines division.
                              Many roads meet here
in me, the traveller and the ways I travel.
All the hills' gathered waters feed my seas
who am the swimmer and the mountain river;
and the long slopes' concurrence is my flesh
who am the gazer and the land I stare on;
and dogwood blooms within my winter blood,
and orchards fruit in me and need no season.
But sullenly the jealous bones recall
what other earth is shaped and hoarded in them.

Where's home, Ulysses? Cuckolded by lewd time
he never found again the girls he sailed from,
but at his fireside met the islands waiting
and died there, twice a stranger.
                              Wind, blow through me
till the nostalgic candles of laburnum
fuse with the dogwood in a single flame
to touch alight these sapless memories.
Then will my land turn sweetly from the plough
and all my pastures rise as green as spring.

Dust

This sick dust, spiralling with the wind,
is harsh as grief's taste in our mouths
and has eclipsed the small sun.
The remnant earth turns evil,
the steel-shocked earth has turned against the plough
and runs with wind all day, and all night
sighs in our sleep against the windowpane.

Wind was kinder once, carrying cloud
like a waterbag on his shoulder; sun was kinder,
hardening the good wheat brown as a strong man.
Earth was kinder, suffering fire and plough,
breeding the unaccustomed harvest.
Leaning in our doorway together
watching the birdcloud shadows,
the fleetwing windshadows travel our clean wheat
we thought ourselves rich already.
We counted the beautiful money
and gave it in our hearts to the child asleep,
who must never break his body
against the plough and the stubborn rock and tree.

But the wind rises; but the earth rises,
running like an evil river; but the sun grows small,
and when we turn to each other, our eyes are dust
and our words dust.
Dust has overtaken our dreams that were
wider and richer than wheat under the sun,
and war's eroding gale scatters our sons
with a million other grains of dust.

O sighing at the blistered door, darkening the evening star,
the dust accuses. Our dream was the wrong dream,
our strength was the wrong strength.
Weary as we are, we must make a new choice,
a choice more difficult than resignation,
more urgent than our desire of rest at the end of the day.
We must prepare the land for a difficult sowing,
a long and hazardous growth of a strange bread,
that our son's sons may harvest and be fed.

FROM

Woman to Man

1949

Love was the most ancient of all the gods, and existed before everything else, except Chaos, which is held coeval therewith. ... The summary or collective law of nature, or the principle of love, impressed by God upon the original particles of all things, so as to make them attack each other and come together, by the repetition and multiplication whereof all the variety in the universe is produced, can scarce possibly find full admittance in the thoughts of men, though some faint notion may be had thereof.

FRANCIS BACON
The Wisdom of the Ancients

WOMAN TO MAN

T he eyeless labourer in the night,
  the selfless, shapeless seed I hold,
builds for its resurrection day—
silent and swift and deep from sight
foresees the unimagined light.

This is no child with a child's face;
this has no name to name it by:
yet you and I have known it well.
This is our hunter and our chase,
the third who lay in our embrace.

This is the strength that your arm knows,
the arc of flesh that is my breast,
the precise crystals of our eyes.
This is the blood's wild tree that grows
the intricate and folded rose.

This is the maker and the made;
this is the question and reply;
the blind head butting at the dark,
the blaze of light along the blade.
Oh hold me, for I am afraid.

WOMAN'S SONG

O move in me, my darling,
  for now the sun must rise;
the sun that will draw open
the lids upon your eyes.

O wake in me, my darling.
The knife of day is bright
to cut the thread that binds you
within the flesh of night.

Today I lose and find you
whom yet my blood would keep—
would weave and sing around you
the spells and songs of sleep.

None but I shall know you
as none but I have known;
yet there's a death and a maiden
who wait for you alone;

so move in me, my darling,
whose debt I cannot pay.
Pain and the dark must claim you,
and passion and the day.

WOMAN TO CHILD

You who were darkness warmed my flesh
where out of darkness rose the seed.
Then all a world I made in me;
all the world you hear and see
hung upon my dreaming blood.

There moved the multitudinous stars,
and coloured birds and fishes moved.
There swam the sliding continents.
All time lay rolled in me, and sense,
and love that knew not its beloved.

O node and focus of the world;
I hold you deep within that well
you shall escape and not escape—
that mirrors still your sleeping shape;
that nurtures still your crescent cell.

I wither and you break from me;
yet though you dance in living light
I am the earth, I am the root,
I am the stem that fed the fruit,
the link that joins you to the night.

CONCH-SHELL

Virgin and clean the house is washed, and empty
the wave withdrawing leaves it to my hand.
The spiral passage turns upon itself.
The sweet enclosing curve of pearl
shuts in the room that was the cell of birth,
and is a windless shelter housing nothing.

Delicate argument and hieroglyph
of flesh that followed outward from the germ,
your line resolves the force that set its strength
against the wave's weight and the storm;
maps on my hand the puzzle, the perfection,
the brilliant arch from darkness into darkness.

And here, half-guess, half-knowledge, I contract
into a beast's blind orbit, stare deep down
the cliffs not I have climbed; your prodigal,
probe with my sense your senseless life—
since life, the force that leapt between your poles,
burns forward still in me against the night.

THE MAKER

I hold the crimson fruit
and plumage of the palm;
flame-tree, that scarlet spirit,
in my soil takes root.

My days burn with the sun,
my nights with moon and star,
since into myself I took
all living things that are.

All things that glow and move,
all things that change and pass,
I gather their delight
as in a burning-glass;

all things I focus in
the crystal of my sense.
I give them breath and life
and set them free in the dance.

I am a tranquil lake
to mirror their joy and pain;
and all their pain and joy
I from my own heart make,

since love, who cancels fear
with his fixed will,
burned my vision clear
and bid my sense be still.

PAIN

Manjack home from the wars walked down the street—
bent like a bow his body round its great scar—
and held his head upright. I saw his eyes
flaring and fixed, a tiger or a dark star.

Pain, what is it? The scythe turned under the ribs,
the soft explosion in the belly that means death,
the hornet where were berries, the snake in flowers,
the ice about the heart, the lung that leaks its breath—

that which drives out love, hunger, thirst or hate;
the trap that waits, the precipice past hope
upon whose edge we walk, how delicately—
the loaded whip no shoulders can escape.

Pain, what is it? That which keeps alive
amoebae doubling from the acid; pain
that forces flesh to wisdom: hedge of swords
beside the road from protoplasm to man.

Pain the fierce darkness thrusting at all life
that drives it up to light; pain the black No
that knifes us in blind alleys; pain that can only say
You have chosen wrong; this is no way to go.

Manjack home from the wars walked down the street,
and in his flesh a fire that ate him lean.
Vision of famine, death with blazing eyes,
what shall we do to save ourselves from Pain?

CHILD AND WATTLE-TREE

Round as a sun is the golden tree.
Its honey dust sifts down among the light
to cover me and my hot blood
and my heart hiding like a sad bird
among its birds and shadows.

Lock your branches around me, tree;
let the harsh wooden scales of bark enclose me.
Take me into your life and smother me with bloom
till my feet are cool in the earth
and my hair is long in the wind;
till I am a golden tree spinning the sunlight.

Strong as the sun is the golden tree
that gives and says nothing,
that takes and knows nothing;
but I am stronger than the sun; I am a child.
The tree I am lying beneath is the tree of my heart,
and my heart moves like a dark bird
among its birds and shadows.

THE SISTERS

In the vine-shadows on the veranda,
under the yellow leaves, in the cooling sun,
sit the two sisters. Their slow voices run
like little winter creeks dwindled by frost and wind,
and the square of sunlight moves on the veranda.

They remember the gay young men on their tall horses
who came courting; the dancing and the smells of leather
and wine, the girls whispering by the fire together:
even their dolls and ponies, all they have left behind
moves in the yellow shadows on the veranda.

Thinking of their lives apart and the men they married,
thinking of the marriage-bed and the birth of the first
    child,
they look down smiling. "My life was wide and wild,
and who can know my heart? There in that golden jungle
I walk alone," say the old sisters on the veranda.

SPRING AFTER WAR

Winter and spring the clouds drift in,
and mist is grey as moving sheep
where ewe goes heavy in lamb, and ewe
beside her lamb lies half-asleep,
her narrow sides with milk drawn thin.

How reconcile the alien eyes,
the warring life how reconcile?
On the lean slope and dripping hill
the sheep move slowly, single-file.
Where is it the heart's country lies?

The rope-vines hang where the clouds move.
The scorpion dances in the brain.
The years of death rattle their bones.
The ewe cries in the pitiless rain
the mortal cry of anguished love.

Which is the country, which is true?
How reconcile the treacherous earth,
the gaping flesh how reconcile—
and still move forward to some birth,
as the lamb moves within the ewe?

Within the bones the scorpion lay.
Within the bones the lamb was made.
Within the bones the heart is housed.
The blood that leaps behind the blade
is death or life; is night or day.

The knife goes back into its sheath;
the lamb comes struggling from the womb:
the seeking flesh has found its goal.
The compass heart swings seeking home
between the lands of life and death.

THE CHILD

To be alone in a strange place in spring
   shakes the heart. The others are somewhere else;
the shouting, the running, the eating, the drinking—
never alone and thinking,
never remembering the Dream or finding the Thing,
always striving with your breath hardly above the water.
But to go away, to be quiet and go away,
to be alone in a strange place in spring
shakes the heart.

To hide in a thrust of green leaves
with the blood's leap and retreat
warm in you;
burning, going and returning
like a thrust of green leaves
out of your eyes, out of your hands and your feet—
to turn and to look up,
to find above you the enfolding, the exulting
may-tree
shakes the heart.

Spring is always the red tower of the may-tree,
alive, shaken with bees, smelling of wild honey,
and the blood a moving tree of may;
like a symbol for a meaning; like time's recurrent
   morning
that breaks and beckons, changes and eludes,
that is gone away;
that is never gone away.

CAMPHOR LAUREL

Here in the slack of night
the tree breathes honey and moonlight.
Here in the blackened yard
smoke and time and use have marred,
leaning from that fantan gloom
the bent tree is heavy in bloom.

The dark house creaks and sways;
"Not like the old days."
Tim and Sam and ratbag Nell,
Wong who keeps the Chinese hell,
the half-caste lovers, the humpbacked boy,
sleep for sorrow, or wake for joy.

Under the house the roots go deep,
down, down, while the sleepers sleep;
splitting the rock where the house is set,
cracking the paved and broken street.
Old Tim turns and old Sam groans,
"God be good to my breaking bones";
and in the slack of tideless night
the tree breathes honey and moonlight.

THE GARDEN

Flowers of red silk and purple velvet grew
under the humming may-tree; the huge pines
made night across the grass, where the black snake
went whispering in its coils; and moving sunlight drew
copper fingers through the apple-trees.
Warm is the light the summer day refines,

and warm is she, whom life has made secure.
Walking slow along her garden ways,
a bee grown old at summer's end, she dips
and drinks that honey. All that we endure,
all that we meet and live through, gathers in our old age
and makes a shelter from the cold, she says.

Pulling around her shoulders her Joseph's-coat,
small bright bouquets reflected in her eyes,
this is the night's fit enemy and good friend
who has felt often his black hand at her throat;
and therefore my heart chose her, scarecrow, bag of old
    bones,
Eve walking with her snake and butterfly.

THE WORLD AND THE CHILD

I

This is the child. He has not yet put out leaves.
His bare skin tastes the air; his naked eyes
know nothing but strange shapes. Nothing is named;
nothing is ago, nothing not yet. Death is that which dies,
and goes no farther; for the mere dead he grieves,
and grief has yet no meaning and no size.

Where the wild harebell grows to a blue cave
and the climbing ant is a monster of green light
the child clings to his grassblade. The mountain range
lies like a pillow for his head at night,
the moon swings from his ceiling. He is a wave
that timeless moves through time, imperishably bright.

Yet what is it that moves? What is the unresting hunger
that shapes the soft-fleshed face, makes the bones harden?
Rebel, rebel, it cries. Never be satisfied.
Do not weaken for their grief; do not give in or pardon.
Only through this pain, this black desire, this anger,
shall you at last return to your lost garden.

II

Out of himself like a thread the child spins pain
and makes a net to catch the unknown world.
Words gather there heavy as fish, and tears,
and tales of love and of the polar cold.
Now, says the child, I shall never be young again.
The shadow of my net has darkened the sea's gold.

Yet what is it that draws the net and throws?
Forget to be young, it says; forget to be afraid.
No net is strong enough to hold the world,
nor man of such a sinew ever was made.
What is the world? That secret no man knows:
yet look, beyond the sundazzle, the blinding blade—
was not that the white waterfall from some vast side?

Nets have been breached and men have died in vain.
No net is strong enough to hold the world.
Yet gather in your bleeding hands your net again—
not till Leviathan's beached shall you be satisfied.

NIGHT AFTER BUSHFIRE

There is no more silence on the plains of the moon
and time is no more alien there, than here.
Sun thrust his warm hand down at the high noon,
but all that stirred was the faint dust of fear.

Charred death upon the rock leans his charred bone
and stares at death from sockets black with flame.
Man, if he come to brave that glance alone,
must leave behind his human home and name.

Carry like a threatened thing your soul away,
and do not look too long to left or right,
for he whose soul wears the strict chains of day
will lose it in this landscape of charcoal and moonlight.

THE BULL

In the olive darkness of the sally-trees
silently moved the air from night to day.
The summer-grass was thick with honey-daisies
where he, a curled god, a red Jupiter,
heavy with power among his women lay.

But summer's bubble-sound of sweet creek-water
dwindles and is silent; the seeding grasses
grow harsh, and wind and frost in the black sallies
roughen the sleek-haired slopes. Seek him out, then,
the angry god betrayed, whose godhead passes,

and down the hillsides drive him from his mob.
What enemy steals his strength—what rival steals
his mastered cows? His thunders powerless,
the red storm of his body shrunk with fear,
runs the great bull, the dogs upon his heels.

DREAM

Travelling through a strange night by a strange light
 I sought upon the hill the crimson rose
that without age and in no acre grows;
and I was caught by silence at that sight.

The burning wires of nerves, the crimson way
from head to heart, the towering tree of blood—
who travels here must move, not as he would,
but fed and lit by love alone he may.

O dying tree, I move beneath your shade;
and road of blood, I travel where you lead;
and rose unseen, upon your thorn I bleed;
and in a triple dream a dream I made.

I travel through this night and by this light
to find upon a hill the unsought rose
that out of silence into silence grows;
and silence overtakes me at that sight.

THE CYCADS

Their smooth dark flames flicker at time's own root.
 Round them the rising forests of the years
alter the climates of forgotten earth
and silt with leaves the strata of first birth.

Only the antique cycads sullenly
keep the old bargain life has long since broken;
and, cursed by age, through each chill century
they watch the shrunken moon, but never die,

for time forgets the promise he once made,
and change forgets that they are left alone.
Among the complicated birds and flowers
they seem a generation carved in stone.

Leaning together, down those gulfs they stare
over whose darkness dance the brilliant birds
that cry in air one moment, and are gone;
and with their countless suns the years spin on.

Take their cold seed and set it in the mind,
and its slow root will lengthen deep and deep
till, following, you cling on the last ledge
over the unthinkable, unfathomed edge
beyond which man remembers only sleep.

THE TWINS

Not because of their beauty—though they are slender
as saplings of white cedar, and long as lilies—
not because of their delicate dancing step
or their brown hair sideways blown like the manes of
  fillies—
it is not for their beauty that the crowd in the street
wavers like dry leaves around them on the wind.
It is the chord, the intricate unison
of one and one, strikes home to the watcher's mind.

How sweet is the double gesture, the mirror-answer;
same hand woven in same, like arm in arm.
Salt blood like tears freshens the crowd's dry veins,
and moving in its web of time and harm
and unloved heart asks, "Where is my reply,
my kin, my answer? I am driven and alone."
Their serene eyes seek nothing. They walk by.
They move into the future and are gone.

THE FLOOD

I

Under the olive-trees and in the orange-groves,
in Sunday silence and in the clamour of traffic,
against the sound of the sea and the sound of speeches
and the howling of unattended machines
the talk is beginning.

The labourer thinks and spits and looks aside;
the young girls laugh and look frightened;
the fat man with pale eyes passes on the rumour
although he does not believe it.
The street-corner preacher shouts at his changing crowd
to repent, to repent.

Have you heard the story? Where can it have started?
It was a very old prophecy.
I remember my mother told me. I have never believed it.
How strange these sudden panics are. There's a run on
    money.
Mountain property's gone to a very high figure.
Is it worth buying in?

They pause in the markets; the noise in the Stock Exchange
drops for a second; the bleating of lambs in the abattoirs
dies down; the trams stop running. What are they saying?
Yes, it looks like rain.

II

On the other side of the range the clouds are rising;
dark and heavy brows; wild shapes dissolving
like people seen in a dream, familiar
yet fused, confused, moving in a mute lightning,
and the air soundless.

On the other side of the range. Few of us know
that country—certainly people live there.
Not many. Sensible people live in cities.
Some of us have been there when we were children
but never comfortable.

I can remember the lost ravines, the forests,
the sudden nightfall and the chill of stars,
the loneliness; you could walk there all year long
and never meet a soul. But sometimes out of the darkness
faces, like doppelgangers.

On the other side of the range the clouds are rising.
Sallow the air hangs on spur and valley:
the black trees topple suddenly in a wind-eddy
under the sulphurous crags of cloud. No light
except the lightning.

III

O descent of archaic darkness. O sun gone out.
To us who stare through the darkness into the long rain
no sun returns again.
Where is our awkward Noah, the square family man
broad-based on the nursery floor? Where is dry land?
The desperate animals climb to our treetop shelter
and all about
the waters rise quietly.

They do not choose their victims nor give reason.
Neither the good nor the bad, neither man nor creature
is favoured. This is the forgotten logic of nature.
Those who drift past us, those rain-darkened faces,
all look the same; but out of our dull fear
sometimes we can distinguish the business-man, the seer,
the girl from the corner shop, the tout we saw at the races.
Perhaps they ran indoors to fetch their money.
Perhaps they hoped too long; or were with child.
They drift like logs among the animals.
Is it still rising?

Death has destroyed us. We do not know each other,
but huddled on our islands feel thought dissolve
and love vanish like rain into water.
I have put out my hand and drowned my brother.
His face goes swirling on the current of my mind
and is forgotten.

Near as a nightmare, the cries from the other islands.
Laus Domine, salve me,
Lord, in this thy Day
remember my good deeds. Let the others be washed away,
but I have done no harm. Remember my good deeds.
Laus Domine, salve me.
The voices of journalist, priest and politician,
barrowman, auctioneer and market agent—
I cannot tell their voices from my own.
The waters rise quietly.

IV

Slowly, how slowly,
I who was spread over the winds and waters,
I who was lost in the dark cave
am gathered together.
Is it the aeon-tide of earth
that moves me on its gradual mammoth-shoulder,
or is it you, my darling,
sun of my night, far warmth, who draw me upward?

Slowly, how slowly,
I shall stir now within my crusted earth.
I feel the green, the sap that moves within me,
turn to your touch.
I will be ready for the violence of your kiss,
be ready for the pain and the delight.
Only a little while, a little longer.
Sun of me, life, far love, I climb towards you.

V

You in your brown coat of earth there,
you, lifting out of the earth like a strange tuber,
knobbed and clothed with clay,
I know you and I do not know you.
Now, when I see your brilliant crystal eyes
pierced in the clay, I know you.
You are Man.

How warm is the light; how green has the world grown
     over us!
We lumber through the light, grateful as beasts.
I dreamed we had lost much.
I do not remember
what we have lost. My friend, death and birth are behind
     us;

death, and the flood that rose as it always rises
out of the heart; out of the terrible,
the incessantly dreaming, the implacable heart.
I stand and stare
upon your clay. Uncouth beasts, roots of earth,
we stare with love into each other's eyes.

ELI, ELI

To see them go by drowning in the river—
soldiers and elders drowning in the river,
the pitiful women drowning in the river,
the children's faces staring from the river—
that was his cross, and not the cross they gave him.

To hold the invisible wand, and not to save them—
to know them turned to death, and yet not save them;
only to cry to them and not to save them,
knowing that no one but themselves could save them—
this was the wound, more than the wound they dealt him.

To hold out love and know they would not take it,
to hold out faith and know they dared not take it—
the invisible wand, and none would see or take it,
all he could give, and there was none to take it—
thus they betrayed him, not with the tongue's betrayal.

He watched, and they were drowning in the river;
faces like sodden flowers in the river—
faces of children moving in the river;
and all the while, he knew there was no river.

THE BUILDERS

Only those coral insects live
that work and endure under
the breakers' cold continual thunder.
They are the quick of the reef
that rots and crumbles in a calmer water.
Only those men survive
who dare to hold their love against the world;
who dare to live and doubt what they are told.
They are the quick of life;
their faith is insolence; joyful is their grief.

This is life's promise and accomplishment—
a fraction-foothold taken.
Where dark eroding seas had broken,
the quick, the sensitive, the lover,
the passionate touch and intergrowth of living.
Alive, alive, intent,
love rises on the crumbling shells it shed.
The strata of the dead
burst with the plumes and passions of the earth.
Seed falls there now, birds build, and life takes over.

THE MIRROR AT THE FUN FAIR

This dark grotesque, this my familiar double
 I meet again among the lights and sawdust.
This is the changeling head that weights my shoulders,
the sidelong china smile that masks my trouble:
and there is no escape in the brass music,
no loss of self among the moving crowd.
Ah, my clown-lover, how shall we dissemble?

I do not fear the small rat-teeth of time
that gnaw my matchwood beauty. I do not fear
the splintering blow of death who waits behind me.
These are the foe, the faces in this frame,
the twisted images that from the mirror
grimace like hatred, wrenching us awry
till love's a club-foot pander, sly and lame.

Look in the mirror. Silent, unleashed and savage,
the nameless crowd sways in its coil and waits.
Look, we are caught; look, we are lost and homeless.
The gunman crowd watches to do us damage.
The crowd repeats, repeats our crooked faces;
our bird-thin hands, our desperate eyes that stare,
and, "Hate," each lover cries to his companion.
"O hate that is my pain. O desolate fear."

THE BUSHFIRE

Upon the burning mountain stands the palm.
 Deeper was its grove than the heart's night,
and hung with green the spring rose under it.
Hidden in miles of leaves stood the great palm,
that column of a thousand years.

Too sharp, too bright
burned this winter's sun. The wind's fine fever
withered and pierced. O time that brings us harm,
undoes our knowledge, dries up our sap and love—
upon the burning mountain burns the palm
within the burning grove.

"I am that which is not able to be whole,"
says the fire; "and therefore I devour
seeking the absolute I do not find.
This strength that falls to ash within the palm
grew through a million days, is eaten in an hour,
and in its death I die." All the faint voices
within the fire-voice whimper Death; the small
flames murmur and are gone. "I am that word
that, emptied by the nightfall, inward turned,
you from your depths have heard."

"I am that which is unbuilt but to renew,"
says the palm. "I was time's living scale,
and that alone in me is given to fire.
Also, I scaled time; here upon his crest
I toss my fronds of flame. It is the eaten shell
only that vanishes, fibre and leaf that fall.
I am the Thing, thought's crystal residue.
Worm and flame at my heart in their fierce love
touch me not, nor know me. I burn alone
within the burning grove."

THE UNBORN

I

I know no sleep you do not stand beside.
You footless darkness following where I go,
you lipless drinker at my drowsy breast—
yet whom I must deny I have denied.
The unpossessing is the unpossessed.

Slight is the foothold from the well of night,
the stair is broken and the keys are lost,
and you whom I have wrecked are wrecked indeed;
and yet you stand upon the edge of sight,
and I have known no path you have not crossed.

The shadow wakeful on my sleeping arm
stares from the hidden depths far under birth.
How like a diamond looks the far-off day,
that crystal that reflects your darkened dream,
that bubble of sunlight broken and blown away.
O gift ungiven. O uncreated earth.

II

Not even tears were mine,
not even death;
not even the dazzling pain
of one first breath.

I never knew the sleep
of the warm womb.
The end of my beginning
was dumb; was dumb.

Only the foot of the stair
I felt, being blind.
Then came the touch of fear
time now can never mend.

My name was a dark sound
that made no word.
Terror alone spoke it
and nothing heard.

Neither awake nor asleep
on the rack of dark I lie,
hearing my own not-voice.
"What was I? I? I?"

NIGHT

Standing here in the night
we are turned to a great tree,
every leaf a star,
its root eternity.

So deeply goes its root
into the world's womb,
so high rises its stem
it leaves for death no room.

We are turned to a great tree
hung with heavy fruit,
torn by the winds of time
and the worm at the root.

Come back to the kind flesh,
to love and simple sight.
Let us forget awhile
that we create the night;

Out of this dark of time
alive and human, come.
Brief is the warm day
wherein we have our home.

THE CITY ASLEEP

Night like decay crumbles the mask of stone.
Rain like a giant room shuts being in
and sleep undoes the knot of sight and nerve.
When we are most, then we are least alone;

for are these faces not identical?
The stone mask fallen and the flesh laid open,
they are the naked and continuing seed
whence city and engine spring, their victim and their will.

Now out of the cold and the destroying night,
out of the grip of stone, now, my beloved,
move, and sleep. Let fall the shield of fear.
No enemy watches; sleep has swallowed sight—

sleep, that drinks the separate and alone,
till under the dark lies smoothed a senseless flesh,
simple and vacant, the untouched quick of life
where lover, brother and murderer still are one.

Now like the rain led deeper underground,
my brother of flesh, sleepwalker, murderer,
kind brother of flesh, we must descend through stone
towards the buried water, speechless and blind.

We are the white grave-worms of the grave.
We are the eyeless beginning of the world.
Oh, blind, kind flesh, we are the drinking seed
that aches and swells towards its flower of love.

THE KILLER

T he day was clear as fire,
 the birds sang frail as glass,
when thirsty I came to the creek
and fell by its side in the grass.

My breast on the bright moss
and shower-embroidered weeds,
my lips to the live water
I saw him turn in the reeds.

Black horror sprang from the dark
in a violent birth,
and through its cloth of grass
I felt the clutch of earth.

O beat him into the ground
O strike him till he dies,
or else your life itself
drains through those colourless eyes.

I struck again and again.
Slender in black and red
he lies, and his icy glance
turns outward, clear and dead.

But nimble my enemy
as water is, or wind.
He has slipped from his death aside
and vanished into my mind.

He has vanished whence he came,
my nimble enemy;
and the ants come out to the snake
and drink at his shallow eye.

METHO DRINKER

Under the death of winter's leaves he lies
who cried to Nothing and the terrible night
to be his home and bread. "Oh take from me
the weight and waterfall of ceaseless Time
that batters down my weakness; the knives of light
whose thrust I cannot turn; the cruelty
of human eyes that dare not touch nor pity."
Under the worn leaves of the winter city
safe in the house of Nothing now he lies.

His white and burning girl, his woman of fire,
creeps to his heart and sets a candle there
to melt away the flesh that hides the bone,
to eat the nerve that tethers him in Time.
He will lie warm until the bone is bare
and on a dead dark moon he wakes alone.
It was for Death he took her; death is but this
and yet he is uneasy under her kiss
and winces from that acid of her desire.

STARS

Oh storm of honey-bees,
out of what fields do you come?
From what chill flowers of night
is your gold honey drawn,
and to what hive is your flight
tending for ever home?

O flight of golden birds
or swarm of motes in a beam
or fish in a dark sea—
she to whom I cling
and he who fathered me
fly with you into a dream.

A child who travels asleep—
wrapped in his golden hair,
caught to her breast—I lie.
O swarm of honey-bees
to what far hive do you fly?
for we, too, follow there.

THE OLD PRISON

The rows of cells are unroofed,
a flute for the wind's mouth,
who comes with a breath of ice
from the blue caves of the south.

O dark and fierce day:
the wind like an angry bee
hunts for the black honey
in the pits of the hollow sea.

Waves of shadow wash
the empty shell bone-bare,
and like a bone it sings
a bitter song of air.

Who built and laboured here?
The wind and the sea say
—Their cold nest is broken
and they are blown away.

They did not breed nor love.
Each in his cell alone
cried as the wind now cries
through this flute of stone.

THE BONES SPEAK

Great images of silence haunt me
in the visible darkness bowed in unseen stone.
It is a thousand years and all are one:
great rocks of silence lie upon my tongue
and idols carved by no man rule this cave.

Ah, into what a silence our fear ran:
man with his woman fled from woman and man
into the untenanted hollow of this cave.
Who then was left alive? Is there a world alive?

And the rock fell, and we dissolved in night
and walked the ceaseless maze of emptiness
hollow-socketed, alone, alone;
her once sweet flesh impersonal as stone,
for love is lost in terror, child of sight.

Not even voices then, not even weeping.
The pulse, that only memory of time,
crumbled to darkness. Is it that we are sleeping?
Is it that darkness has become our home?
Great images of silence haunt me.

Yet from this universe of vacancy
always I hear the river underground,
the ceaseless liquid voices of the river
run through these bones that here lie loose together,
a quiver, a whispering, a promise of sound.

The river whose waters move toward the day,
the river that wears down our night of stone—
I hear its voice of fall and flood deny
the reign of silence and the realm of bone;
its mining fingers work for this cave's ruin.

It is a dark root groping in our death
to change dry silence into wine and bread;
to alter the long winter of the dead
into the swinging vine, the flowering wreath.

LETTER TO A FRIEND

I

I have sat down by the river
with you in my mind.
Now at last we have time to meet, here
where by the swift river
palms toss their hair and the witchfire convolvulus
burns and entangles the eyes.
Tonight the moon will be full,
the cloud bright;
and the nightbird will speak,
the air and the tree be silent.

Underground death lies. I must tread lightly
the time-bomb world. Overhead it hangs—
a cloud, a shade, a smoke—
the dust of bodies moving
far and tormented on the high air.
Everywhere it settles, blows and rises
and finds no rest.
The polar ice receives it,
the thin and homeless dust that moves as the winds
  move.

Now I shall be your mourner.
Those who are given to death
cannot weep, for their blood is dry.
Those who are given to fear
cannot live, for they are a dry fountain.
Those who are given to grief know grief only.
It is because of the joy in my heart
that I am your fit mourner.

I sit among leaves.
The flowers enwrap me, the sun
delights me, the cloud is bright.
It is because of these things
that I weep for you, friend.

II

The small waves endlessly vanish on the shore.

Now all of us who live
are in our lives an elegy;
are in our lives an eternal speech
with the dead; the mourner speaks to the mourned,
the murderer speaks to the murdered.
To you whom I have killed,
you whom I have seen die
(and my tears were useless),
you with whom I have died—
to you at least I should speak the truth.
With you at least I should share my heart.

The small waves grow,
gather strength and run forward.
Having come out of Nothing, they desire All.
Like the waves you are broken.
You who were all are made nothing,
returned to the river.

Did you fear the darkness
as it rose in you and over you?

III

Black is the night; it spreads and rises
from its home in the sea-bottom
day cannot touch. Not even
the deepsea fish without eyes move there,
and the dead men's bones cannot reach it.

All we know of it is darkness,
and the old legend of the sea-monster
thrust upward from those vast pressures
blind and in pain, seeking
death or birth, the sea bloody.
Only a legend, and darkness.

Darkness the enemy, flowering upwards
from the sea-depth, from the earth bottom,
enfolded you; night has eaten
your blood and your bones and your words;
night the old enemy, rising
to swallow the light of our day.

IV

The light falls from the sky,
the lamp fades on the hill.
The voice of the river
grows in the darkness clearer and louder.
On my face is the breath of night
and the hands of the night on my hands.

Night is our daily ritual,
the ritual ending of our day.
The sun goes underseas; the river voices
tell interminably of what we have forgotten.
What the voice says is spoken in a language
the bending branch writes, held by wind on sand,
the flying bird scrawls on the planes of air;
and sliding into sleep, our vanishing speech
is in that tongue, the night-talk of the world,
the less-than-childish language.

In the night, in the loss of light,
tree is tree no longer; is our lost self,
luminous, menacing, leaning alive above us
and hung like fruit with moons.
This is the thing that was before names were,
before thought is;
hung with tongues of leaves towers the wild thing
dark in our loss of light,
alive in our night of sleep.

V

In the depth where we sink and sway
like weed broken from rock,
we are one with the dead, immobile,
clamped between pressure and pressure,
with the tongue locked,
the eyes empty.

It will be here the god speaks.
While we are caught under these waters,
empty of thought and ambition,
empty of knowledge and speech,
empty of pain and delight,

we shall stare with our waiting eyes
not in wonder or fear
(being lost to fear or wonder)
on the blind and night-wrapped monster,
the lost legend, the old serpent.
Where we are one with the dead,
it will be here the god speaks.

VI

The sun moves to be born out of the sea;
the heart moves to waken from its silence.
I am not water nor stone,
I am not air nor fire
says the heart. I am no other creature.
I have come out of nothing and desire all.
This is the voice of the joy in my heart
as I see on the river
the light of the risen sun.

Only my joy is your mourner.

For the world's loss and terror,
for the night of unbearable grief,
for the child who died burning,
for the man wrecked, for the woman
crippled and made sterile;
for the friends who betrayed each other,
for the lovers who killed each other,
there is no other healer.

For the death that fell on you
there is no other answer.

To you at last I can speak the truth;
all is a shadow, except the joy in my heart.

MIDNIGHT

Darkness where I find my sight,
shadowless and burning night,
here where death and life are met
is the fire of being set.

Watchman eye and workman hand
are spun of water, air and sand.
These will crumble and be gone,
still that darkness rages on.

As a plant in winter dies
down into the germ, and lies
leafless, tongueless, lost in earth
imaging its fierce rebirth;

And with the whirling rays of the sun
and shuttle-stroke of living rain
weaves that image from its heart
and like a god is born again—

so let my blood reshape its dream,
drawn into that tideless stream;
that shadowless and burning night
of darkness where I find my sight.

FLAME-TREE IN A QUARRY

From the broken bone of the hill
stripped and left for dead,
like a wrecked skull,
leaps out this bush of blood.

Out of the torn earth's mouth
comes the old cry of praise.
Still is the song made flesh
though the singer dies—

flesh of the world's delight,
voice of the world's desire,
I drink you with my sight
and I am filled with fire.

Out of the very wound
springs up this scarlet breath—
this fountain of hot joy,
this living ghost of death.

WONGA VINE

Look down; be still.
The sunburst day's on fire,
O twilight bell,
flower of the wonga vine.

I gather you
out of his withering light.
Sleep there, red;
sleep there, yellow and white.

Move as the creek
moves to its hidden pool.
The sun has eyes of fire;
be my white waterfall.

Lie on my eyes like hands,
let no sun shine—
O twilight bell,
flower of the wonga vine.

NIGHT AND THE CHILD

In the morning the hawk and the sun flew up together;
the wildhaired sun and the wild bird of prey.
Now both are fallen out of the treacherous sky.
One holds a bullet as leaden as the lid of his eye
and one from the west's red beaches fell to the western
    water.
O hawk and sun of my morning, how far you are gone
    down.

The night comes up over you, faceless and forbidden,
over the hawk sunk in earth and the sun drunk by the sea;
and who can tell, the child said, no matter what they say—
who can be sure that the sun will rise on another day?
For he died in his blood on the water as the hawk died,
    and is hidden.
How far under the grey eyelid the yellow eye is gone.

Who can be sure, the child said, that there will be a
    waking?
Now I am given to the night and my soul is afraid.
I would people the dark with candles and friends to stay by
    my side
but the darkness said, Only in my heart can you hide.
I said to the dark, Be my friend; but the dark said, I am
    nothing,
and now I must turn my face to the sea of Nothing and
    drown.

And no one could reach me or save me out of that deadly
    dream
until deep under the sea I found the sleeping sun.
With the sun asleep in my arms I sank and was not and
    was gone
even as the hawk was gone after the noise of the gun.
I who run on the beach where the morning sun is warm
went under the black sea, and rose with the sun, and am
    born.

THE BLIND MAN

I THE DUST IN THE TOWNSHIP

Under the Moreton Bay fig by the war memorial
blind Jimmy Delaney sits alone and sings
in the pollen-coloured dust; and Jimmy Delaney
coloured like the dust, is of that dust
three generations made. Sing for the dust
then, Jimmy, thin and strange as old fiddle-strings
or the dry wires of grass-stems stretched in the thrust
of a winter westerly; and if it's true
black Mary's your father's mother, none better than you
can speak in the voice of the forgotten dust.

Horrie Delaney came here first with cattle,
and shook the dust out of its golden sleep;
the golden sleep of eternal generation.
Grass, wattle- and messmate-tree and earth;
death bearing life, and both come out of earth.
Deeper than the shadows of trees and tribes, deep
lay the spring that issued in death and birth.
Horrie Delaney with his dogs and his gun
came like another shadow between the earth and the sun
and now with the tribes he is gone down in death.

Dick Delaney the combo cleared these hills.
Easily the bush fell and lightly, now it seems
to us who forget the sweat of Dick Delaney,
and the humpy and the scalding sunlight and the black
hate between the white skin and the black.
The smoke sang upward, the trees vanished like dreams
and the long hills lie naked as a whipped back.
Greed and hunger tear at the marrow-bone
and the heart in the breast hangs heavy as a great gold
   stone.
Under the marred earth, his bones twist on that rack.

Yellow Delaney is the third of that name
and like the yellow dust, he finds no rest.
Landless and loveless he went wandering
with his despised white girl, and left no track
but the black mark of a campfire. How can they die
who live without a country? He does not die
though like the night curlew the blood mourns in his breast
and gets no answer. Under the tenantless sky
he lives by his traps in the lost ranges; he
is the brain-fever bird calling from a rung tree
that time is a cracked mask and day a golden lie.

Under the Moreton Bay fig by the war memorial
Jimmy Delaney the blind man sits and sings
where the wind raises dry fountains of faded gold.
No one has loved or sung of the unregarded dust.
Dance upright in the wind, dry-voiced and humble dust
out of whose breast the great green fig-tree springs,
and the proud man, and the singer, and the outcast.
All are but shadows between the earth and the sun
sings Jimmy Delaney, sitting where the dust-whirls run,
columns of dancing dust that sink at last.

And yet those men, this fallen dust, these shadows
remembered only by the blind man whose songs none hear
sting him in the noon sunlight as a hornet stings.
The conqueror who possessed a world alone,
and he who hammered a world on his heart's stone,
and last the man whose world splintered in fear—
their shadows lengthen in the light of noon;
their dust bites deep, driven by a restless wind.
O singer, son of darkness, love that is blind,
sing for the golden dust that dances and is gone.

II   COUNTRY DANCE

The dance in the township hall is nearly over.
Hours ago the stiff-handed wood-cheeked women
got up from the benches round the walls
and took home their aching eyes and weary children.
Mrs McLarty with twenty cows to milk
before dawn, went with the music stinging
like sixty wasps under her best dress.
Eva Callaghan whose boy died in the army
sat under the streamers like a house to let
and went alone, a black pot brimming with tears.
"Once my body was a white cedar, my breasts the buds on
    the quince-tree,
that now are fallen and grey like logs on a cleared hill.
Then why is my blood not quiet? what is the good
of the whips of music stinging along my blood?"

The dance in the township hall is nearly over.
Outside in the yard the fire like a great red city
eats back into the log, its noisy flames fallen.
Jimmy Dunn has forgotten his camp in the hills
and sleeps like a heap of rags beside a bottle.
The young boys sit and stare at the heart of the city
thinking of the neon lights and the girls at the corners
with lips like coals and thighs as silver as florins.
Jock Hamilton thinks of the bally cow gone sick
and the cockatoos in the corn and the corn ready to pick
and the wires in the thirty-acre broken.
Oh, what rats nibble at the cords of our nerves?
When will the wires break, the ploughed paddocks lie open,
the bow of the fiddle saw through the breast-bone,
the dream be done, and we waken?

Streamers and boughs are falling, the dance grows faster.
Only the lovers and the young are dancing
now at the end of the dance, in a trance or singing.
Say the lovers locked together and crowned with coloured
     paper:
"The bit of black glass I picked up out of the campfire
is the light that the moon puts on your hair."
"The green pool I swam in under the willows
is the drowning depth, the summer night of your eyes."
"You are the death I move to." "O burning weapon,
you are the pain I long for."

Stars, leaves and streamers fall in the dark dust
and the blind man lies alone in his sphere of night.

Oh, I,
red centre of a dark and burning sky,
fit my words to music, my crippled words to music,
and sing to the fire with the voice of the fire.
Go sleep with your grief, go sleep with your desire,
go deep into the core of night and silence.
But I hold all of it, your hate and sorrow,
your passion and your fear; I am the breath
that holds you from your death.
I am the voice of music and the ended dance.

I cannot tell your voice from the voice of the dust,
the stinging river of drought that runs with the wind;
for the dust cries with a child's voice as it goes past,
telling of the blood that falls, and the death of the mind.
If you would speak to me, do not forget I am blind.

I am the singing man who pours dust in the palm of his
    hand.
It is as dark as dry blood or as bright as the dust of gold.
I do not need to know the colours of earth, who am blind.
Your voice is the voice of the dust that weeps at the world's
    end—
of a child among violent masks, weeping the death of the
    world.

Who will gather the dust to a sphere, who will build us a
    world?
Who will join atom to atom, the waiting seed to the seed?
Who will give the heat of the sun to death's great grave of
    cold,
and deliver the countries of the heart, in the womb of a
    dust-grain furled?
Who will join lover to loved, and raise from the ash the
    blazing bird?

We two, the singer and the crying child, must feed
that whirling phantom on the wind of the world's end.
Only these two can join the sperm to the golden seed—
the tears of a child that fall for the dust at the world's end
and the song of the singer of love, whom the wasps of the
    dust made blind.

IV   LOST CHILD

Is the boy lost? Then I know where he is gone.
He has gone climbing the terrible crags of the Sun.

The searchers go through the green valley, shouting his
    name;
the dogs are moaning on the hill for the scent of his track;
but the men will all be hoarse and the dogs lame
before the Hamiltons' boy is found or comes back.
Through the smouldering ice of the moon he is stumbling
    alone.
I shall rise from my dark and follow where he is gone.

I heard from my bed his bugle breath go by
and the drum of his heart in the measure of an old song.
I shall travel into silence, and in that fierce country
when we shall meet he will know he has been away too
    long.
They are looking for him now in the vine-scrub over the
    hill,
but I think he is alone in a place that I know well.

Is the boy lost? Then I know where he is gone.
He is climbing to Paradise up a river of stars and stone.

V   BLIND MAN'S SONG

No one but a child or a fool dares
to listen to silence, or to the words of this song.
Silence goes back into the man who hears
and carries all the sorrow was ever in his ears
and all the fear he has gathered all his life long:
and this song is a fool's song.

The old man and the young man saw me lie
like a yellow snake in the dust when the dust was still.
The whispering song of the wind or the snake sang I
and the old man turned his head away and went by,
and the young man set his horse full speed at the hill;
but the song went on still.

I have the tune of the singer who makes men afraid.
I repeat the small speech of the worm in the ground,
and out of the depths of the rock my words are made.
I have laid my ear to the dust, and the thing it said
was Silence. Therefore I have made silence speak; I found
for the night a sound.

So no one but a fool or a lonely child
will turn his head to listen to my song.
I am the yellow snake with a dark, a double tongue,
speaking from the dust to the two rulers of the world.

Thou perceivest the Flowers put forth their precious Odours;
And none can tell how from so small a centre comes such sweet,
Forgetting that within that centre Eternity expands Its ever-during doors ...

BLAKE, *Milton* (fo. 31, ll. 47–50)

DARK GIFT

The flower begins in the dark
where life is not.
Death has a word to speak
and the flower begins.

How small, how closely bound
in nothing's net
the word waits in the ground
for the cloak earth spins.

The root goes down in the night
and from the night's mud
the unmade, the inchoate
starts to take shape and rise.

The blind, the upward hand
clenches its bud.
What message does death send
from the grave where he lies?

Open, green hand, and give
the dark gift you hold.

Oh wild mysterious gold!
Oh act of passionate love!

FIRE AT MURDERING HUT

I   THE GRAVE

You who were the snake hidden under my house,
   the breath of the bushfire—
are you come to take me again like a storm in the night,
oh storm of my desire?
Are you come to take me like a knife in the breast
after this silent century?
You will find me this time lying alone.
It has been a long time you have left me with the rose-tree,
the wandering mist and the stone.

Lay down your fire beside my frost again,
against my stone your blade.
I have been too long alone in the drought and the rain—
it is all true as you said.
Come now and take me—
dig with the blade of your heart into the grave and wake
     me,
and this time you will find me lying alone.
I have been here too long with the white rose-tree,
the wandering mist and the stone.

II   THE FIRE

Are you one of the old dead, whisperer under my feet?
I stamp on your shallow earth
like a red bird, my song is the last message of love,
which is the news of death.
Now I shall eat even your white roses, and eat
the dry moss on your stone.
Neither love nor death come to the dead, nor does flesh
grow on the bared bone.

But look, I am beautiful, I dance on your grave
like a lover's ghost.
I dance with your tree of roses, I whirl my blade
till they fall into black dust.
And though I am not your lover and am not love
I shall set before I am gone
a kiss on the rose-root to travel down to your breast;
the last message of love, the fire's black stain
to wear like a badge over your white breastbone.

III   THE STONE

Cruel was the steel in the hand that split my sleep
and branded me with pain.
Why did I not lie for ever out of time's way,
cold, quiet and deep?
Now I am delivered to the fire again
and set naked in the track of merciless day
for the years to fret me, those instruments of love
that will eat my stone away.

You, the poor nakedness that lies beneath—
the bone that love left bare—
I hear you call on him, the terrible one,
the eater even of death.
If I were hidden in earth, I should lie quiet there
and forget the summoning cry of the wild sun,
and forget the fire that would lay open my heart
for love to tear.

Why can you not lie quiet as the knife
that rots beside your bone?
It is because the stone that life has once possessed
is ever starved for life.
And that is why I am afraid of the stab of the sun
and the rain's hands beating my breast.
Fire, do not open my heart. I do not wish to wake
to the cruel day of love. Leave me my rest.

THE CEDARS

The dried body of winter is hard to kill.
Frost crumbles the dead bracken, greys the old grass,
and the great hemisphere of air goes flying
barren and cold from desert or polar seas
tattering fern and leaf. By the sunken pool
the sullen sodom-apple grips his scarlet fruit.

Spring, returner, knocker at the iron gates,
why should you return? None wish to live again.
Locked in our mourning, in our sluggish age,
we stand and think of past springs, of deceits not yet
    forgotten.
Then we answered you in youth and joy; we threw
open our strongholds and hung our walls with flowers.
Do not ask us to answer again as then we answered.

For it is anguish to be reborn and reborn:
at every return of the overmastering season
to shed our lives in pain, to waken into the cold,
to become naked, while with unbearable effort
we make way for the new sap that burns along old
    channels—
while out of our life's substance, the inmost of our being,
form those brief flowers, those sacrifices, soon falling,
which spring the returner demands, and demands for ever.

Easier, far easier, to stand with downturned eyes
and hands hanging, to let age and mourning cover us
with their dark rest, heavy like death, like the ground
from which we issued and towards which we crumble.
Easier to be one with the impotent body of winter,
and let our old leaves rattle on the wind's currents—
to stand like the rung trees whose boughs no longer
    murmur
their foolish answers to spring; whose blossoms now are
the only lasting flowers, the creeping lichens of death.

Spring, impatient, thunderer at the doors of iron,
we have no songs left. Let our boughs be silent.
Hold back your fires that would sear us into flower again,
and your insistent bees, the messengers of generation.
Our bodies are old as winter and would remain in winter.
So the old trees plead, clinging to the edge of darkness.
But round their roots the mintbush makes its buds ready,

and the snake in hiding feels the sunlight's finger.
The snake, the fang of summer, beauty's double meaning,
shifts his slow coils and feels his springtime hunger.

TRAIN JOURNEY

Glassed with cold sleep and dazzled by the moon,
out of the confused hammering dark of the train
I looked and saw under the moon's cold sheet
your delicate dry breasts, country that built my heart;

and the small trees on their uncoloured slope
like poetry moved, articulate and sharp
and purposeful under the great dry flight of air,
under the crosswise currents of wind and star.

Clench down your strength, box-tree and ironbark.
Break with your violent root the virgin rock.
Draw from the flying dark its breath of dew
till the unliving come to life in you.

Be over the blind rock a skin of sense,
under the barren height a slender dance ...

I woke and saw the dark small trees that burn
suddenly into flowers more lovely than the white moon.

TRANSFORMATIONS

I   FAIRYTALE

The witch has changed the Prince into a toad.
That slender girl, so thistledown, so fair,
that subtle face that stole him from his home,
that voice, that dance that brightened all the air—
how could they turn to darkness and a snare?
His feet are bound and cannot find his road.
He is held fast where help may never come.

The wizard chains the Princess in a swan.
Oh cruel snow, cold as your thousand years,
where only her sad eyes are golden still!
He holds a crystal jar to catch her tears;
her wings may beat the air, but no wind hears.
Now love will never trace where she is gone
or find the castle on the guarded hill.

The Prince remembers nothing but his pain:
how all the woven knowledge he had won
fell down like the quenched flame of a tall fire
into this tiny space—all life undone.
A toad hiding in crannies from the sun
with agony and a jewel for a brain
he has forgotten pity and desire.

The Princess thinks of nothing but her grief;
how she must crouch within that alien bone,
all wit and will subdued into a bird,
all memory, all hope and beauty gone.
She thrusts her beak into the lake alone
whose courtiers called her lips a scarlet leaf;
and she would mourn, if she but knew the word.

Only his kiss might strip her dark away.
Only her love might tear away his night.
Bird-eye and toad-eye blinded with thick tears
like rain on window-panes, forget their sight.
Prince, she is here, the beautiful, the bright—
Princess, your lover here is locked away.
Oh, do not weep alone your thousand years!

II MYTH

A god has chosen to be shaped in flesh.
He has put on the garment of the world.
A blind and sucking fish, a huddled worm,
he crouches here until his time shall come,
all the dimensions of his glory furled
into the blood and clay of the night's womb.
Eternity is locked in time and form.

Within those mole-dark corridors of earth
how can his love be born and how unfold?
Eternal knowledge in an atom's span
is bound by its own strength with its own chain.
The nerve is dull, the eyes are stopped with mould,
the flesh is slave of accident or pain.
Sunk in his brittle prison-cell of mud
the god who once chose to become a man
is now a man who must become a god.

III THE PLAY

Now all the years his bargain bought are gone.
Midnight is near, and soon the clock will strike,
the devil will come, and Faustus must be damned.
What have his famous art and knowledge done
who feels within him rise the fiery lake?
He and the prince of hell are left alone.

Destruction eats the edges of his rage;
and soon the door will open on the night
his soul is bound to. Hear the angels first.
They step from light and darkness to the stage
to stand upon his left hand and his right.
What words shall he record on their last page?

But he's for neither angel, being both.
They hold their quarrel only in his mind.
The clock will strike in him; it is his blood
that streams in heaven, his voice that speaks in wrath.
He is the door and that which waits behind.
In him divides the hell-and-heavenward path.

All this his magic taught him year by year,
until the contract seemed an antique dream
and he alone stood builder of his world.
But now the Time he made draws in too near
and whirls him from that world into its stream
that leads to midnight's fall, and his old fear.

Mountains and hills, come, come and fall on me!
But they are weightless figures in a play.
He and his soul alone stand face to face,
and in all art there is no mystery
will change the stroke of midnight into day
or hold the door against the turning key.

Helen's the picture of a girl who died,
the world he ruled, less than a cardboard scene—
and he, his instrument and victim both.
What is it triumphs, then, and what's denied?
Darkness and light alone remain. Between
the trapped rat turns his head from side to side.

Is nothing left to say that might be worth
the breaking of his pride, that brittle sword?
The Lucifer whom he created makes
his knowledge useless and usurps his earth;
and he is snared between death's final word
and the more difficult agony of rebirth.

THE JOURNEY

He was the man they chose to fly alone
to search at the end of the sea for the Blessed Isles.
Often enough reported, still unknown,
they had survived untouched, forgotten, so late,
because of a lost chart and a million miles;
but now they must come under the care of the State.
It was he, the single-minded airman, whom they chose
to place on the maps again the land of the lost rose.

The mission was secret, but at the aerodrome
a great official waited among his guard,
gave him his orders and messages from home,
spoke of the honour to him of such a choice,
and hinted at promotion and reward.
Then from the amplifiers rang out the Voice—
the eternal indisputable Voice that everywhere
follows the farmer, the citizen, the man of the air—

The Voice that knows the mind of everyone,
and through the clustered trumpets in street and square
is daily magnified, cold and busy as a machine-gun
with bulletin, prophecy, threat, denunciation—
"Here is a special message. One of our men of the air
is setting out today to an unmapped destination
to further the State's plans. The people of the State will
   now
join their thoughts to wish him all that the fates allow."

There were a million miles of sea and cloud.
The dials moved calmly, the polished instruments
followed instructions, the Voice in his ear was loud.
He hung on the Voice, a foetus hung on its cord.
Its level stream was rippled with incidents—
the presentation of a medal, a civil award,
a flash from a traitor's trial, the sudden familiar noise
of a firing-party's rifles, and again the Voice.

But up from the cloud-floor a forest began to grow—
branched and wonderful trees climbed dazzling in light,
thrusting him upwards. The plane scaled peaks of snow
so high that ice began to weight his wings
and he dived again into blinding moving white.
And now in that country of nothings shaped like things
the Voice faltered, fading to silence in his ear
and leaving him suddenly alone with fear.

O Lord of the terrors of silence, open your hand:
O Voice, return and fill my emptiness!
He dropped through mist treacherous as quicksand
where the voices of nothing wove their silent song.
He fought with the radio, trembling in distress,
but nothing was wrong, he could find nothing wrong.
Then from the floors of cloud he fell, and below
lay the lovely immaculate archipelago.

On the great breast-like curve of eternity
those islands hung like pearl. Their hills and shores
were shining shadows answered in a still sea.
Then he looked up before the plane, and found
the edge of the air—the cliff where time and cause
at eternity's edge disputed their last ground.
He would turn back, but frightened and without a guide
his desperate hands were slow. The plane fell from the
   cliffside.

How appalling is the terror and the weight of love!
In the explosion of that instant's revelation
the body is lost that washes under the wave
and all is lost but the knowledge of that death.
The islands of the saints stir not from contemplation.
Above their hills light blazes, and beneath
the angel clouds whose image fills the sea
the bones of the dead hold their vision of eternity.

ERODED HILLS

These hills my father's father stripped,
    and beggars to the winter wind
they crouch like shoulders naked and whipped—
humble, abandoned, out of mind.

Of their scant creeks I drank once
and ate sour cherries from old trees
found in their gullies fruiting by chance.
Neither fruit nor water gave my mind ease.

I dream of hills bandaged in snow,
their eyelids clenched to keep out fear.
When the last leaf and bird go
let my thoughts stand like trees here.

OLD HOUSE

Where now outside the weary house the pepperina,
    that great broken tree, gropes with its blind hands
and sings a moment in the magpie's voice, there he stood
    once,
that redhaired man my great-great-grandfather,
his long face amiable as an animal's,
and thought of vines and horses.
He moved in that mindless country like a red ant,
running tireless in the summer heat among the trees—
the nameless trees, the sleeping soil, the original river—
and said that the eastern slope would do for a vineyard.

In the camp by the river they made up songs about him,
songs about the waggons, songs about the cattle,
songs about the horses and the children and the woman.
These were a dream, something strayed out of a dream.
They would vanish down the river, but the river would
    flow on,
under the river-oaks the river would flow on,
winter and summer would burn the grass white
or red like the red of the pale man's hair.
In the camp by the river they made up those songs
and my great-great-grandfather heard them with one part of
    his mind.

And in those days
there was one of him and a thousand of them,
and in these days none are left—
neither a pale man with kangaroo-grass hair
nor a camp of dark singers mocking by the river.
And the trees and the creatures, all of them are gone.
But the sad river, the silted river,
under its dark banks the river flows on,
the wind still blows and the river still flows.
And the great broken tree, the dying pepperina,
clutches in its hands the fragments of a song.

DROUGHT YEAR

That time of drought the embered air
    Burned to the roots of timber and grass.
The crackling lime-scrub would not bear
the Mooni Creek was sand that year.
The dingoes' cry was strange to hear.

I heard the dingoes cry
in the whipstick scrub on the Thirty-mile Dry.
I saw the wagtail take his fill
perching in the seething skull.
I saw the eel wither where he curled
in the last blood-drop of a spent world.

I heard the bone whisper in the hide
of the big red horse that lay where he died.
Prop that horse up, make him stand,
hoofs turned down in the bitter sand—
make him stand at the gate of the Thirty-mile Dry.
Turn this way and you will die—
and strange and loud was the dingoes' cry.

FLOOD YEAR

Walking up the driftwood beach at day's end
I saw it, thrust up out of a hillock of sand—
a frail bleached clench of fingers dried by wind—
the dead child's hand.

And they are mourning there still, though I forget,
the year of flood, the scoured ruined land,
the herds gone down the current, the farms drowned,
and the child never found.

When I was there the thick hurling waters
had gone back to the river, the farms were almost drained.
Banished half-dead cattle searched the dunes; it rained;
river and sea met with a wild sound.

Oh with a wild sound water flung into air
where sea met river; all the country round
no heart was quiet. I walked on the driftwood sand
and saw the pale crab crouched, and came to a stand
thinking, A child's hand. The child's hand.

OLD MAN

Before the coming of that arrogant and ancient kingdom
something is waiting to be done, something should be
   said.
The very old man has lost the clues that led
into the country of his mind, its people are all dead.
He stumbles through the days of bright and sorrowful
   winter.

The stubble of the corn is raked together and burning
with a sweet smoke that brings a memory to his mind.
He stands on the ploughed earth's edge where the smoke
   lifts on the wind,
red flame on red earth beckons, but his eyes are blind;
and rocketing up the high wind, magpies are singing.

There is something to be said yet, a word that might be
   spoken
before the flames blacken and the field is sown again.
Blade and weed will grow over it after the spring rain,
weed and worm will riot in the country of the brain,
but now in the wind on the bared field a word crouches in
   the open.

Catching at the turns of smoke where the breeze wanders
he leans on the fence, the old old man gone queer,
waiting for the word or his death to come near.
If he can catch either of them, his eyes will suddenly
   clear—
but the figureless smoke moves on like mist over windows.

Put up the hare, good dog, in a fury of yelling.
Let the red field and the red flame open to watch you run
violent in your intent to the smoky winter sun.
Put up the hare, good dog; catch him before he is gone—
the last hare on the place, perhaps, there's no telling.

But the winter wind brings ice to fill the sky with winter,
and the hare crouches and eludes and the smoke turns
  aside.
The old man coughs in the eddies, forgetful and red-eyed;
there is no clue to his mind now and all his friends have
  died.
He must wait for the coming of that arrogant and ancient
  kingdom.

BOTANICAL GARDENS

U nder the miraculous baptism of fire
  that bows the poinciana tree, the old man drab as a
  grub
burrows with his spade. Alas, one's whole life long
to be haunted by these visions of fulfilled desire.

"Alas," he cries, leaning alone on the wet bar of the pub,
"to find them flourishing, clambering, gesturing in the
  mind—
the sweet white flesh of lilies, the clutching lips of the vine,
the naked flame-trees, their dark limbs curved and strong.

"Oh terrible garden to which my small grey life is food—
oh innocent passionate stare recurring year after year.
Great purple clematis, cassias draped in their golden hair,
they root in the soil of my days, they are drunk with my
  heart's blood.

"Tear out of your hearts the dreadful beauty of flowers.
Walk your dark streets alone but without fear.
Go back to your death in life not caring to live or die,
and forget the crazy glance of the flowers out of a time
  gone by."

BIRDS

Whatever the bird is, is perfect in the bird.
Weapon kestrel hard as a blade's curve,
thrush round as a mother or a full drop of water
fruit-green parrot wise in his shrieking swerve—
all are what bird is and do not reach beyond bird.

Whatever the bird does is right for the bird to do—
cruel kestrel dividing in his hunger the sky,
thrush in the trembling dew beginning to sing,
parrot clinging and quarrelling and veiling his queer eye—
all these are as birds are and good for birds to do.

But I am torn and beleaguered by my own people.
The blood that feeds my heart is the blood they gave me,
and my heart is the house where they gather and fight for
    dominion—
all different, all with a wish and a will to save me,
to turn me into the ways of other people.

If I could leave their battleground for the forest of the bird
I could melt the past, the present and the future in one
and find the words that lie behind all these languages.
Then I could fuse my passions into one clear stone
and be simple to myself as the bird is to the bird.

LION

Lion, let your desert eyes
turn on me.
Look beyond my flesh and see
that in it which never dies;

that which neither sleeps nor wakes—
the pool of glass
where no wave rocks or breaks,
where no days or nights pass.

Your shining eyes like the sun will find
an image there
that will answer stare for stare
till with that gaze your gaze is blind.

Though you wear the face of the sun
in the mortal gold of your eyes,
yet till that Lord himself dies
this deeper image will live on.

It is the crystal glance of love
earth turns on sun as the two move.
It is the jewel I was given
in exchange for your heaven.

THE ORANGE-TREE

The orange-tree that roots in night
draws from that night his great gold fruit,
and the green bough that stands upright
to shelter the bird with the beating heart.

Out of that silent death and cold
the tree leaps up and makes a world
to reconcile the night and day,
to feed the bird and the shining fly—

a perfect single world of gold
no storm can undo nor death deny.

SANDY SWAMP

From the marble-dazzling beaches
or the tame hills where cattle pasture
the eye that ranges never reaches
the secret depth of that storm-cloud
the bitter and thorny moor
that sets its bar between
hill's green and sea's glitter.

No visiting traveller crosses
by the pale sandy tracks that vanish
under the banksias hung with mosses.
In yellow evenings when the sea sounds loud
night rises early here,
and when white morning sings
here clings the darkness longest.

Who walks this way, then? Only
the rebel children who fear nothing
and the silent walker who goes lonely,
silence his goal, out of the holiday crowd.
And these, if they go far,
will find the clustering moons and stars of white
that jealous night saves for her wanderers.

PHAIUS ORCHID

Out of the brackish sand
see the phaius orchid build
her intricate moonlight tower
that rusts away in flower.

For whose eyes—for whose eyes
does this blind being weave
sand's poverty, water's sour,
the white and black of the hour

into the image I hold
and cannot understand?
Is it for the ants, the bees,
the lizard outside his cave,

or is it to garland time—
eternity's cold tool
that severs with its blade
the gift as soon as made?

Then I too am your fool.
What can I do but believe?
Here like the plant I weave
your dying garlands, time.

RAIN AT NIGHT

The wind from the desert over mountain and plain
gathered the loose unhappy dust
and set it running like a ghost from door to door again—
like the heart's red ghost
it ran to accuse me of the murder of the heart.
O little voice of the dry dust at the windowpane,
I wept for you before I slept
till in the night came on the undreamed-of rain.

Out of the seed of night and the divided dust
and the clouds of rain
what thrones are made, and stand up there in the east
to hold the sun!
What pure and shining altars rise in the night—
altars set with the ritual of love—the first
god that broke out when night's egg woke—
the blind and divine son of dust and night.
In the fierce rites of the flowers now, heart and heart's
    murderer rest.

EDEN

This is the grief of the heart—
  that it can never be
closed in one flesh with its love,
like the fruit hung on Eve's tree:

This is the lament of the flesh—
that it must always contain
the uncompleted heart,
greedy of love and pain.

—This is not what I desired—
the flesh in anguish cries;
—the gift that was made to me
in my lost Paradise,

where in predestined joy
and with a shock like death,
the two halves of my being
met to make one truth.

Yet where the circle was joined
the desperate chase began;
where love in love dissolved
sprang up the woman and man,

and locked in the pangs of life
sway those unwilling selves
till the circle join again
and love in love dissolves.

SONG FOR WINTER

When under the rind we felt the pressure of the bud
then we forgot all, being caught beyond ourselves.
    Grow in us now that we are left alone.

When in the morning light our flowers first blew open
we stood in the bright spray of the glory of our blood.
    Shine in us now, left bare since our delight is gone.

When the flower fell we knew the growth of the fruit
and we devoted our desires to the fulfilment of time.
    Set your eternity in us, now that our night comes
      on.

When autumn sweetened the sap, then we were crowned.
O lovely burdens breaking the branch, straining the root!
    Hang on us stars, moons and the absolute light
      of the sun.

When the fruit fell we were more lonely than the cold
and childless rock that waits its far-off day.
    Be now the knowledge of the root of our despair.

All we have made was made by what we do not know
and the worn tool is rusted and grows old.
Now that truth strips us naked to the winter's blow
give us your depthless dark, your light brighter than the
   brightness of the air.

SONNET FOR CHRISTMAS

I saw our golden years on a black gale,
our time of love spilt in the furious dust.
"O we are winter-caught, and we must fail,"
said the dark dream, "and time is overcast."
—And woke into the night; but you were there,
and small as seed in the wild dark we lay.
Small as a seed under the gulfs of air
is set the stubborn heart that waits for day.
I saw our love the root that holds the vine
in the enduring earth, that can reply,
"Nothing shall die unless for me it die.
Murder and hate and love alike are mine";
and therefore fear no winter and no storm
while in the knot of earth that root lies warm.

THE POOL AND THE STAR

Let me be most clear and most tender;
let no wind break my perfection.
Let the stream of my life run muted,
and a pure sleep unbar
my every depth and secret.

I wait for the rising of a star
whose spear of light shall transfix me—
of a far-off world whose silence
my very truth must answer.
That shaft shall pierce me through
till I cool its white-hot metal.

Let move no leaf nor moth;
sleep quietly, all my creatures.
I must be closed as the rose is
until that bright one rises.
Then down the fall of space
his kiss the shape of a star
shall wake the dark of my breast.

For this I am drawn from far—
for this I am gathered together.
Though made of time and of waters
that move even while I love
I shall draw from the living day
no hour as pure, as bright,
as this when across the night
he stoops with his steady ray
and his image burns on my breast.

ALL THINGS CONSPIRE

All things conspire to hold me from you—
even my love,
since that would mask you and unname you
till merely woman and man we live.
All men wear arms against the rebel—
and they are wise,
since the sound world they know and stable
is eaten away by lovers' eyes.

All things conspire to stand between us—
even you and I,
who still command us, still unjoin us,
and drive us forward till we die.
Not till those fiery ghosts are laid
shall we be one.
Till then, they whet our double blade
and use the turning world for stone.

OUR LOVE IS SO NATURAL

Our love is so natural,
　the wild animals move
gentle and light on
the shores of our love.

My eyes rest upon you,
to me your eyes turn,
as bee goes to honey,
as fire to fire will burn.

Bird and beast are at home,
and star lives in tree
when we are together
as we should be.

But so silent my heart falls
when you are away,
I can hear the world breathing
where he hides from our day.

My heart crouches under,
silent and still,
and the avalanche gathers
above the green hill.

Our love is so natural—
I cannot but fear.
I would reach out and touch you.
Why are you not here?

SONG FOR EASTER

Who is it singing on the hill at morning,
　and who runs naked down the beach at evening,
and who is ferried by the starless sea
to wake again upon the wave of morning?

O, said the girl, it is my love:
and the boy said, it is the secret that I seek:
and the man drawing nets, it is the sun:
and the child said, it is myself: and all
of them joined hands beneath the moon of Easter.

But, love, you are my secret and my sun.
It is for you I make my song of Easter.

THE FLAME-TREE

How to live, I said, as the flame-tree lives?
—to know what the flame-tree knows; to be
prodigal of my life as that wild tree
and wear my passion so?
That lover's knot of water and earth and sun,
that easy answer to the question of baffling reason,
branches out of my heart this sudden season.
I know what I would know.

How shall I thank you, who teach me how to wait
in quietness for the hour to ask or give:
to take and in taking bestow, in bestowing live:
in the loss of myself, to find?
This is the flame-tree; look how gloriously
that careless blossomer scatters, and more and more.
What the earth takes of her, it will restore.
These are the thanks of lovers who share one mind.

SONG

When cries aloud the bird of night
then I am quiet on your breast.
When storms of darkness quench the trees
I turn to you and am at rest:
and when the ancient terrors rise
and the feet halt and grow unsure,
for each of us the other's eyes
restore the day, the sickness cure.

You, who with your insistent love
dissolved in me the evil stone
that was my shield against the world
and grew so close it seemed my own—
gave, easily as a tree might give
its fruit, its flower, its wild grey dove—
the very life by which I live;
the power to answer love with love.

TWO HUNDRED MILES

From the front of this house a road runs
and I am already gone.
Across the miles of moons and suns
I am running already.

Down the hill to the bridge,
over the bridge to the town,
through the town to the plain,
up the range and down.

O back to my red mountain
and along the red road,
and at the green gate
I put down my load.

All I want is to see you.
Nothing matters at all;
not the buds on the peach-tree,
or the new leaf on the fern,
or the hyacinth if it is flowering,
or the spring green on the hill.
I have come so far; why have I come?
Only because you are my home.

LEGEND

The blacksmith's boy went out with a rifle
and a black dog running behind.
Cobwebs snatched at his feet,
rivers hindered him,
thorn-branches caught at his eyes to make him blind
and the sky turned into an unlucky opal,
and he didn't mind.
I can break branches, I can swim rivers, I can stare out any
    spider I meet,
said he to his dog and his rifle.

The blacksmith's boy went over the paddocks
with his old black hat on his head.
Mountains jumped in his way,
rocks rolled down on him,
and the old crow cried, "You'll soon be dead."
And the rain came down like mattocks.
But he only said
I can climb mountains, I can dodge rocks, I can shoot an
    old crow any day,
and he went on over the paddocks.

When he came to the end of the day the sun began falling.
Up came the night ready to swallow him,
like the barrel of a gun,
like an old black hat,
like a black dog hungry to follow him.
Then the pigeon, the magpie and the dove began wailing
and the grass lay down to pillow him.
His rifle broke, his hat blew away and his dog was gone
and the sun was falling.

But in front of the night the rainbow stood on the
    mountain,
just as his heart foretold.
He ran like a hare,
he climbed like a fox;
he caught it in his hands, the colours and the cold—
like a bar of ice, like the column of a fountain,
like a ring of gold.
The pigeon, the magpie and the dove flew up to stare,
and the grass stood up again on the mountain.

The blacksmith's boy hung the rainbow on his shoulder
instead of his broken gun.
Lizards ran out to see,
snakes made way for him,
and the rainbow shone as brightly as the sun.
All the world said, Nobody is braver, nobody is bolder,
nobody else has done
anything to equal it. He went home as bold as he could be
with the swinging rainbow on his shoulder.

NURSERY RHYME FOR A SEVENTH SON

You must begin by leaving home;
and that is not easy.
Home is so faithful, so calm,
a shelter from the cold wind
that calls to the frightened, the weak and the lazy,
"Come; you must come."

The wind will blow you to the witch,
and the witch is your danger.
Remember the trick of the latch,
and be careful with questions.
When she gives you your answer, don't wait any longer—
go, and keep watch.

The witch will send you to the wall,
and the wall is your barrier.
You will not see it at all
if you don't walk boldly,
until with a grip like warm flesh it will seize you and bury
    you
before you can call.

If you hack at the flesh with your sword
it will weep like your mother.
Like a snake it will spring, like a cord
it will choke you to silence.
You never will cross it—one fold will give way to
    another—
till you find the right word.

The wall is the way to the wood,
and the wood is your death.
You must go by the darkest road
where the voices whisper.
They will steal from you your sight and your speech and
    breath—
you will drown in a night like a flood.

It will cover you deeper in cold
than your heart can measure.
You will lose the sword that you hold
and all that you own.
And after that you will find your heart's true treasure,
your love and your gold.

THE CICADAS

On yellow days in summer when the early heat
   presses like hands hardening the sown earth
into stillness, when after sunrise birds fall quiet
and streams sink in their beds and in silence meet,
then underground the blind nymphs waken and move.
They must begin at last to struggle towards love.

For a whole life they have crouched alone and dumb
in patient ugliness enduring the humble dark.
Nothing has shaken that world below the world
except the far-off thunder, the strain of roots in storm.
Sunk in an airless night they neither slept nor woke
but hanging on the tree's blood dreamed vaguely the
   dreams of the tree,
and put on wavering leaves, wing-veined, too delicate to
   see.

But now in terror overhead their day of dying breaks.
The trumpet of the rising sun bursts into sound
and the implacable unborn stir and reply.
In the hard shell an unmade body wakes
and fights to break from its motherly-enclosing ground.
These dead must dig their upward grave in fear
to cast the living into the naked air.

Terrible is the pressure of light into the heart.
The womb is withered and cracked, the birth is begun,
and shuddering and groaning to break that iron grasp
the new is delivered as the old is torn apart.
Love whose unmerciful blade has pierced us through,
we struggle naked from our death in search of you.

This is the wild light that our dreams foretold
while unaware we prepared these eyes and wings—
while in our sleep we learned the song the world sings.
Sing now, my brothers; climb to that intolerable gold.

ISHTAR

When I first saw a woman after childbirth
the room was full of your glance who had just gone
away.
And when the mare was bearing her foal
you were with her but I did not see your face.

When in fear I became a woman
I first felt your hand.
When the shadow of the future first fell across me
it was your shadow, my grave and hooded attendant.

It is all one whether I deny or affirm you;
It is not my mind you are concerned with.
It is no matter whether I submit or rebel;
the event will still happen.

You neither know nor care for the truth of my heart;
but the truth of my body has all to do with you.
You have no need of my thoughts or my hopes,
living in the realm of the absolute event.

Then why is it that when I at last see your face
under that hood of slate-blue, so calm and dark,
so worn with the burden of an inexpressible knowledge—
why is it that I begin to worship you with tears?

THE PROMISED ONE

I lived in a wind of ghosts; a storm of hands
beat at my flesh. The Lazarus at my gate
demanding life, redoubled his demands—
I being rich beyond reason, warm in my coat of time
for which the dead weep and the unborn wait.
Now, beggar and ghost, child in the shell of night,
fasten on my warm blood and drink your fate.

You were the promised one time told me I must choose,
who lay until now buried under my blood's tree.
And you have been the dream each night renews—
the runner on lonely roads, whose face is turned away;
the footprint vanishing under the twilight sea.
Pursuer and pursued, we meet in one.
I draw you out of my dream into the sun.
Child, beggar, ghost, inherit life of me.

A SONG TO SING YOU

When I went out in early summer
    the creeks were full
and the grass growing;
the bat's-wing coral-tree stood in flower
and the lake of my heart
was clear and peaceful.

I began to make a song
to sing you some day.

It was a still song,
green and quiet,
like the new grass growing,
the full creek flowing,
the heron in the pool
and the tree in flower.

Flow in silence
clear river,
flower in hope
my flowering tree.

Work on in me
past and future,
the race of man
and the world to be.

This song I made
in early summer
while the creeks sang
and the wind blew.

My heart made it,
my blood bore it,
my tongue spoke it,
the song of the child yet to be born.

The creek washed it,
the sun blessed it,
the dove sang it,
the song of the child yet to be born.

WAITING WARD

Some wore fear like a wound,
some wore hope like a flower.
Some waited for the touch of joy
and some for the summons of terror;

But I would have her remembered,
the girl with the red hair.
She wore fear like a flower
and carried death like a child.

All the other women
overmastered by life
contained besides their terror
that terror's gentle answer;

she was the ace of spades,
she knew the future early—
the girl who sang and smiled
and carried a black secret.

Ageless face of stone
beaten by senseless air,
no birds come any longer
to nest in your hollows.
The sun that rises on you
cannot undo your night.

Face of grey stone
I have turned you into a mountain
to oppose in me for ever
the world of pleasure and grievance,
the world of winning and losing.

THE WATCHER

Lie quiet in the silence of my heart.
I watching thee am turned into a cloud;
I guarding thee am spread upon the air.

Lie quietly; be covered by my love.
I will be rain to fall upon your earth;
I will be shade to hold the sun from you.

I am the garden beyond the burning wind,
I am the river among the blowing sand;
I am the song you hear before you sleep.

In being these, I lose myself in these.
I am the woman-statue of the fountain
out of whose metal breasts continually
starts a living water; I am a vase
shaped only for my hour of holding you.

This drought is but to turn me to a cloud.
This heat but casts my shadow cooler on you.
Turn to my breast your fever, and be still.

FULL MOON RHYME

There's a hare in the moon tonight,
crouching alone in the bright
buttercup field of the moon;
and all the dogs in the world
howl at the hare in the moon.

"I chased that hare to the sky,"
the hungry dogs all cry.
"The hare jumped into the moon
and left me here in the cold.
I chased that hare to the moon."

"Come down again, mad hare,
we can see you there,"
the dogs all howl to the moon.
"Come down again to the world,
you mad black hare in the moon,

"or we will grow wings and fly
up to the star-grassed sky
to hunt you out of the moon,"
the hungry dogs of the world
howl at the hare in the moon.

To a Child

When I was a child I saw
a burning bird in a tree.
I see became *I am*,
I am became *I see*.

In winter dawns of frost
the lamp swung in my hand.
The battered moon on the slope
lay like a dune of sand;

and in the trap at my feet
the rabbit leapt and prayed,
weeping blood, and crouched
when the light shone on the blade.

The sudden sun lit up
the webs from wire to wire;
the white webs, the white dew,
blazed with a holy fire.

Flame of light in the dew,
flame of blood on the bush
answered the whirling sun
and the voice of the early thrush.

I think of this for you.
I would not have you believe
the world is empty of truth
or that men must grieve,

but hear the song of the martyrs
out of a bush of fire—
"All is consumed with love;
all is renewed with desire."

TWO SONGS FOR THE WORLD'S END

I

Bombs ripen on the leafless tree
under which the children play.
And there my darling all alone
dances in the spying day.

I gave her nerves to feel her pain,
I put her mortal beauty on.
I taught her love, that hate might find
its black work the easier done.

I sent her out alone to play;
and I must watch, and I must hear,
how underneath the leafless tree
the children dance and sing with Fear.

II

Lighted by the rage of time
where the blind and dying weep,
in my shadow take your sleep,
though wakeful I.

Sleep unhearing while I pray—
Should the red tent of the sky
fall to fold your time away,
wake to weep before you die.

Die believing all is true
that love your maker said to you.
Still believe
that had you lived you would have found
love, world, sight, sound,
sorrow, beauty—all true.
Grieve for death your moment—grieve.

The world, the lover you must take,
is the murderer you will meet.
But if you die before you wake
never think death sweet.

DROUGHT

The summer solstice come and gone,
now the dark of the moon comes on.
The raging sun in his pale sky
has drunk the sap of the world dry.
Across the plains the dustwhirls run
and dust has choked the shrivelling tree.

This is my world that dies with me,
cries the curlew in the night.
I have forgotten how the white
birdfooted water in the creek
used in spring to call and speak.
All is fallen under the sun
and the world dies that once I made.

The strength that brandished my green blade,
the force uncoiling from the cell,
drains like water from a wrecked well,
says the dried corn out of the earth.
The seed I cherished finds no birth.

Now the dark of the world comes on.

UNKNOWN WATER

No rain yet, and the creek drying, and no rain coming;
and I remember the old man, part of my childhood,
who knew all about cattle and horses. In the big drought,
he said, the mares knew when their milk gave out,
and I've seen a mare over the dead foal
with tears coming out of her eyes. She kept on standing;
she wouldn't go near water or look for grass,
and when the rain came she stayed where the foal died,
though we dragged it away and burned it.

Old man, go easy with me.
The truth I am trying to tell is a kind of waterhole
never dried in any drought. You can understand that;
you lived by a water not like the cattle drank,
but the water you knew of is dried up now. All dried,
and the drought goes raging on. Your own sons and
    daughters
have forgotten what it is to live by a water
that never dries up. But I know of another creek.
You will not understand my words when I tell of it.

You do not understand me; yet you are part of me.
You understand the cattle and the horses
and knew the country you travelled in, and believed
what everyone believed when you were a child.
And I believed in you, and otherwise in nothing,
since the drought was coming, that dried up your
    waterholes;
and I still believe in you, though you will not understand
    me.

For the country I travelled through was not your kind of
    country;
and when I grew I lost the sound of your stories
and heard only at night in my dreams the sound of dogs
and cattle and galloping horses. I am not you,
but you are part of me. Go easy with me, old man;
I am helping to clear a track to unknown water.

WALKER IN DARKNESS

The country where he lives is the country of no sight,
and no-man's-field is the black earth turned by his
    blade.
Men stand like trees asleep, a shade in a shade;
their fruit ripens and falls in the hot sun of the night
for him to find and eat.

The sea he swims in is the sea where other men drown;
the shore he walks is the white sand of their bones.
The forest is full of monsters and mad ferns,
and no man comes there but those who die, who mourn,
or who desire to be born.

Walker in darkness, the sun has gone out in my mind.
You carry your heart like a star, like a lamp in your hand.
But where shall I look for my light, and how shall I find
my heart in your dark land?

THE ANCESTORS

That stream ran through the sunny grass so clear—
more polished than dew is, all one lilt of light.
We found our way up to the source, where stand
the fern-trees locked in endless age
under the smothering vine and the tree's night.

Their slow roots spread in mud and stone,
and in each notched trunk shaggy as an ape
crouches the ancestor, the dark bent foetus,
unopened eyes, face fixed in unexperienced sorrow,
and body contorted in the fern-tree's shape.

That sad, pre-history, unexpectant face—
I hear the answering sound of my blood, I know
these primitive fathers waiting for rebirth,
these children not yet born—the womb holds so
the moss-grown patience of the skull,
the old ape-knowledge of the embryo.

Their silent sleep is gathered round the spring
that feeds the living, thousand-lighted stream
up which we toiled into this timeless dream.

THE FOREST PATH

When the path we followed began to tend downwards—
how it came about we hardly now remember—
we followed still, but we did not expect this,
the loss of self, the darkness and the forest.

Turning to each other in fear and question,
we saw in place of the column of the human body
the bole of tree overgrown, eaten by fern and lichen,
and heard instead of answer the wind in far-off leaves.

And when night fell the dark was scarcely closer.
We were afraid, straining in the bond of earth,
the nightmare weight, while round us lay that silence,
in which water somewhere fell with its own rhythm;
in which wind somewhere thrust against the height of
   leaves.

Familiar yet in terror; and the snake uncoiling
his venom out of our hollow hearts, and the bird
springing suddenly unseen from the upper branches
   singing—
all familiar as though remembered before birth
or expected dumbly after death.
Yet when the path led downwards we did not think of this.

And if we had not been afraid—if terror had not
taken over our minds and cruelty our hearts—
would we have found perhaps in the bewildering dark
not the death we thought of at first and almost hoped to
   find,
but the birth we never expected or desired?

Darkness of water falling in its own rhythm,
and underfoot the quiet corpse and seed
each strive to their own invisible consummation.

THE LOST MAN

To reach the pool you must go through the rain-forest—
   through the bewildering midsummer of darkness
lit with ancient fern,
laced with poison and thorn.
You must go by the way he went—the way of the bleeding
hands and feet, the blood on the stones like flowers,
under the hooded flowers
that fall on the stones like blood.

To reach the pool you must go by the black valley
among the crowding columns made of silence,
under the hanging clouds
of leaves and voiceless birds.
To go by the way he went to the voice of the water,
where the priest stinging-tree waits with his whips and
    fevers
under the hooded flowers
that fall from the trees like blood,

you must forget the song of the gold bird dancing
over tossed light; you must remember nothing
except the drag of darkness
that draws your weakness under.
To go by the way he went you must find beneath you
that last and faceless pool, and fall. And falling
find between breath and death
the sun by which you live.

THE TRAVELLER AND THE ANGEL

When I came to the strength of my youth
    I set out on my journey;
and on the far side of the ford
the angel waited.

His voice—himself invisible—
rang through my carefree thought—
"I am the first of your tasks.
Learn now your own strength."

And his hand on my shoulder
was like an awakening—
the challenge of his touch lit up
delight on delight in me.

How long it was that we wrestled
I hardly know—time waited
while through defeat on defeat
I reached my triumph.

Full-tested, the pride of my youth,
strained to each farthest limit,
found its strength made greater,
its courage tried and proved;

and all that fight was joy.
Shall I ever know joy fiercer?—
feeling the subtle angel
shift from one trial to another.

Marvellously and matched like lovers
we fought there by the ford,
till, every truth elicited,
I, unsurpassably weary,

felt with that weariness
darkness increase on my sight,
and felt the angel failing
in his glorious strength.

Altering, dissolving, vanishing,
he slipped through my fingers,
till when I groped for the death-blow,
I groped and could not find him.

But his voice on the air
pierced the depths of my heart.
"I was your strength; our battle
leaves you doubly strong.

"Now the way is open
and you must rise and find it—
the way to the next ford
where waits the second angel."

But weak with loss and fear
I lie still by the ford.
Now that the angel is gone
I am a man, and weary.

Return, angel, return.
I fear the journey.

THE GATEWAY

Through the gateway of the dead
(the traveller is speaking)
I kept my pride.
Stepping between those awful pillars
I knew that I myself
had imagined, acted,
and foreseen everything as it was here.

In the land of oblivion
among black-mouthed ghosts,
I knew my Self
the sole reality.

But this was not permitted;
the way went farther.
Stepping down
by the shadows of the river,
even that river
(soundless, invisible)
vanished; and the path dissolved,
and I, upon it.
Self, my justification,
sole lover, sole companion,
slipped from my side.

To say that I recall that time,
that country,
would be a lie; time was not,
and I nowhere.
Yet two things remain—
one was the last surrender,
and the other the last peace.
In the depth of nothing
I met my home.

All ended there;
yet all began.
All sank in dissolution
and rose renewed.

And the bright smoke
out of the pit of chaos
is the flowing and furious world.

And the mind's nightmare
is the world's sweet wellspring
(the traveller said).

The Two Fires

This world, which is the same for all, no one of gods or men has made; but it was ever, is now, and ever shall be an ever-living Fire, with measures of it kindling, and measures going out.

HERAKLEITOS, (Frag. 20, ed. Bywater) Burnet, *Early Greek Philosophy*, p. 134

THE TWO FIRES

A mong green shades and flowering ghosts, the
    remembrances of love,
inventions of the holy unwearying seed,
bright falling fountains made of time, that bore
through time the holy seed that knew no time—
I tell you, ghosts in the ghosts of summer days,
you are dead as though you never had been.
For time has caught on fire, and you too burn:
leaf, stem, branch, calyx and the bright corolla
are now the insubstantial wavering fire
in which love dies: the final pyre
of the beloved, the bridegroom and the bride.
These two we have denied.

In the beginning was the fire;
Out of the death of fire, rock and the waters;
and out of water and rock, the single spark, the divine
    truth.
Far, far below, the millions of rock-years divide
to make a place for those who were born and died
to build the house that held the bridegroom and the bride.
Those two, who reigned in passion in the flower,
whom still the hollow seasons celebrate,
no ritual now can recreate.
Whirled separate in the man-created fire
their cycles end, with the cycle of the holy seed;
the cycle from the first to the last fire.
These too time can divide;
these too have died.

And walking here among the dying centuries—
the centuries of moss, of fern, of cycad,
of the towering tree—the centuries of the flower—
I pause where water falls from the face of the rock.
My father rock, do you forget the kingdom of the fire?
The aeons grind you into bread—
into the soil that feeds the living and transforms the dead;
and have we eaten in the heart of the yellow wheat
the sullen unforgetting seed of fire?

And now, set free by the climate of man's hate,
that seed sets time ablaze.
The leaves of fallen years, the forest of living days,
have caught like matchwood. Look, the whole world burns.
The ancient kingdom of the fire returns.
And the world, that flower that housed the bridegroom and
    the bride,
burns on the breast of night.
The world's denied.

THE PRECIPICE

A t last it came into her mind, the answer.
She dressed the children, went out and hailed the
    driver.
There she sat holding them; looking through the window;
behaving like any woman, but she was no longer living.

To blame her would mean little; she had her logic,
the contained argument of the bomb, not even tragic,
to which each day had made its small addition
ending at last in this, which was completion.

There was no moon but she had brought her torch
and the dark of the mountain forest opened like flesh
before her purpose; possessed and intent as any lover
she fled along the path, the children with her.

So reaching the edge at last and no less certain
she took the children in her arms because she loved them
and jumped, parting the leaves and the night's curtain.

Now, and for years to come, that path is seared
by the blazing headlong torrent of their direction;
and we must hold our weathercock minds from turning
into its downward gale, towards destruction.

SILENCE

S ilence is the rock where I shall stand.
The silence between this and the next breath,
that might be—is not yet—death;
the silence between lover and lover
that neither flesh nor mind bridge over;
the silence between word and word,
in which the truth waits to be heard;
the silence between world and world
in which the promise first was sealed;
the heart's silence between beat and beat,
in which myself and silence meet.

Silence is the rock where I shall stand.
Oh, when I strike it with my hand
may the artesian waters spring
from that dark source I long to find.

RETURN

A far-off boat moves on the morning sea.
That broad and equal monotone of light
is drawn to focus; purpose enters in.
Its unity becomes duality,
and action scars perfection like a pin.

The mind in contemplation sought its peace—
that round and calm horizon's purity,
which, known one instant, must subsist always.
But life breaks in again, time does not cease;
that calm lies quiet under storms of days.

So moves in me time's purpose, evil and good.
Those silent tracts eternity may give;
but the lame shadow stumbles at my back,
still sick for love; the battle of flesh and blood
will hardly come to quiet while I live.

WEST WIND

The leaves that hurry on this black wind too early out of
    time
remind me that I am sad and tell me the reason why;
for to love in a time of hate and to live in a time of death
is lonely and dangerous as the last leaf on the tree
and wrenches the stem of the blood and twists the words
    from truth.

I am not afraid of you, snake in the flowering bush;
I am not afraid of the crow that sharpens his beak for his
    day.
But, legions of the living dead, your death has pulled me
    awry,
you withered by unseasonable winter, torn by the wind's
    lash;
for I am one of your kind and when you die I die.

I feel my mineral bones draw downward to the dark,
and the water and salt of my flesh flow out towards the
    wave;
and the legions of the living dead blow through me with
    my breath,
crying, "You will find no rest in time or being; forget to
    be—
blow as we do down the black wind into an easy grave."

WESTERN STAR

See, that is Venus shining.
Her clear sad light
falls like a thread of dew
to cool the droughts of the heart.

How long we have forgotten
in the neon night
the ritual phases of love!
Venus, too late,

too late, most lovely, most sad,
you touch our sight.
Your still small dew cannot quench
the hellfire blaze of the heart.

TWO GENERATIONS

What do you learn of the world? I hold your hand,
and country flower and city face
leave signs in you, and you become
interpreter to griefs I cannot mend—
your time's not mine, your place strange to my place.
We share this only—this that you will grow to
understand—
the intolerable bright destruction of all time and place.

This is what I can neither bear nor heal
for you—that the fierce various street,
the country tower of tree and bell of bird,
are blown aside a little by the venomous wind
that twitches at the curtain over hell:
are blown aside a little and reveal
what you and I and all men dare not meet—
the seen invisible, the soundless heard,
the wavering ghost of fire that fumes behind.
And the world settles back. But our eyes meet;
and then my eyes must fall.

What do you learn of the world? I hold your hand;
but even my touch is cancelled by that wind;
because the wind is my own breath,
whispering that the heart of man condemns the world to
death.

SEARCHLIGHT PRACTICE

So simple the hour seems,
the night so clear;
if sight could teach us peace
we might learn here

to set ourselves aside,
to be alone,
to let the earth bear us
like a flower or a stone;

to let the hands fall,
the mind forget;
to move like trees in the wind;
to be the night.

Escape the angel? Escape
the bond, the curse?

Great swords in front of the stars
spring up and cross.

FOR THE LOVED AND THE UNLOVED

Love in his alteration
invents the heart to suit him:
its season, spring or autumn,
depends on his decision.

The rose he sets his light in
increases by his brooding.
What colour the sepal's hiding
not even the tree is certain.

The bud bowed in and folded
round love's illumination
works by a light no vision
into our world has welded;

and nerve and artery follow
a track no mind is treading:
and what's the compass guiding
the far-returning swallow?

The roads unwind within us.
It is not time's undone us,
but we ourselves, who ravel
the thread by which we travel.

DIALOGUE

Above the child the cliffs of the years tower.
He dares not stop to play, he must climb higher.
The rotting ladders sway beneath his weight
and the winds rise and cry and storm comes nearer.
Oh, passionate gazer, oh enraptured hearer,
oh eager climber, perhaps you climb too late.

Perhaps from the stone peak worn down and trodden
by worshipping generations, the view is hidden.
Nothing but thundering storm and blowing mist
will greet you; and the night will come to blind you
and the last ladder crumble and break behind you—
oh wait, my darling. The world you seek is lost.

Even if the cloud parted and in the dying
light of evening you saw that landscape lying,
you would see a paper map, a country of lost hopes;
seas scrawled by a million courses, ink-dried rivers,
and deserts littered with the bones of the world's lovers.
Turn back, my darling. Play for ever on these gentle slopes.

—"You do not know. You cannot hear the call,
nor see the face that leans from the cliff-wall.
You must not hold me, though you speak in kindness.
There waits, hidden beyond the known and charted,
World, the secret one, the flower-hearted—
her terrible innocence the measure of your blindness."

The Man beneath the Tree

Nothing is so far as truth;
nothing is so plain to see.
Look where light has married earth
through the green leaves on the tree.

Nothing is so hard as love—
love for which the wisest weep;
yet the child who never looked
found it easily in his sleep.

Nothing is as strange as love—
love is like a foreign land.
Yet its natives find their way
natural as hand-in-hand.

Nothing is so bare as truth—
that lean geometry of thought;
but round its poles there congregate
all foliage, flowers and fruits of earth.

Oh, love and truth and I should meet,
sighed the man beneath the tree;
but where should our acquaintance be?
Between your hat and the soles of your feet,
sang the bird on top of the tree.

Cyclone and Aftermath

Hooded shadows out of a universe of weeping
crouch on the gale through the rack of trees; repetitive
of disaster, procession of fugitives. Vanishing
downhill each on the vanishing heel of the other
they form and are gone.

                    Nothing else visible
but the despair of trees against wind.
                    Navigators
wise to this coast are careful of these months,
but there is nothing that the tall rose-gums,
annually betrayed by summer's languors
into an overplus of leaves, can do about it.
Misfortune ruins their pride. They implore and gesture—
bent on the wheel, spring up in a moment's mercy
and with flung arms accuse her, betrayer, destroyer,
from whose inescapable injustice the hooded shadows fly.

Drenched flowers, bruised unripe fruit, limb wrenching the
    wound—
all that summer contrived of cunning ornament
tossed drowning, the old witch is furious still,
aiming and pelting water and air in unbreathable mixture,
till entity fades to ghost, labouring to hold a shape
against the universal wet—a shape that frays into water,
bruises into water at a touch, snaps at a pull.

This is her cruelty—that she has hung decay
like lace over the laughing brides of summer.
Fungus and mould spread their webs in the hush when the
    wind has fallen
and the tree fallen; the tall tree that meditated
dance after dance for white limbs crossing in winds
is dissolved in intent silence;
that lovely building debased, that tower pulled down.

This is her wisdom: she is not one thing nor the other.
Praise her if you like in the season of flower and serenity,
for it is hers: reproach her, oppressor of those
weeping swift-running shadows: it's she you are speaking of.

But look for her, too, when evening darkens and wind
    drops.
The shattered flowers melt into industrious earth;
the heron watches the pool, the high clouds stand
arena for the light's farewell. She is that figure
drawing the twilight's hood about her:
that wise woman from the land past joy or grief.

FOR PRECISION

Yet I go on from day to day, betraying
    the core of light, the depth of darkness—
my speech inexact, the note not right,
never quite sure what I am saying—

on the periphery of truth. Uphold me now,
pure colours, blacks, whites, bells on the central tone,
middays, midnights. I wander among cross-lights.
Let me be sure and economical as the rayed
suns, stars, flowers, wheels: let me fall as a gull, a hawk

through the confusions of foggy talk,
and pin with one irremediable stroke—
what?—the escaping wavering wandering light,
the blur, the brilliance; forming into one chord
what's separate and distracted; making the vague hard—
catching the wraith—speaking with a pure voice,
and that the gull's sole note like a steel nail
that driven through cloud, sky, and irrelevant seas,
joins all, gives all a meaning, makes all whole.

NAMELESS FLOWER

Three white petals float
above the green.
You cannot think they spring from it
till the fine stem's seen.

So separated each from each,
and each so pure,
yet at the centre here they touch
and form a flower.

Flakes that drop at the flight of a bird
and have no name,
I'll set a word upon a word
to be your home.

Up from the dark and jungle floor
you have looked long.
Now I come to lock you here
in a white song.

Word and word are chosen and met.
Flower, come in.
But before the trap is set,
the prey is gone.

The words are white as a stone is white
carved for a grave;
but the flower blooms in immortal light,
Being now; being love.

BREATH

I turned to the dark window;
outside were stars and frost.
My breath went out to the night
shaped like a cloud or a mist.
Small and soulless ghost,
what was it my heart meant
that, watching the way you went,
it moved so under my breast?

SCRIBBLY-GUM

The cold spring falls from the stone.
I passed and heard
the mountain, palm and fern
spoken in one strange word.
The gum-tree stands by the spring.
I peeled its splitting bark
and found the written track
of a life I could not read.

FLYING-FOX ON BARBED WIRE

Little nightmare flying-fox
  trapped on the cruel barbs of day
has no weapon but a wing
and a tiny scream.
Here's a patch of night, a thing
that looks by daylight like a hoax;
dawn wouldn't let it fly away
with its kin into a dream,
but stabbed with a pin its velvet hand
and hung it in a hostile land.

Imp from the world of upside-down,
here's some darkness in a bag
to foil your frightened needle-bite.
Now we can untie
from the staring stake of pain
your black claw on its velvet rag.
Scramble, silent, out of the light
and hang by your feet in the kind-leaved tree.
Gargoyle, thief, forget your grief
and go to your country night; and we,
accomplice to day's enemy,
too must forget
that we and the Devil ever met.

GUM-TREES STRIPPING

S ay the need's born within the tree,
and waits a trigger set for light;
say sap is tidal like the sea,
and rises with the solstice-heat—
but wisdom shells the words away
to watch this fountain slowed in air
where sun joins earth—to watch the place
at which these silent rituals are.

Words are not meanings for a tree.
So it is truer not to say,
"These rags look like humility,
or this year's wreck of last year's love,
or wounds ripped by the summer's claw."
If it is possible to be wise
here, wisdom lies outside the word
in the earlier answer of the eyes.

Wisdom can see the red, the rose,
the stained and sculptured curve of grey,
the charcoal scars of fire, and see
around that living tower of tree
the hermit tatters of old bark
split down and strip to end the season;
and can be quiet and not look
for reasons past the edge of reason.

Seven Songs from a Journey

I   Carnarvon Range

Carnarvon Creek
and cliffs of Carnarvon,
your tribes are silent;
I will sing for you—
each phrase
the size of a stone;
a red stone,
a white stone,
a grey,
and a purple;
a parrot's cry
from a blossoming tree,
a scale of water
and wavering light—
each word a sign
to set on your cliffs,
each phrase a stone
to lie in your waters.
A white orchid
from the cave's shade,
a fish from your waters
clearer than green—
I shall take these two
in exchange for a song,
Carnarvon Creek
and cliffs of Carnarvon.

II Brigalow Country

When the metal-blue moon
plays tunes on the hut-roof,
and the long slope darkens
with its brigalow tribe,
then Margery dances,
awkward as an emu—
dances for the useless
coin of the moon.

Haunted and alone
with the tribe of the brigalows,
their steel-coloured leaves
as curved as a skinning-knife,
her sidelong eye
as queer as the moonlight,
Margery dances
to the singing of the dingoes.

Living lost and lonely
with the tribe of the brigalows,
don't want to stay
but never can go.
Never get no money
for when I go hungry,
never get no kisses
for when I feel sad—
rooted like the brigalows
until I'm dead.

When the bright tin moon
plays tunes on the hut-roof
Margery dances
in her long pale hair.
And the tribe of the brigalows
drop their shadows
like still black water,
and watch her there.

III NIGHT

The contours of night are like
the contours of this rock,
and worn by light as by water.

The pin-sharp stars drag
their thin bright trails across it.
The moon's pale creek and the floods
of the sunlight erode it;
and round its secret flanks
the currents of the living—
plant, beast, man, and god—
swirl their phosphorescence.

Night is what remains
when the equation is finished.
Night is the earth's dream
that the sun is dead.
Night is man's dream
that he has invented God—
the dream of before-creation;
the dream of falling.

Night blocks our way, saying,
I at least am real.

The contours of night are like
the contours of this rock.

IV THE PROSPECTOR

Full moon's too bright for sleeping;
I'll watch her rise
on the range where no bird's speaking
except in the crow's voice—
on the land to be won by love only;
and here there's none
but the fire's black kiss, and the lonely
print of skull and bone.

Rise up and walk, old skeleton.
But no: lie still.
Let no phase of the moon disturb you,
no heats recall.
Let the bones dream on, the kind dream
that was their last—
dream the mirage's river
has quenched the world's thirst.

Full moon's too bright for sleeping—
too white the sky.
And foreign to this country
restless I lie.
But you, moon—you're no stranger.
You're known here, moon;
drawing your mad hands over
rock, dust and bone.

V   CANEFIELDS

The coloured girl leans on the bridge,
folding her sorrow into her breast.
Her face is a dark and downward mirror
where her eyes look, and are lost.

The old land is marshalled under
the heavy regiment of green cane;
but by the lagoon the paperbarks
unroll their blank and tattered parchment,
waiting for some unknown inscription
which love might make in ink-dark water.

And in that water the great lily
sets her perfect dusk-blue petals
in their inherited order of prayer
around that blazing throne, her centre.
There time shall meet eternity
and her worship find its answer.

Mountain, wall and tree
bear witness against our lives,
being scrawled with obsolete slogans—
initialled by clumsy knives:
No one has marked the sea.

Below high tide you can stand
as though you stood in the sky.
No sign on the clean sand
will stay to remember you by.

Sea, anonymous pilgrim
made free of time and place,
from the unhistoried poles
and the shores of Asia and Greece

you carry no memory,
you bear no symbol or gift,
except the unshaped bone,
the silver splinter of raft.

And though you beckon and play,
we will not stay here long.
We will snatch back the child
who trusts too far to your song.

The sea cleans everything,
a sailor said to me:
and these white empty shells
come out of the scour of the sea.

VII MOUNT MARY

The solitary mountain is as tall as grief—
a figure in an estranged landscape, drawing
her biblical blue cloak across her shoulders.
Age and the sun have worn her barren;
even the one small creek of her tears is drying;
and the crows haunt her, crying her name,
like birds blackened by hell-fire—crying and flying.

The mountain sits among rocks, and over her head
noonday's white skull-moon hangs dead.
Nothing is left for her to dream on, virgin
and widow, except the few small pools of her tears,
rock-bound and sunk, that will not reach the sea.

But by those pools I found two trees in flower.
One wept long branches full of withering stars,
and one, naked of leaves, held up a crown;
a great fierce blossom yellow as the sun
taken out of the sky at his heat's thirsty noon.

SANCTUARY

The road beneath the giant original trees
sweeps on and cannot wait. Varnished by dew,
its darkness mimics mirrors and is bright
behind the panic eyes the driver sees
caught in headlights. Behind his wheels the night
takes over: only the road ahead is true.
It knows where it is going: we go too.

Sanctuary, the sign said. Sanctuary—
trees, not houses; flat skins pinned to the road
of possum and native cat; and here the old tree stood
for how many thousand years?—that old gnome-tree
some axe-new boy cut down. Sanctuary, it said:
but only the road has meaning here. It leads
into the world's cities like a long fuse laid.

Fuse, nerve, strand of a net, tense
bearer of messages, snap-tight violin-string,
dangerous knife-edge laid across the dark,
what has that sign to do with you? The immense
tower of antique forest and cliff, the rock
where years accumulate like leaves, the tree
where transient bird and mindless insect sing?
The word the board holds up is Sanctuary
and the road knows that notice-boards make sense

but has no time to pray. Only, up there,
morning sets doves upon the power-line.
Swung on that fatal voltage like a sign
and meaning love, perhaps they are a prayer.

AT COOLOOLAH

The blue crane fishing in Cooloolah's twilight
has fished there longer than our centuries.
He is the certain heir of lake and evening,
and he will wear their colour till he dies,

but I'm a stranger, come of a conquering people.
I cannot share his calm, who watch his lake,
being unloved by all my eyes delight in,
and made uneasy, for an old murder's sake.

Those dark-skinned people who once named Cooloolah
knew that no land is lost or won by wars,
for earth is spirit: the invader's feet will tangle
in nets there and his blood be thinned by fears.

Riding at noon and ninety years ago,
my grandfather was beckoned by a ghost—
a black accoutred warrior armed for fighting,
who sank into bare plain, as now into time past.

White shores of sand, plumed reed and paperbark,
clear heavenly levels frequented by crane and swan—
I know that we are justified only by love,
but oppressed by arrogant guilt, have room for none.

And walking on clean sand among the prints
of bird and animal, I am challenged by a driftwood spear
thrust from the water; and, like my grandfather,
must quiet a heart accused by its own fear.

LANDSCAPES

To look at landscapes loved by the newly dead
is to move into the dark and out again.
Every brilliant leaf that lives by light
dies from its hold at last and desires earth's bed:
men and trees and grasses daily falling
make that veil of beauty for her. Slight
aeons of soil on rock, of grass on soil, of men
standing on grass, can't hide her outcrops. Stone—
stone our mother locks in, tongueless, without feeling,
our far blind brothers, future, and past who had no luck
and never was born. And now the newly dead
is lowered there. Now we weep for eyes whose look
is closed on landscapes loved, and at last known.

THE WATTLE-TREE

The tree knows four truths—
earth, water, air, and the fire of the sun.
The tree holds four truths in one.
Root, limb and leaf unfold
out of the seed, and these rejoice
till the tree dreams it has a voice
to join four truths in one great word of gold.

—Oh, that I knew that word!
I should cry loud, louder than any bird.
O let me live for ever, I would cry.
For that word makes immortal what would wordless die;
and perfectly, and passionately,
welds love and time into the seed,
till tree renews itself and is for ever tree—

Then upward from the earth
               and from the water,
then inward from the air
               and the cascading light
poured gold, till the tree trembled with its flood.

Now from the world's four elements I make
my immortality; it shapes within the bud.
Yes, now I bud, and now at last I break
into the truth I had no voice to speak:
into a million images of the Sun, my God.

... AND MR FERRITT

B ut now Mr Ferritt
with his troublesome nose,
with his shaven chin
and his voice like a grief
that grates in dark corners,
moves in his house
and scrapes his dry skin
and sees it is morning.

O day, you sly thief,
now what have you taken
of all the small things
I tie on my life?
The radio serial
whines in the kitchen,
caught in a box,
and cannot get out.
The finch in his cage,
the border of phlox

as straight as a string
drawn up in my garden,
the potted geranium,
all are there.
But day from his cranium
twitches one hair;
and never again
will a hair grow there.
— O day, you sly thief,
how you pluck at my life,
frets Mr Ferritt;
but there, he must bear it.

Outside the fence
the wattle-tree grows.
It tosses; it shines;
it speaks its one word.
Beware, beware!
Mr Ferritt has heard.
— What are axes for?
What are fences for?
Who planted that wattle-tree
right at my door?
God only knows.
All over the garden
its dust is shaken.
No wonder I sneeze
as soon as I waken.

O world, you sly thief;
my youth you have taken,
and what have you given
who promised me heaven,
but a nagging wife
and a chronic catarrh,
and a blonde on the pictures
as far as a star?

And wild and gold
as a film-star's hair
that tree stands there,
blocking the view
from my twenty-perch block.
What are axes for,
what are fences for
but to keep this tree
away from my door?

And down came the tree.
But poor Mr Ferritt
still has hay-fever.
Nothing will cure it.

FLESH

I THE HAND

Put your hand out, and hold it still, and look.
Like something wild picked up and held too long
it loses truth; light fades on the stopped wing.
Infinite cleverness pivoted on a clever stalk,
it lives in time and space, and there is strong;
but draw it outside doing into being,
it pales and withers like a sea-star dying.

The hand is drawn from the flesh by its own uses.
Powers unchannelled, shapes unshaped await it;
and what has long since happened and been completed
lies in it and directs its bone and chooses
stress and muscle. Textures thrust to meet it,
for it is their answer; stuff that cannot move
moves under the hand that is all it knows of love.

Do not look at me, the hand says. I am not true
except as means. I am the road, the bridge,
not starting-point nor goal nor traveller.
I am not you, the doer, nor what you do.
I am extension; I am your farthest edge.
I am that which strokes the child's hair, tenderly—
    tenderly—
and drives the nail into the hand stretched on the tree.
My shape is action. Look away. Do not look at me.

II THE BODY

I am the depth below. You would do well
to look down, sometimes. I can be your tree,
solid in the gale—if you consent to be flower,
seed, and fruit. But you don't believe in me
except as crass and suffering and to be suffered,
or instrument of your uncertain love.

I am your notion of hell
and your tool for discovering heaven. But perched on me
you lean out with your arrogant polished eye—
trying to be God. Look down; remember where you are.
I am the strata that reach from earth to star
and the great cliff down which your father Adam fell.

You would do well to look down.
More was built into me than quickset night.
God walked through all my ages. He set in me
the key that fits the keyhole; use it right
and eternity's lightning splits the rock of time.
And there I was begun and so begotten
in that unspeakable heart of flame.
From that light where flesh on flesh was welded
the world itself unfolded.
Look down through me on the light you have forgotten.

I am your blundering kind companion.
I am your home that keeps out bitter weather.
I am the perilous slow deposit of time's wisdom.
You are my threat, my murder. And yet, remember.
I am yourself. Come, let us live together.

III   THE FACE

The face turns inward and down
on the head's bud;
curves to its inner world
of shaping flesh and blood;
is closed like an eyelid; blind;
is made before its mind.

Birth draws the stalk out straight
and the face wakes.
Naked in a passion of light
its long composure breaks.
It writhes to regain sleep;
but life has stung too deep,

and flesh has now become
time's instrument
for the first task that is set
and the easiest learnt.
Two shapes obsess it; need,
and the need satisfied.

The mirror answers the face:
an animal in a cave
that lusts and tastes and sings.
A hill that breathes the air;
a glance that looks for love;
two crystals where all things
leech at the panes and stare.

What shall the face pursue
that drinks all time and event
and changes as it drinks?
What was it the flesh meant
foreshadowing in the womb
the person not yet come?

The face that turns to the world
opens itself to ask.
Look at it now, before
it learns it is a mask:
for eyes take light like dew
while their glance is new.

It takes out of the air
all it can know.
Whatever look turns on it,
that look it will grow.
So some learn love, and some
can never find a home.

The face becomes its world.
It is the moving field
printed by days grown common
and the unmastered night—
by unacknowledged need
and fear of its own deed:

yet knows that there have been,
flowering the world's dull years,
faces more true than stars
and made of purer light;
and they may happen again.
O may they happen again.

THE CUP

Silence is harder, Una said.
If I could be quiet I might come true
like the blue cup hung over the sink,
which is not dead,
but waiting for someone to fill it and drink.

Una said, Silence can reach my mouth:
but a long way in my trouble lies.
The look in my eyes, the sound of my words
all tell the truth:
they spring from my trouble like a flight of birds.

Let silence travel, Una said,
by every track of nerve and vein
to heart and brain, where the troubles begin.
Then I shan't be dead,
but waiting for something to come in.

TWO OLD MEN

I

The rusty iron hut, the sunk slab chimney,
the china-roses running wild in grass untended,
the path gone under, the paneless windows blank—
but they are not deserted. Not quite deserted.

Hidden by those pink roses, beside that jarred grey door,
Matt Freestone sits. All day? Perhaps all night;
for night and day are one. And looks? If he is there at all,
he watches the wild young river. Green gorge, blue spur,
run back into the cleft sky. He drinks the sunlight's
mazed and heavy honey, the river's rush, the wrangle
of edged slate shingle on rock. His white hair blows
round a face like a china rose, like an old, old child,
sins washed in river and air, mind washed away.

And as he sits his name
becomes himself, a stone, a smooth free stone
harassed by nothing but the flood's brown fretting manes of
    water.

And we, the travellers on the road and somewhere bound,
wonder where we are bound, to what wheel's round—
since he is free, not owning nor desiring,
not thinking nor fearing, not counting and not daring.
Age and life lived unchain him, set before him
his time of silent freedom. What need now to be human?
The rose, the river shade him. He is a stone.

II

Old Gustav sings on Endless Creek,
"The spotted-gums are stripping down,
the yellow box in flower again,
all as it was in the old joy
that time first made when time was long,
and I a boy—and I a boy.

"Love is various as the sea,
and many shapes can death put on.
May not the white-ant love the tree?
and the strangler-fig has a woman's arms.
Whatever made the world, it seems,
will not change till time is done.

"As innocent as the yellow-box flower,
as deadly as the brown snake's fang,
it has the thunder's word to speak,
and the weebill's tiny song.
It grows in me with sorrow and joy.
It sets the cancer in my side.
And it will bring, when I have died,
the box to flower on Endless Creek
as once it flowered, and I a boy."

TO A CHILD OUTSIDE TIME*

In the legendary years long past, of the flowering tree,
when first you stirred in my dreams,
no face limited the look you turned on me.
Only your gentle weight upon my arms
stayed like a blessing far into the day.
My fruit, fall from me now—hang no longer there
stretched on my body's cross, withered by my breath's
    furnace-air.

The buds of the flowering tree wavered away
grey and vanishing like the smoke from the rifles.
All my veins' branches withered
as the blood gathered into the shelter of my heart—
as in the shelter of my own death I hid—
hid myself and came out living.

Oh forgive me that when I knew my seven-times-sentenced
    life
reserved and saved from all that death
to be your prison, gentle one—unseen child—
for love of you I denied you the food of my flesh.

---

* This poem is based on the case-history of a survivor of the destruction of the Warsaw ghetto, given by Dr H. B. M. Murphy in an article, "Displaced Persons", in the Australian Quarterly, vol. xxiv, No. I.

Forgive my tenderness: forgive my love: forgive.
If I had let you learn to live,
believe that I believed I would deserve
that which, alone, there can be now between us—
the inconsolable silence of your hatred.

FOR A BIRTHDAY

(*to J. P. McK.*)

Bind—that word was spoken,
and there was I bound.
The rope can no more be broken
that then wrapped me round.

Live, I was commanded.
O life, your touch was strange.
There the flesh was founded
that bodies my change.

Act—my blood told me.
And so time began;
time, that now has filled me
with the whole world of man.

Love, from its unknown centre,
spins a silence like thought;
and deep there as the heart can enter
my wholeness I sought.

Decay; upon my body
that summons was served;
and now the flesh speaks sadly,
How can we be saved?

Build, though the world be falling,
that crystal, your truth.
Its eight sides shall be your dwelling
though time take your breath.

IN PRAISE OF MARRIAGES

Not till life halved, and parted
one from the other,
did time begin, and knowledge;
sorrow, delight.
Terror of being apart, being lost,
made real the night.
Seeking and finding made
yesterday, now and tomorrow.
And love was realized first
when those two came together.

So, perilously joined,
lighted in one small room,
we have made all things true.
Out of the I and the you
spreads this field of power,
that all that waits may come,
all possibles be known—
all futures step from their stone
and pasts come into flower.

REQUEST TO A YEAR

If the year is meditating a suitable gift,
I should like it to be the attitude
of my great-great-grandmother,
legendary devotee of the arts,

who, having had eight children
and little opportunity for painting pictures,
sat one day on a high rock
beside a river in Switzerland

and from a difficult distance viewed
her second son, balanced on a small ice-floe,
drift down the current towards a waterfall
that struck rock-bottom eighty feet below,

while her second daughter, impeded,
no doubt, by the petticoats of the day,
stretched out a last-hope alpenstock
(which luckily later caught him on his way).

Nothing, it was evident, could be done;
and with the artist's isolating eye
my great-great-grandmother hastily sketched the scene.
The sketch survives to prove the story by.

Year, if you have no Mother's day present planned;
reach back and bring me the firmness of her hand.

STORM

On the headland's grassed and sheltered side,
out of the wind I crouch and watch
while driven by the seaward ship-destroying storm
races of insane processional breakers come.
A long-dead divine authority reflows the tide
at evening, and already the gnawed hill of beach
alters and shrinks. The waves cry out: Let us be done.

Let us be done with the long submission, the whips—
that hurl us for ever on time's frigid stone
mouthing our ever-repeated plea for an answer and getting
     none.
Let us break free, smash down the land's gate
and drown all questions under a black flood.
Hate, then, the waves cry: hate.

And round each headland of the world, each drenching
  rock,
crowding each wild spray-drop, as in the womb's calm
  lying,
they beat and whirl on the waves, the invisible legion
of momentary crystals, less-than-a-second's-tick
lives, love's first and everywhere creation;
so small, so strong, that nothing of all this mad rock-torn
surge and violence, not the storm's final desperation
touches them,
busy in the unhurt stillness, breeding and dying.

SONG

O where does the dancer dance—
 the invisible centre spin—
whose bright periphery holds
the world we wander in?

For it is he we seek—
the source and death of desire;
we blind as blundering moths
around that heart of fire.

Caught between birth and death
we stand alone in the dark
to watch the blazing wheel
on which the earth is a spark,

crying, Where does the dancer dance—
the terrible centre spin,
whose flower will open at last
to let the wanderer in?

WILDFLOWER PLAIN

The angry granite,
the hungry range,
must crumble away,
must melt and change;
forget the single
iron word
that no voice spoke
when no ear heard,
and learn this thorny,
delicate, tender
speech of the flower
as last surrender.
This various speech
that covers over
the gravel plain
like the words of a lover.

Blue orchid gentle
as skies seen early;
blown purple iris
so quick to wither;
tea-tree falling
on water-lily;
heath, boronia,
many another,
can but spring
where rock makes way.
Let rock be humble.
Let it decay.
Let time's old anger
become new earth,
to sign to the heart
the truth of death.

THE HARP AND THE KING

Old king without a throne,
    the hollow of despair
behind his obstinate unyielding stare,
knows only, God is gone:
and, fingers clenching on his chair,
feels night and the soul's terror coming on.

Bring me that harp, that singer. Let him sing.
Let something fill the space inside the mind,
that's a dry stream-bed for the flood of fear.
Song's only sound; but it's a lovely sound,
a fountain through the drought. Bring David here,
said the old frightened king.

Sing something. Comfort me.
Make me believe the meaning in the rhyme.
The world's a traitor to the self-betrayed;
but once I thought there was a truth in time,
while now my terror is eternity.
So do not take me outside time.
Make me believe in my mortality,
since that is all I have, the old king said.

I sing the praise of time, the harp replied:
the time of aching drought when the black plain
cannot believe in roots or leaves or rain.
Then lips crack open in the stone-hard peaks;
and rock begins to suffer and to pray
when all that lives has died
and withered in the wind and blown away;
and earth has no more strength to bleed.

I sing the praise of time and of the rain—
the word creation speaks.
Four elements are locked in time;
the sign that makes them fertile is the seed,
and this outlasts all death and springs again,
the running water of the harp-notes cried.

But the old king sighed obstinately,
How can that comfort me?
Night and the terror of the soul come on,
and out of me both water and seed have gone.
What other generations shall I see?
But make me trust my failure and my fall,
said the sad king, since these are now my all.

I sing the praise of time, the harp replied.
In time we fail, alone with hours and tears,
ruin our followers and traduce our cause,
and give our love its last and fatal hurt.
In time we fail and fall.
In time the company even of God withdraws
and we are left with our own murderous heart.

Yet it is time that holds,
somewhere although not now,
the peal of trumpets for us; time that bears,
made fertile even by those tears,
even by this darkness, even by this loss,
incredible redemptions—hours that grow,
as trees grow fruit, in a blind holiness,
the truths unknown, the loves unloved by us.

But the old king turned his head sullenly.
How can that comfort me,
who sees into the heart as deep as God can see?
Love's sown in us; perhaps it flowers; it dies.
I failed my God and I betrayed my love.
Make me believe in treason; that is all I have.

This is the praise of time, the harp cried out—
that we betray all truths that we possess.
Time strips the soul and leaves it comfortless
and sends it thirsty through a bone-white drought.
Time's subtler treacheries teach us to betray.
What else could drive us on our way?
Wounded we cross the desert's emptiness,
and must be false to what would make us whole.
For only change and distance shape for us
some new tremendous symbol for the soul.

FROM

Birds

1962

for Meredith

THE PEACOCK

S hame on the aldermen who locked
the Peacock in a dirty cage!
His blue and copper sheens are mocked
by habit, hopelessness and age.

The weary Sunday families
along their gravelled paths repeat
the pattern of monotonies
that he treads out with restless feet.

And yet the Peacock shines alone;
and if one metal feather fall
another grows where that was grown.
Love clothes him still, in spite of all.

How pure the hidden spring must rise
that time and custom cannot stain!
It speaks its joy again—again.
Perhaps the aldermen are wise.

THE BLUE WRENS AND THE BUTCHER-BIRD

S weet and small the blue wren
whistles to his gentle hen,
"The creek is full, the day is gold,
the tale of love is never told.
Fear not, my love, nor fly away,
for safe, safe in the blackthorn-tree
we shall build our nest today.
Trust to me, oh trust to me."

Cobwebs they gather and dry grass,
greeting each other as they pass
up to the nest and down again,
the blue wren and the brown wren.
They seek and carry far and near,
down the bank and up the hill,
until that crystal note they hear
that strikes them dumb and holds them still.

Great glorious passion of a voice—
sure all that hear it must rejoice.
But in the thorn-bush silent hide
the nest-builders side by side.
"The blue wren's nestlings and his wife,
and he himself, that sprig of blue,
I shall kill, and hang them safe—
the blackthorn spears shall run them through."

Still and still the blue wren
sits beside his cowering hen.
There they wait like stone by stone
until the butcher-bird is gone.
Then soft and sweet the blue wren
twitters to his anxious hen,
"Trust to me, oh trust to me;
I know another blackthorn-tree."

EGGS AND NESTLINGS

The moss-rose and the palings made
a solemn and a waiting shade
where eagerly the mother pressed
a sheltering curve into her nest.

Her tranced eye, her softened stare,
warned me when I saw her there,
and perfect as the grey nest's round,
three frail and powdered eggs I found.

My mother called me there one day.
Beneath the nest the eggshells lay,
and in it throbbed the triple greed
of one incessant angry need.

Those yellow gapes, those starveling cries,
how they disquieted my eyes!—
the shapeless furies come to be
from shape's most pure serenity.

WINTER KESTREL

Fierce with hunger and cold
all night in the windy tree
the kestrel to the sun cries,
"Oh bird in the egg of the sea,

"break out, and tower, and hang
high, oh most high,
and watch for the running mouse
with your unwearying eye;

"and I shall hover and hunt,
and I shall see him move,
and I like a bolt of power
shall seize him from above.

"Break from your blue shell,
you burning Bird or God,
and light me to my kill—
and you shall share his blood."

CURRAWONG

The currawong has shallow eyes—
bold shallow buttons of yellow glass
that see all round his sleek black skull.
Small birds sit quiet when he flies;
mothers of nestlings cry *Alas!*
He is a gangster, his wife's a moll.

But I remember long ago
(a child beside the seldom sea)
the currawongs as wild as night
quarrelling, talking, crying so,
in the scarlet-tufted coral-tree;
and past them that blue stretch of light,

the ocean with its dangerous song.
Robber then and robber still,
he cries now with the same strange word
(*currawong—currawong*)
that from those coxcomb trees I heard.
Take my bread and eat your fill,
bold, cruel and melodious bird.

THE SWAMP PHEASANT

The swamp pheasant was wide awake
when the dawn-star came up new.
He scrambled up the garden gate
and made green tracks in the web-white dew.

All round the lawn he ran and peered;
he found a lizard under a stone;
he found a tiny wart-eyed toad—
one scuffle and it was gone.

Then out came our cat Violet,
one eye half-closed from many a fight.
He combed from his whisker a mouse's fur,
and breathed the air with calm delight.

The swamp pheasant looks and sees
a tiger made in pheasant-size—
runs to the fence and scrambles out,
while Violet squints his scornful eyes.

And I lean out and laugh to see
that queer old woman cross the street,
holding her brown skirts high behind
and scuttling on her long black feet.

THORNBILLS

Their tiny torrent of flight
sounds in the trees like rain,
flicking the leaves to the light—
a scattered handful of grain,
the thornbills little as bees.

I hear in the blowing trees
the sudden tune of their song.
Pray that the hawk not sees,
who has scanned the wind so long
for his small living food.

Oh let no enemies
drink the quick wine of blood
that leaps in their pulse of praise.
Wherever a trap is set
may they slip through the mesh of the net.
Nothing should do them wrong.

BLACK-SHOULDERED KITE

Carved out of strength, the furious kite
shoulders off the wind's hate.
The black mark that bars his white
is the pride and hunger of Cain.
Perfect, precise, the angry calm
of his closed body, that snow-storm—
of his still eye that threatens harm.
Hunger and force his beauty made
and turned a bird to a knife-blade.

EGRETS

Once as I travelled through a quiet evening,
I saw a pool, jet-black and mirror-still.
Beyond, the slender paperbarks stood crowding;
each on its own white image looked its fill,
and nothing moved but thirty egrets wading—
thirty egrets in a quiet evening.

Once in a lifetime, lovely past believing,
your lucky eyes may light on such a pool.
As though for many years I had been waiting,
I watched in silence, till my heart was full
of clear dark water, and white trees unmoving,
and, whiter yet, those thirty egrets wading.

"DOVE—LOVE"

The dove purrs—over and over the dove
    purrs its declaration. The wind's tone
changes from tree to tree, the creek on stone
alters its sob and fall, but still the dove
goes insistently on, telling its love
        "I could eat you."

And in captivity, they say, doves do.
Gentle, methodical, starting with the feet
(the ham-pink succulent toes
on their thin stems of rose),
baring feather by feather the wincing meat:
        "I could eat you."

That neat suburban head, that suit of grey,
watchful conventional eye and manicured claw—
these also rhyme with us. The doves play
on one repetitive note that plucks the raw
helpless nerve, their soft "I do. I do.
        I could eat you."

MIGRANT SWIFT

Beneath him slid the furrows of the sea;
    against his sickle-skill the air divided;
he used its thrust and current easily.

He trusted all to air: the flesh that bred him
was worn against it to a blade-thin curving
made all for flight; air's very creatures fed him.

Such pride as this, once fallen, there's no saving.
Whatever struck him snapped his stretch of wing.
He came to earth at last, Icarus diving.

Like a contraption of feathers, bone and string,
his storm-blue wings hung useless. Yet his eyes
lived in his wreckage—head still strove to rise
and turn towards the lost impossible spring.

APOSTLE-BIRDS

Strangers are easily put out of countenance,
and we were strangers in that place;
camped among trees we had no names for;
not knowing the local customs.

And those big grey birds, how they talked about us!
They hung head-down from branches and peered.
They spread their tawny wings like fans,
and came so close we could have touched them;
staring with blunt amusement.
It was ridiculous to feel embarrassed.

Of that camp I remember the large wild violets,
the sound of the creek on stones,
the wind-combed grass, the tree-trunks
wrinkled and grey like elephant-legs all round us;
and those apostle-birds, so rude to strangers,
so self-possessed and clannish,
we were glad when they flew away.

PARROTS

Loquats are cold as winter suns.
Among rough leaves their clusters grow
like oval beads of cloudy amber,
or small fat flames of birthday candles.

Parrots, when the winter dwindles
their forest fruits and seeds, remember
where the swelling loquats grow,
how chill and sweet their thin juice runs,

and shivering in the morning cold
we draw the curtains back and see
the lovely greed of their descending,
the lilt of flight that blurs their glories,

and warm our eyes upon the lories
and the rainbow-parrots landing.
There's not a fruit on any tree
to match their crimson, green and gold.

To see them cling and sip and sway,
loquats are no great price to pay.

MAGPIES

A long the road the magpies walk
with hands in pockets, left and right.
They tilt their heads, and stroll and talk.
In their well-fitted black and white

they look like certain gentlemen
who seem most nonchalant and wise
until their meal is served—and then
what clashing beaks, what greedy eyes!

But not one man that I have heard
throws back his head in such a song
of grace and praise—no man nor bird.
Their greed is brief; their joy is long.
For each is born with such a throat
as thanks his God with every note.

WOUNDED NIGHT-BIRD

Walking one lukewarm, lamp-black night I heard
a yard from me his harsh rattle of warning,
and in a landing-net of torchlight saw him crouch—
the devil, small but dangerous. My heart's lurch
betrayed me to myself. But I am learning:
I can distinguish: the devil is no bird.

A bird with a broken breast. But what a stare
he fronted me with!—his look abashed my own.
He was all eyes, furious, meant to wound.
And I, who meant to heal, took in my hand
his depth of down, his air-light delicate bone,
his heart in the last extreme of pain and fear.

From nerve to nerve I felt the circuit blaze.
Along my veins his anguish beat; his eyes
flared terror into mine and cancelled time,
and the black whirlpool closed over my head
and clogged my throat with the cry that knows no aid.
Far down beneath the reach of succouring light
we fought, we suffered, we were sunk in night.

THE WAGTAIL

So elegant he is and neat
from round black head to slim black feet!
He sways and flirts upon the fence,
his collar clean as innocence.

The city lady looks and cries
"Oh charming bird with dewdrop eyes,
how kind of you to sing that song!"
But what a pity—she is wrong.

"Sweet-pretty-creature"—yes, but who
is the one he sings it to?
        Not me—not you.

The furry moth, the gnat perhaps,
on which his scissor-beak snip-snaps.

PELICANS

Funnel-web spider, snake and octopus,
    pitcher-plant and vampire-bat and shark—
these are cold water on an easy faith.
Look at them, but don't linger.
If we stare too long, something looks back at us;
something gazes through from underneath;
something crooks a very dreadful finger
down there in an unforgotten dark.

Turn away then, and look up at the sky.
There sails that old clever Noah's Ark,
the well-turned, well-carved pelican
with his wise comic eye;
he turns and wheels down, kind as an ambulance-
    driver,
to join his fleet. Pelicans rock together,
solemn as clowns in white on a circus-river,
meaning: this world holds every sort of weather.

SILVER TERNS

It was a morning blue as ocean's mirror,
    and strong and warm the wind was blowing.
Along the shore a flock of terns went flying,
their long white wings as clean as pearl.

Inland among the boulders of grey coral
their mates upon the eggs sat waiting.
A shoal of fishes hurried by the island
and the terns plunged into the shoal.

The sea was pocked with sudden silver fountains
where the birds dived, so swift and clever;
and some rose with a flash of fish and water
as sunlight broke on splash and scale;

but some, we saw, stayed down and did not rise.
That shoal the big bonito harried,
and they took fish and diving bird together.
One tern rose like a bloodied sail,

and a bonito leapt to make its capture.
All morning it went on, that slaughter,
with white birds diving, obstinate with hunger;
and some would rise, and some would fail.

The morning was as gentle as a pearl,
the sea was pocked with sudden silver fountains;
you would not guess the blood, unless you saw it,
that the waves washed from feather and from scale.

BROWN BIRD

B rown bird with the silver eyes,
fly down and teach me to sing.
I am alone, I will not
touch you or move.
I am only thirsty for love
and the clear stream of your voice
and the brown curve of your wing
and the cold of your silver eyes.

Yet though I hung my head
and did not look or move,
he felt my thirst and was gone.
Though not a word I said,
he would not give me a song.
My heart sounded too strong;
too desert looked my love.

BLACK COCKATOOS

Each certain kind of weather or of light
has its own creatures. Somewhere else they wait
as though they but inhabited heat or cold,
twilight or dawn, and knew no other state.
Then at their time they come, timid or bold.

So when the long drought-winds, sandpaper-harsh,
were still, and the air changed, and the clouds came,
and other birds were quiet in prayer or fear,
these knew their hour. Before the first far flash
lit up, or the first thunder spoke its name,
in heavy flight they came, till I could hear
the wild black cockatoos, tossed on the crest
of their high trees, crying the world's unrest.

RAINBOW-BIRD

Once in a winter killing as its war,
and settled in the heart as sharp as sleet,
under a trellised rose hook-thorned and bare
that twined its whips and flogged the cruel air,
the rainbow-bird lay fallen at my feet.

Yes, fallen, fallen like the spring's delight,
that bird that turned too late to find the spring.
The cold had struck him spinning from its height;
his cobweb-plumes, his breast too neat and slight
to beat that wind back, and his twisted wing.

And I stood looking. All of me was chilled.
My face was silent as a mask of wood,
and I had thought my very core was killed.
But he in his soft colours lay more cold
even than my heart. He met me like a word
I needed—pity? love?—the rainbow-bird.

BLACK SWANS

Night after night the rounding moon
rose like a bushfire through the air.
Night after night the swans came in—
the lake at morning rocked them there.

The inland fired the western wind
from plains bared by a year-long drought.
Only the coastal lakes were kind
until that bitter year ran out.

Black swans shadowed the blaze of moon
as they came curving down the sky.
On hills of night the red stars burned
like sparks blown when the wind is high.
On rushing wings the black swans turned
sounding aloud their desolate cry.

NIGHT HERONS

It was after a day's rain:
the street facing the west
was lit with growing yellow;
the black road gleamed.

First one child looked and saw
and told another.
Face after face, the windows
flowered with eyes.

It was like a long fuse lighted,
the news travelling.
No one called out loudly;
everyone said "Hush."

The light deepened; the wet road
answered in daffodil colours,
and down its centre
walked the two tall herons.

Stranger than wild birds, even,
what happened on those faces:
suddenly believing in something,
they smiled and opened.

Children thought of fountains,
circuses, swans feeding;
women remembered words
spoken when they were young.

Everyone said "Hush";
no one spoke loudly;
but suddenly the herons
rose and were gone. The light faded.

LYREBIRDS

Over the west side of this mountain,
that's lyrebird country.
I could go down there, they say, in the early morning,
and I'd see them, I'd hear them.

Ten years, and I have never gone.
I'll never go.
I'll never see the lyrebirds—
the few, the shy, the fabulous,
the dying poets.

I should see them, if I lay there in the dew:
first a single movement
like a waterdrop falling, then stillness,
then a brown head, brown eyes,
a splendid bird, bearing
like a crest the symbol of his art,
the high symmetrical shape of the perfect lyre.
I should hear that master practising his art.

No, I have never gone.
Some things ought to be left secret, alone;
some things—birds like walking fables—
ought to inhabit nowhere but the reverence of the heart.

SATIN BOWER-BIRDS

In summer they can afford their independence,
down in the gullies, in the folds of forest;
but with the early frosts they're here again—
hopping like big toy birds, as round as pullets,
handsomely green and speckled, but somehow comic—
begging their bread. A domestic,
quarrelling, amateur troupe.

Ordinary birds with ordinary manners,
uninteresting as pigeons;
but, like the toad, they have a secret.
Look—the young male bird—
see his eye's perfect mineral blaze of blue.
The winter sea's not purer
than that blue flash set in a bird's head.

Then I remember
how ritually they worship that one colour.
Blue chips of glass, blue rag, blue paper,
the heads of my grape-hyacinths,
I found in their secret bower; and there are dances
done in the proper season,
for birth, initiation, marriage and perhaps death.

Seven years, some say, those green-brown birds
elect blue for their colour
and dance for it, their eyes round as the sea's horizons,
blue as grape-hyacinths.

And when those seven years are served?
See, there he flies, the old one,
the male made perfect—
black in the shadow, but in the caressing sun
bluer, more royal than the ancient sea.

BRUSH TURKEY

Right to the edge of his forest
the tourists come.
He learns the scavenger's habits
with scrap and crumb—
his forests shrunk, he lives
on what the moment gives:
pretends, in mockery,
to beg our charity.

Cunning and shy one must be
to snatch one's bread
from oafs whose hands are quicker
with stones instead.
He apes the backyard bird,
half-proud and half-absurd,
sheltered by his quick wit,
he sees and takes his bit.

Ash-black, wattles of scarlet,
and careful eye,
he hoaxes the ape, the ogre,
with mimicry.
Scornfully, he will eat
thrown crust and broken meat
till suddenly—"See, oh see!
The turkey's in the tree."

The backyard bird is stupid;
he trusts and takes.
But this one's wiles are wary
to guard against the axe:
escaping, neat and pat,
into his habitat.
Charred log and shade and stone
accept him. He is gone.

And here's a bird the poet
may ponder over,
whose ancient forest-meanings
no longer grant him cover;
who, circumspect yet proud,
like yet unlike the crowd,
must cheat its chucklehead
to throw—not stones, but bread.

THE KOEL

One spring when life itself was happiness,
he called and called across the orange-trees
his two strange syllables; and clouds of perfume
followed along the hesitating breeze.

And when he calls, the spring has come again,
and the old joy floods up in memory.
Yet his sad foster-kin cannot forget
the wrong he does them—Cain from his infancy.

Dark wary rebel, migrant without a home
except the spring, bird whom so many hate,
voice of one tune and only one—yet come.
In fear yet boldly, come and find your mate.
Against their anger, outcast by them all,
choose your one love and call your single call—
the endless tale you cannot cease to tell,
half-question, half-reply—*Koel! Koel!*

EXTINCT BIRDS

Charles Harpur in his journals long ago
(written in hope and love, and never printed)
recorded the birds of his time's forest—
birds long vanished with the fallen forest—
described in copperplate on unread pages.

The scarlet satin-bird, swung like a lamp in berries,
he watched in love, and then in hope described it.
There was a bird, blue, small, spangled like dew.
All now are vanished with the fallen forest.
And he, unloved, past hope, was buried,

who helped with proud stained hands to fell the forest,
and set those birds in love on unread pages;
yet thought himself immortal, being a poet.
And is he not immortal, where I found him,
in love and hope along his careful pages?—
the poet vanished, in the vanished forest,
among his brightly tinted extinct birds?

DOTTEREL

Wild and impermanent
    as the sea-foam blown,
the dotterel keeps its distance
and runs alone.

Bare beach, salt wind,
its loved solitude,
hold all that it asks
of shelter and food.

I saw its single egg
dropped in the sand,
with neither straw nor wall
to warm or defend;

and the new-hatched chick,
like a thistle's pale down,
fled and crouched quiet
as sand or as stone.

Water's edge, land's edge
and edge of the air—
the dotterel chooses
to live nowhere.

It runs, but not in fear,
and its thin high call
is like a far bugle
that troubles the soul.

LORY

On the bough of blue summer
hangs one crimson berry.
Like the blood of a lover
is the breast of the lory.

The blood-drinking butcher-birds
pray and sing together.
They long to gather from his breast
the red of one feather.

But "The heart's red is my reward,"
the old crow cries
"I'll wear his colour on my black
the day the lory dies."

The Forest

A DEDICATION

L ost in a desolate country,
I travelled far to find
what only you could give me—
the equal heart and mind
that answer love in kind.

And now while you lie sleeping,
awake but not alone,
I make this midnight blessing,
because the years have grown
to truths beyond my own.

The heart can blaze with candour
as though it housed a star;
but this my midnight splendour
is not my own to wear:
it lights by what you are.

THE BEASTS

The wolf's desires pace through his cage
and try the long-neglected bars.
There is a meaning in his eyes,
a knowledge in his rage.

A life withheld by iron and stone
stays perfect in the lion's skin.
Nightmares have night to plunder in
and make their message known.

Therefore the wolf and lion rise
to prey upon my sighing sleep.
There is a purpose in their eyes
and in the tears I weep.

Their famine's ambush waits to kill
within my heart's dark hinterland.
It is my unlaid fear until
I take love's food in either hand,

and travel searching through the wild
till beast and man are reconciled.

THE FOREST

When first I knew this forest
its flowers were strange.
Their different forms and faces
changed with the seasons' change—

white violets smudged with purple,
the wild-ginger spray,
ground-orchids small and single
haunted my day;

the thick-fleshed Murray-lily,
flame-tree's bright blood,
and where the creek runs shallow,
the cunjevoi's green hood.

When first I knew this forest,
time was to spend,
and time's renewing harvest
could never reach an end.

Now that its vines and flowers
are named and known,
like long-fulfilled desires
those first strange joys are gone.

My search is further.
There's still to name and know
beyond the flowers I gather
that one that does not wither—
the truth from which they grow.

FIVE SENSES

Now my five senses
gather into a meaning
all acts, all presences;
and as a lily gathers
the elements together,
in me this dark and shining,
that stillness and that moving,
these shapes that spring from nothing,
become a rhythm that dances,
a pure design.

While I'm in my five senses
they send me spinning
all sounds and silences,
all shape and colour
as thread for that weaver,
whose web within me growing
follows beyond my knowing
some pattern sprung from nothing—
a rhythm that dances
and is not mine.

THE NAUTILUS

Some queer unshaped uncoloured animal,
much like a moment's pause of smoke or mist,
was yet so made that nothing less
than this hard perfect shape involving it
would do to speak its meaning in the world.

Out of its birth it came with this.
The smallest spiral holds the history
of something tiny in the battering sea,
that carried on its obstinate gathering,
till the years swelled in it to one last perfect
ballooning curve of colour laid by colour.
All was implicit in its hold on time.

Say that the thing was slave to its own meaning
and the unconscious labour of its body.
The terms were these, that it could never guess
how it conspired with time to shroud itself—
a splendid action common to its kind
but never known in doing.

Not even the end of making gave the meaning.
The thing it made was its own self, enclosed it,
and was the prison that prevented sight.
Yet though death strands its emptied spiral,
this sweet completion puts a term to time;
and that, I take it, was the bargain.

PRAISE FOR THE EARTH

The writer in the lighted room
is not single nor alone:
but let him drop his pen and turn
and see the towering universe
wheel its faint lights in the far gloom,
then all the work that time has done
still leaves the heart companionless.

So gather in the golden dead
till all we own is harvested.
While world's our own and our heart's food,
no need to fear eternity.
Little the time that's left for love
between the poised and the broken wave;
let us, who hang like a wave on the sea,
praise all the dead and all who live.

Q TO A

Oh why so fill me
with such delight and terror,
only to leave me
empty of all but sorrow?
        It was my pleasure.

Once you replied
most clear and ever truthful,
who now are silent.
Must I alone be faithful?
             Your question is your answer.

Was I deceived then,
and was it my own echo
I heard and loved then?
My heart is woe to fear so.
             Where found you then your treasure?

In love, it was in love
I found my rest,
And that my own heart gave.
             Put there your trust.

THE LAKE

All day the candid staring of the lake
holds what's passing and forgets the past.
Faithful to cloud and leaf, not knowing leaf nor cloud,
it spreads its smooth eye wide for something's sake.
All daylight's there; and all the night at last
drops threads of light from star to under-star.

Eye of the earth, my meaning's what you are.
You see no tree nor cloud. That's what I take
out of your waters in this net I cast—
the net where time is knotted by the word,
that flying needle. Lakes and eyes at last
drain dry, but the net-maker still must make.

What lover's shuttle flew when all began?
Who chose the images this net can draw?—
sun, moon and cloud, the hanging leaves and trees,
and leaning through, the terrible face of man:
my face. I looked, and there my eyes met eyes,
lover to lover. Deep I looked, and saw.

INTERPLAY

What is within becomes what is around.
 This angel morning on the world-wide sea
is seared with light that's mine and comes from me,
and I am mirror to its blaze and sound,
as lovers double in their interchange.

Yet I am not the seer, nor world the sight;
I am transcended by a single word—
Let there be light—and all creation stirred.
I am that cry alone, that visioned light,
its voice and focus. It's the word that's strange.

Look how the stars' bright chaos eddies in
to form our constellations. Flame by flame
answers the ordering image in the name.
World's signed with words; there light—there love begin.

DRY STORM

The uninhabited mountains stand up green,
 naked with rock or clothed with an old forest
where vines and thorns tangle in damp and dark
among the trunks and boulders. Curls of fern
and coils of water over leaves and rock
pattern the snake's long body, hide from harm
moth, bird and lizard. From those ancient turrets
tonight thrusts up the cloud of this dry storm.

Spring's months are thirsty. The valley's crops are sown
and the seed waits. But nothing comes tonight
except the thrust of lightning. There is sound;
but it is thunder circling, here and gone,
and not the increasing rain. Long since it rained,
and now the grass is dry, ready to burn,
and farmers fear the lightning. The cloud's heart
is torn wide open, but it means no rain.

O ease our restlessness. Wild wandering dark,
vague hurrying depths of storm, pause and be full,
and thrust your fullness into our desire
till time release us, till we sleep. And wake
to a cool sky and a soaked earth left bare
to drink its light in peace.
                                    But this storm's dry,
and dries us with its passion; and means ill,
reared from dark forests to a darker sky.

A CHILD'S NIGHTMARE

The holy image dwells within,
    bequeathed by time from man to man.
It rages in us while we can
support its fires and yet not burn.
And children learn, as the years pass,
the char of that insatiate flame
that melts the towering universe
into a symbol and a name.

Earth is a sad yet glittering star.
Bodied in beast and man and bird,
she seeks her vision and her fear,
old Chaos and the shaping Word;
and we who travel on her path
hold ecstasy and nightmare both.

So you come running from your dreams
where flame and shadow one by one
reveal and darken all that's known,
to sob and tremble in my arms.

BACHELOR UNCLE

When you came visiting
    the house was sour and strange.
Time past was all betrayed
by unknown youth and change.
And in the children's glance
that turned from you and ran,
you saw instead of yourself
an empty cross old man,
alien, denied by all
but the old clocks on the wall.
Ticking as brittle and dry
as an ageing artery
they spoke time's cruelty.

So you took down each clock,
undid its insect-shell,
till spring and coil and wheel
littered your room's cold cell;
and, disarticulate,
old time your enemy
ran mad with chime and bell
of sick machinery.
And day by day you sat
intent and desolate,
with sharpened lip and eye—
an old clock gone awry.

Then it was time to pack—
time to be gone again.
You put the wheels together,
oiled them all with a feather,
and set and took them back.
Time's true and must be told
to the meticulous second;
and your week's work was reckoned
a service due to pride,
neat-handed though grown old.

THE GRAVES AT MILL POINT

Alf Watt is in his grave
These eighty years.
From his bones a bloodwood grows
With long leaves like tears.

His girl grew weary long ago;
She's long lost the pain
Of crying to the empty air
To hold her boy again.

When he died the town died.
Nothing's left now
But the wind in the bloodwoods:
"Where did they go?

"In the rain beside the graves
I heard their tears say
—This is where the world ends;
The world ends today.

"Six men, seven men
Lie in one furrow.
The peaty earth goes over them,
But cannot blind our sorrow—"

"Where have they gone to?
I can't hear or see.
Tell me of the world's end,
You heavy bloodwood tree."

"There's nothing but a butcher-bird
Singing on my wrist,
And the long wave that rides the lake
With rain upon its crest.

"There's nothing but a wandering child
Who stoops to your stone;
But time has washed the words away,
So your story's done."

Six men, seven men
Are left beside the lake,
And over them the bloodwood tree
Flowers for their sake.

OLD WOMAN'S SONG

The moon drained white by day
lifts from the hill
where the old pear-tree, fallen in storm,
puts out some blossom still.

Women believe in the moon.
This branch I hold
is not more white and still than she
whose flower is ages old;

and so I carry home
this branch of pear
that makes such obstinate tokens still
of fruit it cannot bear.

AGE TO YOUTH

The sooty bush in the park
is green as any forest
for the boy to lie beneath,
with his arms around his dearest;

the black of the back street
is washed as any cloud
when the girl and the boy
touch hands among the crowd.

No, nothing's better than love,
than to want and to hold:
it is wise in the young
to forget the common world:

to be lost in the flesh
and the light shining there:
not to listen to the old
whose tune is fear and care—

who tell them love's a drink
poisoned with sorrow,
the flesh a flower today
and withered by tomorrow.

It is wise in the young
to let heart go racing heart,
to believe that the earth
is young and safe and sweet;

and the message we should send
from age back to youth
is that every kiss and glance
is truer than the truth;

that whatever we repent
of the time that we live,
it is never what we give—
it is never that we love.

DOUBLE IMAGE

The long-dead living forest rose
as white as bone, as dark as hair.
In rage the old protagonists
fought for my life; and I was there.

My kinsman's flesh, my kinsman's skull
enclosed me, and our wounds were one.
The long-dead forest reeled and sank
before that bitter night was done—

before we struck and tore again
the jumping flesh from out his hide,
and drank the blood that ran and slowed
to show the moment when he died.

O curve of horror in the claw,
and speech within the speechless eye—
when one must die, not knowing death,
and one knows death who cannot die.

They run from me, my child, my love,
when in those long-dead forests caught
I pace. My tears behind his eyes,
my kinsman dreams of what is not—

dreaming of knowledge and of love
in agony he treads his path.
I bud in him, a thorn, a pain,
and yet my nightmare holds us both.

I drink his murder's choking blood,
and he in ignorance sheds my tears.
The centuries bind us each in each—
the tongueless word, the ignorant ears.

Till from those centuries I wake,
naked and howling, still unmade,
within the forests of my heart
my dangerous kinsman runs afraid.

JUDAS IN MODERN DRESS

Not like those men they tell of, who just as suddenly
walk out of life, from wife and fire and cooking-pot
and the whole confusion, to sit alone and naked
and move past motion; gaze through dark and day
with eyes that answer neither. Having completed their
   journey
they are free to travel past the end of journeys.
But I stepped out alone.
"I reject the journey; it was not I who chose it.
I worked for one end only,
to find the key that lets me through the door
marked Exit. I have found it and I use it."

There is a tale I heard a wise man tell,
how, tattered with age, beneath a fruiting tree
a seeker sat, and heard in God's great silence
another traveller, caught in the nets of self,
weeping between anguish and ecstasy,
and over a thousand miles stretched out one hand
to pluck him back again into the Way.

But I was one the saints knew not at all.
A mocking man, a sad man-animal
rejecting world and sense
not for God's love, but man's intelligence;
as though a hog looked through a human eye
and saw the human world as dunged as its own sty,
foul ante-room to death. Like that I saw
the abattoir ahead, and smelt the soil
soaked under me with blood. No place for me.

And wise in my own way I worked to find
the weak place in the palings of the Real—
the gap between the Word
and its Creation, the act and the conception—
and forced my way between those married two,
set time against eternity, struggled through,
slipped through annihilation, still being I.

What violence those great powers did to me
as I escaped between, I have forgotten.
But swinging clear I saw the world spin by
and leave me, empty as an insect-shell,
beyond the chance of death, and outside time.

I had the choice. Once I had infinite choices—
all the variety of light and shadow
that sprang to being when Choice first was made.
Now I have knowledge only. Knowledge, and eyes
to watch the worlds cross their eternities.

Times after times the saving word is spoken.
Times after times I feel it wither me.
The fools of time live on and never hear,
and I who hear have chosen not to answer.
It beats against me till my ears are broken.

Times after times I see my death go by
and cannot reach it even with a prayer.
Indeed, since I am neither Here nor There
I cannot live, and therefore cannot die.

Times after times my lips begin to form
the word that I renounced, and close again.
The worlds pass jostling, and their makers dream
immortal life betrayed to daily pain—
the pain that I denied.

I still deny it.

O sweet, sweet, sweet the love in human eyes—
the tree of blossom dressed to meet the bee,
all white, all radiant, golden at the heart.
Halt there, at your Creation! And it dies,
dies into rotting fruit, and tyrannous seed.
If it spring up again, so much the worse.
That was the curse on Eden, Adam's curse.
The curse by which my heart will not abide.

If I am Judas, still my cause is good.
I will not move my lips to answer God.

VISION

He who once saw that world beyond the world,
so that each tree and building, stone and face
cracked open like a mask before a flame
and showed the tree, the stone, the face behind it—
walked forever with that beatification.
Waking at night, against the blank of darkness,
knew he contained it; touched hand upon brow
and in his gladness cried "I, even I!"
—knowing the human ends in the divine.

Pride, greed, and ignorance—that world's three veils—
through them he walked and saw what lay beyond;
saw what the human eye was meant to see:
and watched the greedy and the stupid fumble
in a blind fear with intellect and pride—
those blades that cut the ignorant hands that hold them.
So he was sad for victim and oppressor,
for crying child and brute with the slack mouth,
for schemer, clod and safe respectable man
and all who had not seen what he had seen.

And yet these, too, moved in that second world
and stood up real behind the masks of hatred.
The very wound and weapon bled and glittered
as though both steel and flesh were made of light
and men the instruments in some high battle
where God incomprehensibly warred on God.

Wherefore he closed his eyes and hands, and prayed
vision and action know their proper limits,
and knowledge teach him more humility.

MOTH

The great moth winged with many eyes
frets from his breast its silver dust.
Caught in the net my lamp has cast
he beats and circles till he dies.

His life was set on some true path
until his kind inhabited night
betrayed him to a craze of light,
light meaningless and cold like death—

or so I said, who watched him parch
upon his sterile radiant heaven—
a love unjoined, a gift ungiven—
strange failure in the eternal search:

and so turned back my pen to prayer
that might be language for a moth:
"O overcome me, Power and Truth;
transmute my ignorance, burn it bare;
so that against your flame, not I
but all that is not You, may die."

REASON AND UNREASON

When I began to test my heart,
its laws and fantasies, against the world,
the pain of impact made me sad.
Where heart was curved the world ran straight,
where it lay warm the world came cold.
It seemed my heart, or else the world, was mad.

Could I reject arithmetics,
their plain unanswerable arguings,
or find a cranny outside categories,
where two and two made soldiers, love or six?
My heart observed the silence round its songs,
the indifference that met its stories;

believed itself a changeling crazed,
and bowed its head to every claim of reason;
but then stood up and realized
when work is over love begins its season;
each day is contraried by night
and Caesar's coin is paid for Venus' rite;

and knew its fantasies, since time began,
outdone by earth's wild dreams, Plant, Beast and Man.

FOR MY DAUGHTER

The days begin to set
your difference in your face.
The world has caught you up
to go at the world's pace.
Time, that is not denied,
as once from my heart it drew
the blood that nourished you,
now draws you from my side.

My body gave you then
what was ordained to give,
and did not need my will.
But now we learn to live
apart, what must I do?
Out of my poverty
what new gift can there be
that I can find for you?

Love was our first exchange—
the kindness of the blood.
Animals know as much,
and know that it is good.
But when the child is grown
and the mouth leaves the breast,
such simple good is past
and leaves us more alone.

So we grow separate
and separate spend our days.
You must become your world
and follow in its ways;
but out of my own need,
not knowing where nor how,
I too must journey now
upon a different road.

While love is innocent
the lion walks beside.
But when the spell's undone
and where the paths divide,
he must be tamed, or slain,
or else the heart's undone.
The path I walk upon
leads to his den again.

When I shall meet with him
I pray to wrestle well;
I pray to learn the way
to tame him, not to kill.
Then he may be my friend,
as Una's once, in love,
and I shall understand
what gifts are mine to give.

NAMING THE STARS

Now all the garden's overcome with dark,
its flowers transplanted, low to high,
become night's far-off suns, and map in hand
we find where Sirius and Canopus stand
and trace our birth-stars on the zodiac.
Is it not strange that you and I
should write those names like jewels on the sky?

My Twins shine in the north, your red-eyed Bull
runs at Orion, each horn ablaze;
but who are we to claim them? Far and far
they fly, and no star sees his brother star;
not Castor knows his twin among them all,
and Taurus with his Pleiades
is the old figure of a dead man's gaze.

Yet they, like us, are caught in time and cause
and eddied on their single stream.
Earth watches through our eyes, and as we stare
she greets, by us, her far compatriots there,
the wildhaired Suns and the calm Wanderers.
Her ancient thought is marked in every name;
hero and creature mingle in her dream.

On her dark breast we spring like points of light
and set her language on the map of night.

SPORTS FIELD

Naked all night the field
  breathed its dew until
the great gold ball of day
sprang up from the dark hill.

Now as the children come
the field and they are met.
Their day is measured and marked,
its lanes and tapes are set;

and the children gilt by the sun
shoulder one another;
crouch at the marks to run,
and spring, and run together—

the children pledged and matched,
and built to win or lose,
who grow, while no one watches,
the selves in their sidelong eyes.

The watchers love them in vain.
What's real here is the field,
the starter's gun, the lane,
the ball dropped or held;

and set towards the future,
they run like running water,
for only the pride of winning,
the pain the losers suffer,

till the day's great golden ball
that no one ever catches,
drops; and at its fall
runners and watchers

pick up their pride and pain
won out of the measured field
and turn away again
while the star-dewed night comes cold.

So pride and pain are fastened
into the heart's future,
while naked and perilous
the night and the field glitter.

THE DIVER

The diver pausing on the tower
   draws in one breath—
the crest of time, the pride, the hour
that answers death—
and down to where the long pool lies
marks out his curve;
descending light that star-like flies
from air to wave
as autumn falls from trees and eyes,
and youth, and love.

Then from the rocking depths' release,
naked and new
the headfirst man springs up, and sees
all still to do—
the tower to climb, the pause to make,
the fill of breath
to gather in—the step to take
from birth to death.

Then, you who turn and climb the stair
and stand alone—
with you I draw that breath, and dare,
time's worst being known.

THE POET

Simplex Simplicior Simplicissimus
stood like a shouldering crystal under the sun
and changed its light into all the colours of love.
Great heavens, they said to him, look what you've done;
you've turned What Is into There's No Such Thing;
now we must turn it back. And the butterfly's wing
dropped at his feet and the bird sang business only.
Simplex Simplicior Simplicissimus
listened to what they said, bemused and lonely,
but being still what he couldn't help but be,
still flashed scarlet, violet, green, incorrigibly.

And though he is slain and many times over slain,
he is the one who dies to rise again.

READING THOMAS TRAHERNE

Can I then lose myself,
and losing find one word
that, in the face of what you were,
needs to be said or heard?

— Or speak of what has come
to your sad race
that to your clear rejoicing
we turn with such a face?

With such a face, Traherne,
as might make dumb
any but you, the man who knew
how simply truth may come:

who saw the depth of darkness
shake, part and move,
and from death's centre the light's ladder
go up from love to Love.

THE MORNING OF THE DEAD

I   THE MEETING

O ut of the sky that is always astonished by dawn
    move the enormous unconscious clouds,
blindly becoming, being, undoing their being;
like the clouds of sleep that want what they are and no
    more,
untouched by future and past.

That's how I went on my pilgrimage; that's how I walked
(changing, altering, sleepily under the sun of love)
with my hand in the hand of another, to look for a grave,
in the blazing day of a town in the far north,
among pale toppling stones.

And found, under the clouds of the mango-trees,
a thin dark muscular man deep in the soil,
shining with sweat, clay crumbed in his stiff hair;
a man in the service of death which is the service of life;
a man digging a grave.

"What are you looking for?" "A grave, sixty years old."
The grave of somebody dead long before I was born;
the grave of a man I had met as part of myself;
a man silenced by death but speaking still in my life—
my dark grandfather's grave.

But he was not to be found. He had crumbled away,
and the wooden tablet had gone and the rose had gone;
probably some other stranger was buried there now,
bone nudging old bone. But since I had come,
he and I met, in my mind.

He and I met; and the gravedigger dripping with sweat
(putting away a stiff in time for the Saturday racing)
gave us a twist of a smile. Sixty years old?
Cripes, it's a long way to come for a long while ago.
Why can't you leave him alone?

But in that sky that is always under the grave
he and I met, bowed in our sleep like clouds;
touched untouchedly; clouds that melt into each other;
shapes that need not strive, because their event is their
    truth;
found each other in love.

II THE INTERCHANGE

It is the eyes of the dead that memory
most ponders over, seeing a rain of crystals
time-long carrying back to earth their vision;
the insect's towers of eyes; birds' light-filled circles;
the fierce or gentle looks of animals
that half-see meaning.

These reflect light more truly than pools or lakes
relating it to being in a new way,
till earth shuts on them and takes in their sight.
In them light generates some new complexity,
able to answer.

So earth is made of answers, the eyes of the dead.
All those old tribes, dark trees endowed with sight,
found new replies to night and day. Their glances
forged a meaning between man and creature,
creature and nature.

But meaning cannot rest or stay the same.
Meaning seeks its own unthought-of meaning,
murders and is murdered, travels on
into new territory past touch or sight—
is dark entreating light.

What drives us is the dead, their thorned desire.
Their eyes of fury, loss or melancholy
turn on us, light tantalizing darkness,
obscurity seeking simplicity
or midnight's peace.

So though I stood and said, My heart's a rose,
the wheel of life and death still turned. The dead
cry, Bear my children; follow out my thought;
live for me, since you wear my life. Their eyes
reflect no rose, no sun,
till the earth grows
into that perfect fruit where day and night are one.

III THE END

Now all things thinned in perfect clarity
desire to rise in this pure resonant air
beyond themselves and take on purity
past reach of vision—only the essence there,
and that rejoicing.

Becoming seeks for being.
Learning desires so to transcend itself
that nothing's left to learn. Time seeks eternity.
The flesh continually works towards its ending.
Earth stares with all its eyes upon divinity.

Shape making perilous way from shapelessness;
sense budding where the blind rock knew no sense,
language carving all silence into meaning,
and motion taking up so intricate a dance—
yet all corrupt, all dying.

Time's not for weeping.
Time and the world press on. So take life further,
let the thin bubble of blown glass, the passion
of vision that is art, refine, reflect and gather
the moving pattern of all things in consummation
and their rejoicing.

For this is what the dead desire—their meaning.
"I was borne down; my work was left unfinished;
alive I turned to stone; my love was ruined;
ignorance, oppression, pain left my sight tarnished,
my world corrupt and dying.

"Oh make me perfect.
Burn with a fire of sight the substance of my sorrow.
Take what I was and find in it that truth
the universes on their holy journey
watch with their eyes of fire. Illuminate my death.
Till all the dead stand in their essence shining
Time has not learned its meaning."

POEM AND AUDIENCE

No, it's not you we speak to. Don't believe it.
The words go past you to another ear.
Does the look seem to rest on you, or you?
Regard it well, and see: it passes through.
It is not you we look at and we hear.

No, it's not hard to speak. This is an answer—
how blurred, how stumbling, we have bitterly known—
yet answer, to a question. Who could ask
so strange a thing, or set so hard a task?
We cannot answer. The voice is not our own,
and yet its tone's deeper than intimate.

And when, expected and entreated long,
the question comes, we cannot hesitate,
but, turning blindly, put all else away.
Searching ourselves in pain, we yet rejoice
that the implacable awaited voice
asks of us all we feared, yet longed, to say.

AUTUMN FIRES

Old flower-stems turn to sticks in autumn,
clutter the garden, need
the discipline of secateurs.
Choked overplus, straggle of weed,
cold souring strangling webs of root;

I pile the barrow with the lot.
Snapped twig that forgets flower and fruit,
thornbranch too hard to rot,
I stack you high for a last rite.

When twigs are built and match is set,
your death springs up like life; its flare
crowns and consumes the ended year.
Corruption changes to desire
that sears the pure and wavering air,
and death goes upward like a prayer.

FROM

The Other Half

1966

THE OTHER HALF

The self that night undrowns when I'm asleep
travels beneath the dumb days that I give,
within the limits set that I may live,
and beats in anger on the things I love.
I am the cross it bears, and it the tears I weep.

Under the eyes of light my work is brief.
Day sets on me the burdens that I carry.
I face the light, the dark of me I bury.
My silent answer and my other half,
we meet at midnight and by music only.

Yet there's a word that I would give to you:
the truth you tell in your dumb images
my daylight self goes stumbling after too.
So we may meet at last, and meeting bless,
and turn into one truth in singleness.

TO HAFIZ OF SHIRAZ

*The rose has come into the garden,
from Nothingness into Being*

Once I did not know the birds were described,
classified, observed, fixed in their proper localities.
Each bird that sprang from its tree, passed overhead,
  hawked from the bough,
was sole, new, dressed as no other was dressed.
Any leaf might hide the paradise-bird.

Once I believed any poem might follow my pen,
any road might beckon my feet to mapless horizons,
any eyes that I met, any hand that I took, any word that I
    heard
might pierce to my heart, stay forever in mine, open worlds
    on its hinge.
All then seemed possible; time and world were my own.

Now that I know that each star has its path, each bird
is finally feathered and grown in the unbroken shell,
each tree in the seed, each song in the life laid down—
is the night sky any less strange; should my glance less
    follow the flight;
should the pen shake less in my hand?

No, more and more like a birth looks the scheduled rising
    of Venus:
the turn of a wing in the wind more startles my blood.
Every path and life leads one way only,
out of continual miracle, through creation's fable,
over and over repeated but never yet understood,
as every word leads back to the blinding original Word.

THE CURTAIN

It was the curtain, softly rising and falling,
reminded me you were home, who had been so long
    away;
and when I went to wake you, I stood in silence watching
your mouth softened in sleep, the lids where your eyes lay.

So grown you looked, in the same unaltered room,
so much of your childhood you were already forgetting,
while I remembered. Yet in the unforgetting dream
you will come here all your life for renewal and meeting.

It was your breath, so softly rising and falling,
that kept me silent. With your lids like buds unbroken
you watched on their curtain your life, a stream of shadows
   moving.
When I touched your shoulder, I too had a little dreamed
   and woken.

METAMORPHOSIS

The old man sat there, and the running child
   paused to look up beyond him, at the tree,
its trunk gnarled grey with time, the branching wood
crawled through with sap, the upward weave of blood
that frayed against the sky in luminous bud.

The tree was an ancient hand that crooked and curled
to touch the child's silk hair; the hand was a tree,
a branching bone membraned with trembling sense.
The new red leaves unfolded their innocence
towards the light and its never-ending dance.

Released from the dawn of leaves, from the fiery nest,
a bird went up from the tree on delighted wings.
How eagerly after its phoenix the poem springs—
how soon, on the threshold of light, its words are lost.

DESTRUCTION

The poet looked for love itself and found
   the wolf, the lion, the sword, the stormy sea—
those portions of the world's eternity
too great to compass with the eye of man;
and so he found his death in his desire.

And so we thrust our hands against the stone,
and thrust again, until the stone descend,
knowing its fall is certain in the end,
and knowing that our death is part of time
and we are incomplete until it come.

Those terrible images walk through our dreams;
we bend our heads in love before the blow.
The wolf and lion go with us where we go;
the sword is fleshed; the sea is in our blood;
fear is our lover and our ill our good.

So we create the selves we must destroy
before we find the pattern of our joy.

IMAGO
(*A Television Vision*)

G loved, goggled, armoured, the slugfoot creature crawled
up from his mud, out of his element,
the laddered tower, and waited for command.
The mask announced that he had eyes; they bent
upward as ever, asking what light meant;
but he was huddled in himself, close-hauled,
meditating perhaps on his likely end;

or perhaps remembering happier days and nights
when in his underworld he stalked, a kind of king
whom others feared. It was the law down there—
eat or be eaten. Slimed, intent and quartering,
he ate whatever was easy slaughtering.
Then came these orders he obeyed in fear.

Crouching alone above his former world,
he was glad at least of the armour he had grown.
He knew the iron fierceness of his stare;
it had been useful in the life he'd known.
He felt his mask, his cuirass, harden to stone.
Light flashed its orders through the perilous air.

To Another Housewife

Do you remember how we went,
on duty bound, to feed the crowd
of hungry dogs your father kept
as rabbit-hunters? Lean and loud,
half-starved and furious, how they leapt
against their chains, as though they meant
in mindless rage for being fed,
to tear our childish hands instead!

With tomahawk and knife we hacked
the flyblown tatters of old meat,
gagged at their carcass-smell, and threw
the scraps and watched the hungry eat.
Then turning faint, we made a pact,
(two greensick girls), crossed hearts and swore
to touch no meat forever more.

How many cuts of choice and prime
our housewife hands have dressed since then—
these hands with love and blood imbrued—
for daughters, sons, and hungry men!
How many creatures bred for food
we've raised and fattened for the time
they met at last the steaming knife
that serves the feast of death-in-life!

And as the evening meal is served
we hear the turned-down radio
begin to tell the evening news
just as the family joint is carved.
O murder, famine, pious wars ...
Our children shrink to see us so,
in sudden meditation, stand
with knife and fork in either hand.

THE ENCOUNTER

Lord, how the creatures bully me!
Stroke me, the cat says.
My vibrant velvet lit with eyes
asks you to stroke it.

Look at me, says the horse—
my arches of suave muscle,
my round, kind eye, my stride and speed
ask you to fill their need.

And in the rockpools of the shore
creatures like flowers and jewels
wait dumbly for my eyes' translation,
decked for our moment's meeting and no more.

I cannot know my beauty
—say all the creatures—
till you interpret me in god-made words.
Before the falling of your final fire
destroys us all—men, plants and birds—
turn your mad destined eyes this way and see
creation's dew still falling here in me.

Lord, how the earth and the creatures look at me.

AGAINST THE WALL

Knocking his knuckles against the wall
he watched the dust trickle awhile;
a scrap of glass from the mosaic,
the yellow robe of God the Father,
tinkled and fell. The floor's great flower
of tile and stone was cracked. A small
eye of light crossed choir and stall
and that great cave became archaic.
Surprised by this he knocked again.

He knocked again. Silently tilting
the great reredos tottering outward.
The antique wood, the stone uniquely
fashioned, all this by craftsmen finished,
unsigned except by Man, all perished
in one tall flourish of dust. And silting
the heaps of rubble, softly felting
the jags and edges, all fell meekly,
till a smooth hill awaited rain.

Knocking his knuckles against each other,
he sat and wept for rain to fall,
for tears and dust to breed together
the scarlet flower that saves us all—
the blood-red flower that saves us all.

POWER

The lizard swerved aside,
the kestrel missed his dive.
Sprawled on the power-lines,
a shock of wings, he died;
a channel for the spark
that in an instant made
life into death, his wreck
too violent for a bird.

I think of death's excess,
life's helplessness. You Power
that make us die and live,
struck by your force aghast
I turn away; I cower.
How dare I call you love?

And yet I call you, Love.
Summoning, awful voice,
I heard you; my breath failed.
How small, how lost was I,
who now take heart, reply,
try even to rejoice
calling myself your child.

CITY SUNRISE
(for Joyce Wilding)

Unseen fountain of dawn
spreading your searching compassion
up from those springs
unstained by our failure,
your light through the smoke grieves down
grey and accusing.

Night is cleaned out of the corners;
a dark detritus, slyly
crouching in garbage cans,
under soiled beds, in cupboards—
an underarm secret, a look
under brows drawn together.

Night without dew, night sweaty,
hunched under roofs of grime,
cannot be visited
wholly by light's clear springs;
tears are crusted on eyelids
like unappeasing sleep.

And the light hardens.
The blessing fingers of dawn
turn into accurate needles
that measure these faces.
Who looks at the sky? Who sees
his self-same fear in the face of the other?

Nobody. No one relinquishes
his sulky wound, his greed.
And the oppressed ones crying
that men and time are cruel
never learn that the sting going in
holds the poison from other men's sores.

Out of the fountain of dawn
the arm of the sun in impartial glory
touches the grime-covered windows,
the metho bottles, the tears on crusted eyelids.
He is risen and night is undone.
One looks him back here; one
fully believes his glance, his old incredible story
of ever-searching, ever-forgiving dawn.

PRO AND CON

Death when he walks behind me frightens me—
soft-footed skulker in a darkened lane,
adept with silence, knives and treachery,
or the stunning blow, or chilly long indifference
that rots the heart and brain.

Death when I turn my head and see him there
meets me with a look I recognize.
Waking at birth to daylight's ruthless stare,
I cried for it, rebelled against enslaving sense
that opened my stung eyes.

Death whom I meet on main roads casually
turns a hairsbreadth wheel and waves goodbye.
By night we meet in old conspiracy
and conjugate "to love"—past, present, future tense.
I wake, repeating "I"—

"I"—"I"—"I"—the tuner testing one cracked note,
the child with one sore tooth.
Round rings of air melt outward from my throat,
bearing that lying truth.

WISHES

What would I wish to be?
I wish to be wise.
From the swamps of fear and greed
free me and let me rise.
There was a poet once
spoke clear as a well-cast bell.
Rumí his name; his voice
rings perfect still.
O could I make one verse
but half so well!

What do I wish to do?
I wish to love:
that verb at whose source all verbs
take fire and learn to move.
Yes, could I rightly love,
all action, all event,
would from my nature spring
true as creation meant.
Love takes no pains with words
but is most eloquent.

To love, and to be wise?
Down, fool, and lower your eyes.

FOR JACK BLIGHT

Poets are always writing about the sea:
   poets are people who want the sea to be real.
Vanities, smuts and despairs are found in the city;
the country is notorious for stupidity;
inland and littoral are glutted with grey humanity;
so poets require the sea, make the sea real.

For only if it is real can the journey be real.
Otherwise neither ship nor passengers have any meaning;
not even the lovers watching wake and bow-wave
(rainbows are relative). Their faces would be negated
by the watching faces of those who are not in love.

But the lonely poets lean over the rail, get drunk
on wine-dark draughts, create themselves mermaids of foam
who desire to be loved by a poet and find immortality.
Poets observe how the sea's eternity
makes the ship important—real because temporal.
Temporality, skipper, makes a here-and-now point
(neither now nor here) on the chart of a pointless sea
that flows everywhere always. Whatever the passengers say
who prefer the ship to the ocean, the point to the chart,
poets will always be writing about the sea.

BESIDE THE CREEK

Under the wavering water shine the stones,
  rounded in ruby-colours and clouded white.
Once I walked barefoot into that cool
never-ceasing flow. I gathered once
pebbles and ripples, the skimming rounds of light,
and took them home.

                Now I am no such fool,
no such blest and envied stupid child
as to believe those colours, that once dry
gathered dust on a top shelf, heavy and dull
as pages written, pages forgotten and filed.
Here on the bank I sit unmoving; I
know the ungathered alone stays beautiful
and the best poem is the poem I never wrote.

Or so I said, watching the summer through.
But oh—years, time, you hoarsen here a throat
that sang all day without suspecting you;
stiffen the hands that gathered rubies then,
and open now, to show this dubious stone.

THE REAL DREAM

There is intellectual pride in the silence of contemplation.
I have called myself poet, extracted from life its images,
then found myself silenced by that great rock in my way—
the silence before and after me: the oblation
that prefigures my sacrifice: the human and animal visages
that enact their poetry, reflect their night and day.

So one night I sat and wrote of imagined death
while on the black road outside, beyond my knowing,
some small crushed creature suffered a real end,
discovered in fading eyes the slow withdrawal of breath,
the blood leaving the veins, the warmth going,
and all the bent sky meant and could not amend.

And so out of a real dream dreamed below my will
I have woken and felt on my cheek the touch of cold
blown on a wind from a southern plain of ice
untouched, uninhabited. Images known can kill;
and in my warm bed I prayed my way over that field
taking no joy in silence, no pride in that image
of—oh my courted one—your terrible contemplation.

THE TRAP

"I love you," said the child,
but the parrot with its blazing breast and wing
flaunted in the high tree, love's very beckoning,
and would not be beguiled.

Look how first innocence
darkens through shades of knowledge and desire!
—the bait, the trap, the patience! When the wire
snaps shut, his eyes' triumphant insolence!

"I loved it and it would not come to me."
Now love is gone.
Cunning and will undo us. We must be
their prisoners, boy, and in a bitterer cage
endure their lifelong rage.
Look round you. See, the chains on everyone.

Quick, save yourself! Undo
that door and let him go.

HOMECOMING

Spring, and the road is plushed with tender dust;
the house waits near and is expecting him.
Its elm puts on a glory, lit yet dim
with mingled light and leaf; there is a thrust
of irresistible budding. On the road
he walks, head up, just balancing its load;

the scarcely bearable load of bitter self
clamped firm, accepted closer day by day
since he stepped out of doors and went away.
Now, rooms made ready, flowers posed on the shelf,
linen ironed white, joy tremblingly arrayed,
you find yourselves made foolish and betrayed.

Take off your tenderness; let the petals fall.
Only one thing here he will recognize:
behind the glowing elm, the nesting cries
of garden birds, as grey, as stern and tall
as in his childhood, the steel pylon stands
gripping its deadly message in cold hands.

Brother, we dare not fail our load. Now brace
your skeleton's height, and hold. Danger and power
is ours; control and measure. Did we flower
our flowers would kill: but that is not our place.
Winter's perpetual gale we know, no more.
Shoulder the weight. Stride on. Open the door.

PRAYER

Let love not fall from me though I must grow old.
To see the words fade on the fading page,
to feel the skin numbing in fold on fold,
the mind and the heart forgetting their holy rage—

oh no, let me run, till the wind's agues blow
my cinders red again—let me tilt and drain
the last drop of my life before I go.
Let the earth's choirs and messengers not sing in vain.

While every flower swings open its eternal door
and every fruit encloses its timeless seed
let me not watch in spite, caring no more,
but let my heart's old pain tear me until I bleed.

Out in the dark, I know, sing a thousand voices;
and the owl, the poet's bird, and the saint's white moth
blunder against my window, the frog in the rain rejoices.
I pledge to the night and day my life's whole truth.

And you, who speak in me when I speak well,
withdraw not your grace, leave me not dry and cold.
I have praised you in the pain of love, I would praise you
    still
in the slowing of the blood, the time when I grow old.

SCULPTURE

The obstinate block, mere weight, oppressed his hands
that sought and failed to find what lay within—
oppressed his heart that could not compass it.
The shape that waited there was future, fate,
the word he had not learned, the thing that stands
around the corner that we cannot turn.

He left it where it stood, and went away.
Humped in its shroud of future it remained
until its hour and his at last came round.
His time, its space, full-circle met that day;
and for their marriage hammer and chisel rang
strokes that, like notes, upon the marble sang.

Cleaning Day

I carried rubbish down
until the house was clean,
cupboards scoured, shelves ransacked and bare.
High the heap grew;
I struck the match and blew
while the flame sulked against the idle air.

Sheltered, coaxed and fed,
slowly it caught and spread
till I could stand and watch its upward stream—
the gesture, the intent
spiralling, violent
dance that began around the core of flame.

Humble and worn-out things
put up their scarlet wings.
To new and pure sprang up the grey and old;
until a self-made wind
eddied within my mind
and drew it upward in a heat of gold.

O fire the poets know,
I kneel, I strike, I blow.

Clock and Heart

The trap of time surprised my heart—
its hidden teeth of circumstance
that draw the child into the clock
upon the cogs of tick and tock.
No logic, artifice nor chance
could silence my protesting heart.

Then poetry's electing shade
enclosed me with its darkening ray,
left me no face to recognize,
no eyes to meet my searching eyes.
The solitude of poetry
locked me within its second shade.

To light that shade and set me free
no flame had power but human love.
Against my will I caught and burned,
but then the key of time was turned,
the dark ray blazed, and from above
it lit the hour that set me free.

Set free at last in human time—
that long-rejected tyranny—
I found in ordinary love
the solitudes of poetry.

To a Mare

Eager and gentle one,
the grass is springing
green where you used to walk.
The drought is over
and all the birds are singing.
The roads of spring are waiting,
eager and gentle one.

Such simple words as these—
words soft and easy—
I use, but you are dead.
You won't hear what I'm saying,
nor lift your head,
its dark long-tilted eyes,
from where you're lying,
eager and gentle one.

Mare of the clean straight pace,
hide grey as mist or ghost,
what shall I tell your rider,
she who will miss you most?
Only, "All born must die;
all loved be lost?"

Say, Death I do not know.
Life, I know well,
its forward urging thrust
that set me dancing,
the noise of its great show—
grass-tastes, the bit-bar's steel.
Tell her who rode me last
death's only nothing;
death has no taste at all.

EVE TO HER DAUGHTERS

It was not I who began it.
Turned out into draughty caves,
hungry so often, having to work for our bread,
hearing the children whining,
I was nevertheless not unhappy.
Where Adam went I was fairly contented to go.
I adapted myself to the punishment: it was my life.

But Adam, you know …!
He kept on brooding over the insult,
over the trick They had played on us, over the scolding.
He had discovered a flaw in himself
and he had to make up for it.

Outside Eden the earth was imperfect,
the seasons changed, the game was fleet-footed,
he had to work for our living, and he didn't like it.
He even complained of my cooking
(it was hard to compete with Heaven).

So he set to work.
The earth must be made a new Eden
with central heating, domesticated animals,
mechanical harvesters, combustion engines,
escalators, refrigerators,
and modern means of communication
and multiplied opportunities for safe investment
and higher education for Abel and Cain
and the rest of the family.
You can see how his pride had been hurt.

In the process he had to unravel everything,
because he believed that mechanism
was the whole secret—he was always mechanical-minded.
He got to the very inside of the whole machine
exclaiming as he went, So this is how it works!
And now that I know how it works, why, I must have
    invented it.
As for God and the Other, they cannot be demonstrated,
and what cannot be demonstrated
doesn't exist.
You see, he had always been jealous.

Yes, he got to the centre
where nothing at all can be demonstrated.
And clearly he doesn't exist; but he refuses
to accept the conclusion.
You see, he was always an egotist.

It was warmer than this in the cave;
there was none of this fall-out.
I would suggest, for the sake of the children,
that it's time you took over.

But you are my daughters, you inherit my own faults of
    character;
you are submissive, following Adam
even beyond existence.
Faults of character have their own logic
and it always works out.
I observed this with Abel and Cain.

Perhaps the whole elaborate fable
right from the beginning
is meant to demonstrate this; perhaps it's the whole secret.
Perhaps nothing exists but our faults?
At least they can be demonstrated.

But it's useless to make
such a suggestion to Adam.
He has turned himself into God,
who is faultless, and doesn't exist.

REMEMBERING AN AUNT

H er room was large enough—you would say, private
from the rest of the house, until you looked again
and saw it supervised by her mother's window.
She kept there, face to the wall, some of the pictures
she had once painted; in a cupboard she had carved
was closed some music she had wished to play.

Her hands were pricked and blackened. At the piano
she played the pieces her mother liked to hear—
Chopin and Chaminade, In a Persian Market.
Her smile was awkward. When they said to her,
"Why not take up your sketching again? So pretty—"
she was abrupt. For she remembered Rome,
Florence, the galleries she saw at thirty,
she who had won art prizes at local shows
and played to country women from her childhood.

Brushes, paints, Beethoven put aside
(for ignorant flattery's worse than ignorant blame),
she took her stance and held it till she died.

I praise her for her silence and her pride;
art lay in both. Yet in her, all the same,
sometimes there sprang a small unnoticed flame—
grief too unseen, resentment too denied.

FOR JOHN SHAW NEILSON

If I could live like you, John Shaw,
fed on by unseen poetry—
the wise clown in country dress,
the bird that flies into the tree,
the melting of the coloured cloud,
the meeting of the flower and bee—

If I could sing like you, John Shaw,
with such a courteous purity,
I'd give these heavy words away
and need no more to speak for me
than such a voice, so morning-clear,
as in your nursery-tunes I hear.

THE YOUNG WIFE

O come to me out of that house
that traps you in your sleep!
I see your face of a stranger
writhe, and your closed eyes weep.
Wake, wake: you are in danger,
lying beside me, close.

I hear a far door open,
and could not call you home.
Silences wait and deepen.
Still you do not come.

When, when will he return?
I throw my sewing down
and walk from room to room.
This is our house, our own,
well-lit and kept with care.

But no—not ours, but mine.
I opened, he came in
out of the threatening night
where once he walked alone.
Was it not mine to share?

Faster, then, faster—run!
These curtained corridors,
this echo of racing feet—
or is it my heart-beat?

O the enormous house
stretches so far, so far
I am powerless as a ghost.
Our room's inhabited star
blinks out. I am lost. I am lost
in a house long loved and known.

Room after room, all dead,
all hollow—but who withdraws
at the knock of my thundering blood?
From the arch the plaster falls;
dust thickens on old wood.
The shadows mean me harm.

At last, in the dark, our door.
My voice, stumbling, calls
on the talisman of your name.

O bring me out of this house
that traps me in my sleep.
I lie beside you, close;
like you I writhe and weep.

TYPISTS IN THE PHOENIX BUILDING

In tiled and fireproof corridors
the typists shelter in their sex;
perking beside the half-cock clerks
they set a curl on freckled necks.
The formal bird above the doors

is set in metal whorls of flame.
The train goes aching on its rails.
Its rising cry of steel and wheels
intolerably comes, and fails
on walls immaculate and dumb.

Comptometers and calculators
compute the frequency of fires,
adduce the risk, add up the years.
Drawn by late-afternoon desires
the poles of mind meet lust's equators.

Where will the inundation reach
whose cycle we can but await?
The city burns in summer's heat,
grass withers and the season's late;
the metal bird would scorch the touch;

and yet above some distant source,
some shrunken lake or spring gone dry,
perhaps the clouds involve the day
in night, and once again on high
the blazing sun forgets its course,

deep-hidden in that whirling smoke
from which the floods of Nile may fall.
But summer burns the city still.
The metal bird upon the wall
is silent; Shirley and her clerk

in tiled and fireproof corridors
touch and fall apart. No fires
consume the banked comptometers;
no flood has lipped the inlaid floors.

CHILD WITH A DEAD ANIMAL

The thing you saw set your eyes running tears
    faster than words could tell:
the creature changed to thing, kindness to dread,
the live shape chilled, forsaken, left for dead—
    these crowded up to blind your eyes; these fell

and fell till it seemed you'd wash away with tears
    the glimpse you'd had of death
and clear it from your heart. It was not true.
The sight you saw had found its home in you;
    it breathes now in your breath,

sits in your glance. From it those gasping tears
  fell, and will always fall.
They sign you Man, whose very flesh is made
of light's encounter with its answering shade.
  Take then this bread, this wine; be part of all.

NAKED GIRL AND MIRROR

This is not I. I had no body once—
  only what served my need to laugh and run
and stare at stars and tentatively dance
on the fringe of foam and wave and sand and sun.
Eyes loved, hands reached for me, but I was gone
on my own currents, quicksilver, thistledown.
Can I be trapped at last in that soft face?

I stare at you in fear, dark brimming eyes.
Why do you watch me with that immoderate plea—
"Look under these curled lashes, recognize
that you were always here; know me—be me."
Smooth once-hermaphrodite shoulders, too tenderly
your long slope runs, above those sudden shy
curves furred with light that spring below your space.

No, I have been betrayed. If I had known
that this girl waited between a year and a year,
I'd not have chosen her bough to dance upon.
Betrayed, by that little darkness here, and here
this swelling softness and that frightened stare
from eyes I will not answer; shut out here
from my own self, by its new body's grace—

for I am betrayed by someone lovely. Yes,
I see you are lovely, hateful naked girl.
Your lips in the mirror tremble as I refuse
to know or claim you. Let me go—let me be gone.
You are half of some other who may never come.
Why should I tend you? You are not my own;
you seek that other—he will be your home.

Yet I pity your eyes in the mirror, misted with tears;
I lean to your kiss. I must serve you; I will obey.
Some day we may love. I may miss your going, some
    day,
though I shall always resent your dumb and fruitful
    years.
Your lovers shall learn better, and bitterly too,
if their arrogance dares to think I am part of you.

WATER

Water in braids and tumbles, shells of spray,
    heaves of clear glass and solemn greeneyed pools,
eel-coils and quick meanders, goes its way
fretting this savage basalt with its tools,

where from the hot rock-edge I drop my hands
and see their bones spread out like tugging weed,
each finger double-winged with ampersands
that stand above the current's talking-speed.

Such sentences, such cadences of speech
the tonguing water stutters in its race
as may have set us talking each to each
before our language found its proper pace;

since we are channelled by its running stream.
A skin of water glitters on your eye,
and round your skull a halo of faint steam
breathes up to join the spindrift in the sky.

THE BEANSTALK, MEDITATED LATER

What's fortune, that we pray it may be mild?
  The beans I carried home that careless day
I thought were toys, and I a clever child—
but mother scolded, throwing them away:
"The subtlest traps have just such pretty bait."
Well, she was right. That beanstalk reached a sky
where giants cheat us. We must skulk and wait
and steal our fortune back to mock them by.

Who was my father? See where that doubt leads—
the ladder grew so pat out of our garden
perhaps my mother recognized its seeds.
Giants have trampled earth and asked no pardon—
Well, nor did I. He took our family's gold.
I stole it back and saw the giant die.
(Four days to bury him.) Now I've grown old,
but still the giants trample in the sky.

Yes, still I hear them; and I meditate
(old, rich, respected, maudlin—says my son)
upon our generations and our fate.
Does each repeat the thing the last has done
though claiming he rejects it? Once I stood
beside my beanstalk—clever boy—and crowed
I'd killed the giant, Tom Thumb whose luck was good;
but now—what farmer saved the seed I sowed?

For somewhere still that dizzy ladder grows—
pathway for tit-for-tat from here to there—
and what's the traffic on it, no man knows.
Sometimes I hug my gold in pure despair
watching my son—my cocky enemy—
big, ugly, boastful. It's the giant strain
comes out in him, I think. I watch, and he
watches me. The gold is in his brain.

I'll post a proclamation—advertise—
find that farmer, buy his whole year's crop,
burn the lot, and see the last seed dies.
But one seed—yes—I'll plant. That's for my son.
I'll send him up it, wait; and when he's crawled
far enough, I'll lay the axe-blows on
and send him sprawling where his grandpa sprawled.

A DOCUMENT

"Sign there." I signed, but still uneasily.
    I sold the coachwood forest in my name.
Both had been given me; but all the same
remember that I signed uneasily.

Ceratopetalum, Scented Satinwood:
a tree attaining seventy feet in height.
Those pale-red calyces like sunset light
burned in my mind. A flesh-pink pliant wood

used in coachbuilding. Difficult of access
(those slopes were steep). But it was World War Two.
Their wood went into bomber-planes. They grew
hundreds of years to meet those hurried axes.

Under our socio-legal dispensation
both name and woodland had been given me.
I was much younger then than any tree
matured for timber. But to help the nation

I signed the document. The stand was pure
(eight hundred trees perhaps). Uneasily
(the bark smells sweetly when you wound the tree)
I set upon this land my signature.

Camping at Split Rock

Red mounting scales of cliff lead the eye up;
but here the rock has spaces of tenderness
where light and water open its heart. A lip
of narrow green shows where the creek-banks bless
a niche for trees and birds. So many birds!
Outside our tent they cross and recross our patch
of vision, hatch the air and double-hatch
in diving curves and lines. Each curve has words;

each flight speaks its own bird. The slowly strong
deep-thrusting heron's stroke; the glittering
daring rush of the swallow and the long
poise and turn of hawk on a still wing;
the quick low scuttle of wren, the coloured wind
of finches, blue-jay's wide noble rise and fall—
we read each bird from its air-written scrawl,
the bird no stranger than the interpreting mind.

The finger of age-old water splits the rock
and makes us room to live; the age-old word
runs on in language and from obstinate dark
hollows us room for seeing. The birds go by;
but we can name and hold them, each a word
that crystals round a more than mortal bird.

Snakeskin on a Gate

Summer's long heats slowing at January's end
I found by the gate a snake-slough; its dry scales
of horn blew newly-cast in the hot wind
against the hedge, ripped between stem and thorn.
I took it, shivering, and hung it on the gate-rails—

thinking it emblem, if emblems had been needed,
of a time of life like January, double-faced month of
   change,
that looking backward sighs for the dedication's innocence,
then turns too many pages, to find the end of the book.
But its touch was closer than omens: dry, cold, strange.

Dry with life withdrawn; cold with a desert cold;
strange, between two realities, neither alive nor decayed,
the snakeskin blew in the wind on the closed gate;
and I went uneasily, watching, for my life's sake,
for a coil of poisonous dark in the pools of shade.

Then at last I saw him, stretching warm in the sun;
shining; his patterned length clean as a cut jewel.
Set free of its dim shell, his glinting eye
saw only movement and light and had no fear of me.
Like this from our change, my soul, let us drink renewal.

New Guinea Legend:
The Finding of the Moon

I   The Village

This is the village where it happened.
   Dawn pushes aside
the huddling leaves of darkness.
Six huts of mud and palm
crouch in the shadow of the hill.
The moonless crag of night
draws back its height above them.

Six huts of palm and mud,
a fence of sharpened sticks,
a garden of yams
and a swamp of sago.
This is the village.

If the crag of night
let loose one thundering boulder—
if the uncontrollable sky
shook with one big storm—
if the huddling jungle
scowled and moved one finger—
the village would not be there.

Mud would slip back to mud,
plaited palm would fall,
palings and garden sink
under a rush of vines
and a thrust of riotous weed,
the dark life of the village
dissolve into darker jungle.

But clinging to its sulky hill
by six perilous huts
the village hangs, and this
is the village where it happened.

II THE PEOPLE

Who lives in the huts? Come out,
my people; go to your gardens,
for light is descending the hill.
Come out, take up your burdens,
for jungle, your angry mother,
is creeping to break your fences,
and sun, your burning father,
hurls at the hill his lances.

Here come the scolds, the wives,
the makers who must keep
the child at the breast fed
and the child in the womb asleep.
Their voices are bitter and loud,
their hands are never still,
for in their hands is the life
of the six huts on the hill.

Here come the old old women
whose children are born and grown—
fallen breast on belly,
skin shrivelled on bone—
the witches, the clever ones
who managed to survive;
from forty years of living
only these are alive.

Here are the girls and boys
who are not married yet—
the shining ones who fish
for love with a shining net.
And now the warriors come
shaking sleep from their eyes
and shaking the sharpened spear
on which the wild pig dies.

Last come the old old men—
the councillors rough with age,
whose words are water-gourds
to quench the young men's rage—
only the old old men
and the children too young still
to run at the women's heels
to the gardens down the hill.

What, is it you, Aruako,
walking here in a dream?
The young men have gone hunting,
the old men fish in the stream;
the women gather and dig,
the quarrelling children play
in the gardens down the hill
where beats the burning day.

What, is it you, Aruako?
Bachelor, lazy man,
village laughing-stock
since your days began—
womanless wanderer,
empty in sun or rain—
dream your dreams at night.
Dreams by day are vain.

III   ARUAKO SPEAKS

Root out the dream in my breast, for the dream is pain.
Why must I walk alone? Let me be like the rest,
for surely my life is vain. I will go where the rest have
    gone.

And yet I always withdraw; on my shoulder a hand
seems to fall. Can I laugh with the girls? can I go to war
with the young men? I must stand alone; I am always the
    fool.

Life is my hurt. The day burns like a brand and is gone,
night is a sightless murk where the wakeful ghosts mourn.
Man is burdened by the sun and blinded by the dark.

No, leave the dream in my breast, for the dream is true.
I have a girl like fire who lights me to my rest
and shining the night through, redeems the world's despair.

When I walk in the heats of day she is pale as a hill-pool;
when I lie in the brutish dark she takes my breath away.
I choose to be dreamer and fool; let the old men scold as
    they like.

IV   HE WALKS IN THE JUNGLE

Call on, you calling pigeon
by the waterfall.
This is the man who seeks from you
nothing, nothing at all.

Come down, you flying parrot,
drink and have no fear.
This is the man whose hands forget
club and sword and spear.

Under the crimson flower
that hangs above the stream,
the only flower that he sees
is the bloom of his own dream.

Wandering under the moonless
crag of everlasting night,
his ribs cage and shelter
a breathing bubble of white light.

V   THE GIRLS MOCK HIM

Come this way down to the creek, my sister.
Let us go for water to the pool by the fall.
I have seen Aruako's tracks there. Has he
a word to throw at us, or none at all?
Does he think he is clever, this Aruako?
Does he think that nobody sees where he goes?
Must we do his work for him, we do his hunting?
He lolls in a dream, and the whole village knows.

What is he doing at the creek, my sister?
He will not fish or dig, he is never any use.
Perhaps he is making his love with the wind
or carving canoes from the kunai grass.
Does he think we care that he lies by the creek?
If we see him let us tell him our thoughts, my sister.
He dreams of a girl, he talks in his sleep,
the fool, the idler, the backward lover.

Suppose it were you or me in his dream?
I would rather have a blind man, a deaf or a lame,
than wed such a lazy man with not a word to say.
Let us find him by the pool, let us mock and run away.

VI   Aruako is Moved by Their Scorn

Something says it is too early, I am too young;
something says do not act out of pride: wait.
But how can I bear this life? I will dig my grave;
I shall begin my first and last song,
I shall call at once on my long-awaited fate.

Sharpen all the digging-sticks, cut more, bring more.
I have nowhere to look for an answer except in the dark,
the mysterious flesh of the earth. Deep, deep, perhaps here,
perhaps she has gathered the secret ore of the sun,
has melted the daylight down into some bright lake
to mirror my jewel of night, the girl that my song must
    make.

Or is there nothing at last? Do sun and earth engender
nothing between them but the mocked shadows of men,
generation dying into generation, death treading on death?
If you hold no light, dark mother, to light me, then
deep in your body bury me with a falling thunder
and let my name die on a scornful breath,

for I reject you. But if, beyond birth and death and sleep,
you hold some answer, give it. Let my question thrust,
    thrust deep
beyond sleep, beyond death, beyond birth.
I look for night's meaning, earth.

VII   He Despairs of the Search

I am further in darkness here than any man has gone.
Heart fails me here; blood fails.
It is all done.
Depth of my being, you are no more than night;
You are nothing. I am nothing, who sprang from you.

I dreamed of light
to set on the crag of dark, to worship in dark.
The glory I saw was made of my dazzling pain.
In the black heart of this rock
I shall lie down. I was a child, and vain.

I was a fool and questioned like a fool;
now I lose even my madness. I breathe despair,
that absolute emptiness, instead of air.
I have lost her, my light, my girl like a hill-pool.

VIII   THE MOON IS BORN

Darkness frays the edge of self;
all boundaries vanish.
Past the shelving of horizons
memory's suns diminish.

Darkness pours through eye-sockets;
erasing silence
rises higher, mouth-high.
Alone with imminence,
in caves that are no shelter,
by waters that cannot move,
he draws now into his centre,
dreaming light: affirming love.

From depths he dares not know,
by veins that scarcely flow,
light stirs and comes in answer.
Fine as threads where dews condense,
faint as starlight's faintest silver,
light is born within his sense.
Light moves from mist to glow.

IX   THE POET BOASTS

This legend is old as the day the poet was born;
the poet who found and loved the stumbling moon
that travels weeping on the sun's triumphant road,
pursued by shadows, a pale uncertain bride.

Look said the poet, that is my dark face
laid against yours, white girl in the sky-space.
It overcomes your beauty, as you remember
our nights in the forest, our nights of love and slumber.

Yes, said the poet, I have cuckolded even the sun.
I the despised, the lazy singing-man,
once dug from the depths of my heart or the caves of earth
that sleeping child of light waiting her time for birth;

and if now she wrings her hands on her lonely way
and shuns her terrible lord, she weeps for me.
And if she reaches her full impassioned sway
of light and love, it is but for a night and a day.

If others seek her, it is in jealousy
of her maidenhead stolen by idle poetry;
for mine is the power, said the poet; the dreams I wove
have charmed into my shadow the girl that all men love.

Yes, now, my people, my elders, I understand
the meaning of my pain, the song on the empty wind
that stole my wits and left me your wandering fool,
the mock of this village that clings to its cruel hill.

We invent both light and dark: that is man's fate.
And I the chosen one, the moon's lunatic mate,
know well what current in you drove me apart
to dig from my depths the image of man's unfinished heart.

PORTRAIT

It was a heartfelt game, when it began—
polish and cook and sew and mend, contrive,
move between sink and stove, keep flower-beds weeded—
all her love needed was that it was needed,
and merely living kept the blood alive.

Now an old habit leads from sink to stove,
mends and keeps clean the house that looks like home,
and waits in hunger dressed to look like love
for the calm return of those who, when they come,
remind her: this was a game, when it began.

TURNING FIFTY

Having known war and peace
and loss and finding,
I drink my coffee and wait
for the sun to rise.

With kitchen swept, cat fed,
the day still quiet,
I taste my fifty years
here in the cup.

Outside the green birds come
for bread and water.
Their wings wait for the sun
to show their colours.

I'll show my colours too.
Though we've polluted
even this air I breathe
and spoiled green earth;

though, granted life or death,
death's what we're choosing,
and though these years we live
scar flesh and mind,

still, as the sun comes up
bearing my birthday,
having met time and love
I raise my cup—

dark, bitter, neutral, clean,
sober as morning—
to all I've seen and known—
to this new sun.

Two Sides of a Story

I KENNEDY

That obstinate thoughtless proud
   intelligent gay young man
read in his tent by night
from Leichhardt's Journal, and said
"I shall lead these tatterdemalion
convicts and rogues of mine
even through hell outright,
like this proud contrary German.
My heartbeat tells me I can."

Strata of ranges and rivers
stood between him and his vow;
and dark insulted spearmen
hid brooding their hate like lovers,
painted with clay and vermilion;
while the cartwheels dragged too slow
and the rain still fell. But Kennedy,
that stubborn dogmatic proud
gay attractive young man,
held service every Sunday,
saw the right Lesson was read,
and wrote up his Journal carefully.

O see what it is to be born
sixth child of a regular Major
("of fine record")—and to learn
the disciplined trade of surveyor.
See what it is to be British,
poor, self-confident, gay,
with a name to be made, and a way
to find, and an admiration
for a rather impractical Leader.

Now, Edmund, Edmund Kennedy,
so sanguine, hopeful, vernal,
you travel to your infernal
and painfully humbling anguish
with a gentlemanly passion.
Revenge and slow starvation
have tattered your Expedition.
Your sextant lost, and your Journal,
you die in the rain, alone.

Or if not alone, then nearly.
Though commendable, your companion
was only a savage. Dearly
as he cradled your head on his shoulder
from the exquisite grip of your pain,
you remembered public opinion,
your duty, the Expedition,
gave one last gasping order,
and lifting your pencil to paper,
died of your own ambition,
never speaking again.

II   JACKY JACKY

We see you still through a mist of sentiment,
Galmahra, Songman, born at a time so unlucky,
in your tribe's last days, and you the last of their poets,
and doomed to be given the nickname Jacky Jacky.

No one recorded the time and place of your birth,
but the white men had your country when you were young
and called it Jerry's Plains. For what you were worth,
they fed you scraps and taught you a humble tongue.

No one recorded the way you came to reach
Sydney Harbour from your country far on the Hunter,
nor how you came to be listed as thirteenth man
on the solemn Expedition across the water.

And what did you come to feel for Edmund Kennedy?
What was it looked from your eyes at your gay young
    leader—
your gentle bottomless eyes—as, grave and polite,
you found a road for that heavy preposterous cart,
growing more indispensable as the way grew harder?

Faithful, was the word the newspapers used,
and the officials, raking the rags left over
from their hopeful Expedition so gaily farewelled,
the few starved bones and bits of harness-leather.
Faithful—the way these wretched blacks should be;
but seldom are—a model for your people
who sit in their wurlies and mope, and are ungrateful
for our busy invasion, our civilized example.

They too should love and help us. So we gave you
a special medal to be worn for the rest of your days,
and fifty pounds in the Bank for approved expenses;
and we spoke of you with pleased uneasy surprise.

Yes, something, some faintly disgusted incredulity,
clouded our commendation. How odd of Kennedy
to die on so black a breast, in arms so alien.
It seemed somehow to betray a lack of dignity.

But you, Galmahra? I try to see into your eyes,
as frank and dark as the depths of your Hunter River.
You loved him, certainly; you wept as you buried him,
and you wept again, when your own escape was over.

But why? I imagine you slowly gaining hope—
hope that increased as the Expedition failed—
knowing yourself at last the trusted guide:
hope that somehow your life-pain would be healed,

that the smouldering flame in your heart might meet his
    eyes
and be quenched in their comforting blue; that you both
    might ride
through a nightmare country, mutually forgiven,
black logical as white, and side by side.

Surely he would give some word, some confirmation
that you were now his treasure, his Expedition,
since all the others were left behind, or dead?
He began to write—what message?—then dropped his
    head.

Over its burning weight you started to weep.
You scarcely looked at the grouped half-hearted spears,
while his heavy head burned in. Not all your tears
could put that pain out. It seared you terribly deep.

In Maitland Hospital, after, you felt it burning,
a red-hot weight; and cough as you might, it stayed
till the day, years after, when drunk as a paid-up drover
you fell in the campfire. Like an accepted lover
you clasped its logs in your arms and into your heart,
and died at last of your unacknowledged yearning.

Songmen may live their song, if they are lucky.
And you were Galmahra.
            Or were you Jacky Jacky?

THE HISTERIDAE

Coming with righteous fires to burn that afflicting carcass
diligently sought in the backyard thicket
for its awful momentous smell—
oh good God, what a disturbed squad
came rattling their elbowy armours
of pitch-black brandishing jaws and spectral elytra;
lean knights defending a rotting city's wall,
their food and task. Now, neutral fire come save us.

Like the corpse's, my lips snarled back from my teeth
at that apparent attack. Creations of nightmare,
I can look you up in a book: you have place and
    recognition.
Risers out of the pit skirted by restless sleep,
classifying Reason has pinned you; citizens of death,
you are of the Histeridae; knights of a black shore,
you are Hololepta sidnensis Mars.; the entomologist,
lips compressed with care, has put you in his collection.
Natural science has made us safe.

But how, how out of the world, though armed by day
with fire's objective cautery and learned Latin,
am I to carry those weapons to the restless pit
your rattling scuffling jaws defend?
You, long-dead entomologist, like this bush rat,
have found the crumbling edge cave in.
Something of you at least was conceded, given
to the black army. The Histeridae came for you at the end.
Come, exorcising verse. Let's turn away.

FOR ONE DYING

Come now; the angel leads.
All human lives betray,
all human love erodes
under time's laser ray;

the innocent animals
within us and without
die in corrupted hells
made out of human thought.

Green places and pure springs
are poisoned and laid bare—
even the hawk's high wings
ride on a fatal air.

But come; the angel calls.
Deep in the dreamer's cave
the one pure source upwells
its single luminous wave;

and there, Recorder, Seer,
you wait within your cell.
I bring, in love and fear,
the world I know too well

into your hands. Receive
these fractured days I yield.
Renew the life we grieve
by day to know and hold.

Renew the central dream
in blazing purity,
and let my rags confirm
and robe eternity.

For still the angel leads.
Ruined yet pure we go
with all our days and deeds
into that flame, that snow.

THIS TIME ALONE

Here still, the mountain that we climbed
when hand in hand my love and I
first looked through one another's eyes
and found the world that does not die.

Wild fuchsia flowered white and red,
the mintbush opened to the bee.
Stars circled round us where we lay
and dawn came naked from the sea.

Its holy ordinary light
welled up and blessed us and was blessed.
Nothing more simple, nor more strange,
than earth itself was then our rest.

I face the steep unyielding rock,
I bleed against the cockspur's thorn,
struggling the upward path again,
this time alone. This time alone,

I turn and set that world alight.
Unfurling from its hidden bud
it widens round me, past my sight,
filled with my breath, fed with my blood;

the sun that rises as I stand
comes up within me gold and young;
my hand is sheltered in your hand,
the bread of silence on my tongue.

LOVE SONG IN ABSENCE

I sighed for a world left desolate without you,
all certainty, passion and peace withdrawn;
men like furious ants without the ant's humility,
their automatic days led in by mechanical dawn.

Voices all round me witnessed your unknown absence.
The stars clicked through their uncaring motions
because they imaged nothing. An unchecked cruelty
was born of winter and fear. Surgical lesions

hardened round hearts from which you had been removed.
Only museums remained. All difference was equated.
Columns of numbers and coins marched through the living
    flesh.
Relationship died away till all was separated.

You are gone, I said, and since through you I lived
I begin to die. Instruments have no song
except the living breath. You moved in the artery
that withers without blood. You are gone too long.

But as I sighed, I knew: incomprehensible energy
creates us and destroys, all words are made
in the long shadow of eternity.
Their meanings alter even as the thing is said.

And so, "Return," I cried, and at the word
was silent, wondering what voice I heard.

THE VISION

(for J. P. McKinney)

G rowing beyond your life into your vision,
at last you proved the circle and stepped clear.
I used to watch you with a kind of fear,
moving untaught and yet with such precision,
as though on bridgeways tested long before.

There was a sureness in your contemplation,
a purity in that closed look you wore,
as though a godwit, rising from its shore,
followed alone and on its first migration
its road of air across the tumbled sea,

containing its own angel of assurance
that far out there its promised home would be.
So certainly you went, so certainly
the path you trusted gave you travel-clearance.
I strained to follow as it drew you on;

you, tracing out a pattern to its core
through lovely logics of the octagon
and radials' perfect plunging. Then you shone
like winter faces meeting spring once more
as the return of love they once had known.

Yes, I was jealous of your close companion,
your angel being brother to my own,
but you more rapt, more held, and less alone,
given more utterly to your communion
than I, who struggled with my own desire;

not strong enough to bear such invocation
nor pure enough to enter such a fire
I winced and envied. How to move entire
into the very core of concentration?
And now, as then, I would be where you are;

where eyes can close because no longer needed,
and heart be stilled around its inner star;
where all dimensions, neither near nor far,
open and crystalline and wholly-heeded,
dance to a music perfectly discerned.

The maze we travel has indeed its centre.
There is a source to which all time's returned.
That was the single truth your learning learned;
and I must hold to that, who cannot enter,
who move uncertainly and now alone.

What I remember of you makes reply.
Your eyes, your look, remain, all said and done,
the guarantee of blessing, now you're gone.
Time may be gaoler, set until we die;
but you were gaoled, and made your breakaway.

And left a truth, a triumph, as you went,
to prove the path. I touched you where you lay
(for it was not goodbye I had to say)
and made a kind of promise. What it meant
was: I am only I, as I was you;

but you were man, and man is more than man—
is central to the maze where all's made new.
That was the end the path had led you to,
the turning search that ends where it began
yet grows beyond itself into the vision;
blinded, yet moving with a blind precision,
because the end is there, the answer's true.

EURYDICE IN HADES

I knew this long ago, when we first loved;
but time went on so well, I had forgotten
what I saw then: how sudden it would be
when the path fell in,
when hand tore out of hand, and I went down
into this region of clay corridors
below the reach of song.

Now I can never hear you, nor you me.
Down these blind passages condemned to wander,
dreams plague me, and my heart
swings like a rocking-horse a child's abandoned.

Singer, creator, come and pierce this clay
with one keen grief, with one redeeming call.
Earth would relent to hear it, if you sang.

As once I dreamed you came.
Some music-maker led me with your voice
upwards; I still remember
one summoning glance of incandescent light
blue as the days I knew.
I saw his laurel-wreath, his mourning mouth:
he had your very look.

And then I dreamed
the King's long shout of triumph, and a voice
that cried "All's lost". And silence fell.
I grope my way through silences like clouds.
And still that phrase of music always murmurs,
but fainter, farther, like your eyes receding.

Your all-creating, all-redeeming song
fades, as the daylight fades.

HELOISE WAKENING

No, I would not go back there if I could.
The fire, as I recall it, sprang too high,
was something out of reason, passing God.
It fused us to a single blasphemy.

After, I thought: what snatched us to its height
and chars us in our separation now,
was some foreseeing of a fiercer light
than these insipid candles dare allow—

some future not yet possible, some Name
no saint or hermit knows or can conceive …
An easier God's virago, I grow tame
herding these simple nuns, who can believe

that flesh and spirit are not one, but two,
and one a slave to set the other free—
poor fools. We once had other work to do;
or so we thought. But who indeed were we?

It was as though all earth sent up a blaze
made of its very thought, to touch the sun,
and we that upward leap. No nights, no days
in that conjunction.
                              Heloise, have done!

The timid Sister knocking at your door
wakes you, she thinks, to give yourself to God.
Go pray and scold again, His virgin whore,
and swear, you'd not go back there, if you could.

TOOL

When I say, Oh, my love
    there's none to hear the cry
but the opposing dark
that begs, but does not speak,
the rock that hides the spark.

I crowd against that rock
my act, affirm, oppose,
I forge myself as tool
that tempers under toil,
to file this night; to steel

with glitter its dull skin
that somewhere holds a fire
but hugs and hoards it deep.
I practise to make sharp
even my dreams in sleep.

A keen and useful tool
shows shining at its edge
of wear against the world.
The edge is me I wield;
it hones a stony field.

So the unanswering night
begs glitter from my tool.
I chisel, shape and strike
that some replying spark
may set the night alight.

Affirm, oppose and give
brighten and wear my edge.
I strike that there may live
one spark's affirmative
to answer ... oh, my love.

EIGHT-PANEL SCREEN

Here the Sage is setting out.

A simple garment, cloth of blue,
is gathered in his girdle. Bare
head, rope sandals; seven lines
circumscribe him; that will do.
Now the world stands round about:
a path, a tree, a peak in air,
one narrow bridge beneath the pines.

Here's the Boy, three steps behind.

A cooking-pot, a sag-backed horse,
and his master's steps to tread
with a bundle on his back,
a tuft of hair, a stick of course,
rounded face still undefined.
As the Sage goes on ahead
the horse's rope takes up its slack.

Now the path begins to climb.

But the Sage still knows the Way,
sets his profile like a crag
or an eagle; meets the storm,
never waiting to survey
World in a moment's breathing-time.
On go Boy and stolid Nag.
Tao knows neither cold nor warm.

Now the path goes down the hill.

Steadily the Sage descends;
Boy and Horse go patter-clop
past the charcoal-burner's hut
where the crooked pine-tree stands.
On the Sage goes striding still.
Droops the Horse's underlip?
Does Boy falter in his trot?

Now they skirt the mountain-brook.

Past the fishers with their rods,
past the children in their game,
past the village with its smoke
and the ploughman in his clods;
up again the path goes—look!
Boy is dragging, so is Moke,
but to Sage it's all the same.

Up—and this time higher yet.

How, Boy wonders, be a Sage?
How ignore such aching feet
only thinking of the Way?
Wisdom seems to come with age—
if it's wisdom to forget
Stomach's groaning yawn for meat
and keep striding on all day.

Round and round the stairways wind.

Cloud and pine-tree, rock and snows,
surround the Sage's sinewy lope.
Muscles strung to meet the steep,
how his one blue garment blows!
Boy is rather far behind;
Horse is leaning on his rope;
Even Sun sinks down to sleep.

Look! The rest-house, there at last.

Sage sits down to meditate,
Moon accosts the last of day.
Boy brings water, stumbling now;
sees his face there fluctuate—
not so round! More sternly cast!
Patience and the endless Way,
these refine us. *That* is Tao.

POEM

"To break the pentameter, that was the first heave."
Afterwards it wasn't so difficult.
First sentences had to go.
Next, phrases.

Now we stand looking
with some kind of
modesty, perhaps?
at the last
and trickiest
one.

Come on boys it's easy.
Come on.
it's

ADVICE TO A YOUNG POET

There's a carefully neutral tone
you must obey;
there are certain things you must learn
never to say.

The city may totter around you,
the girders split;
but don't take a prophetic stance,
you'll be sorry for it.

The stars may disappear
in a poisonous cloud,
you may find your breath choked out.
Please, not so loud.

Your fingers and hands have turned
into hooks of steel?
Your mind's gone electronic
and your heart can't feel?

but listen, your teachers tell you,
it's not to worry.
Don't stamp or scream; take the Exit door
if you must; no hurry.

No panic, and no heroics,
the market's steady.
No rocking the boat, we beg.

What—sunk already?

AT A POETRY CONFERENCE, EXPO '67

This was the dream that woke me
from nembutal sleep into the pains of grief.

I had no hemisphere, yet all four hemispheres
reeled in a number-neoned sky,
over the grieved and starving, over the wars,
over the counter-clicking business corporations.
And round the cliffs of one grey vertical
squares of uncurtained light
showed all the sad, the human ends of love—
not springtime fulltime love but one-night stands
paid for with juke-box coins. And Sarah Vaughan was
    singing:
"Mist," she sang,
but it was chemical mist
mist from incinerators for the dead,
mist from the dollar-mints and automobiles,
mist from the cities grown
from crystallizing chemicals.

To keep the crowds amused
they calmed them with the curves of lovely fireworks,
each arc exact, prefigured and agreed-on
by chemists and by weapon-builders.

Each in their planned and floodlit window-spaces
the poets stood and beckoned to the crowds.
"Language!" they cried with their wild human breath,
but in the squares beneath the crowds cried "Numbers!"
"Words," cried the poets from their past, "Fires! Forests!"
the chemical greens of plastic leaves behind them.

"Rockets!" the crowds cried. "Wars!"
and every window opened, every poet
began to burn with napalm flames,
and fires detached and fell into the crowds,
fires of a human flesh.
Here a hand fell, opening like a flower,
a firework breast, a glowing genital.

In every mirror-surface of the windows
poets blazed self-reflected
until their hearts at last burned best of all.

But here no woman rescued hearts to carry home
in cherished caskets. Over the squares below
only the flower-children lifted faces
that called out "Pretty! Pretty!"
under the metronomed invisible stars.

You might have thought the flames that fell among them
would light the crowds and scar them to the bone,
but it was only language burning. Only
incinerated words. Few phrases
did more than hang above the crowds
an unaccepted holy ghost, a word
that no one dared to take and speak.

Then the squares darkened and the lifted faces
went grey with ash.

The show is over, cried the amplifiers.
Take home your souvenirs. Those burned-out sticks
are radio-active, ticking like geiger counters,
the spinal cords of poets, bright medullas
and clever cortexes. Hang them on your walls.
They'll do to mark your time.

Midnight is closing-time.
The crowds went drifting
into the metro. Only a few
carried their midnight souvenirs, their burned-out rockets.
The metro doors all closed.

Now under midnight's sign
there's nothing but the dark, the nembutal sleep,
the hemispheres are flattened by Mercator
projections; folded like fans.
The sweepers issue from their corners
and that show's over.

FOR A MIGRANT POET

The wounds of evening open:
day's tongue falls silent.
Windows in factory walls
reflect the red of twilight.
Here, Mariano,
the moment's seagull perches.

Here the world's dying
is carried on in silence.
The voice of love forgetting
and unforgotten
your slow guitar takes up.

Here cries the seagull
blown in from its long beaches
to search for food
in refuse dumps, in garbage—
the scavenging seagull
whose voice opens our wounds;

whose white's unsullied—
the gull from those long beaches
where love went walking.
It searches by the factories
for food, like your guitar.

"I am the seagull
who walks among the rubbish
of a land alien
to poets. I search for food
among the factory's refuse.
That is my poem."

THE CITY

Once again I've applied to the wrong place.
The more I walk round this city
(though I know it, you might say, like I know myself)
the less I like the look of it.

In other places, they say, the slums are going
or scheduled to go at least; but here
a street of deplorable humpies
populated by pensioners
is rotting under the City Hall's very windows.

Look at the news from the other capitals;
Everywhere else it seems they're voting money
for smog-abatement, tree-planting projects,
high-rise apartments, steam-cleaning of public buildings.
But here the air gets darker (I can't stop coughing)
and the river smells like death.

The trees that remain are blighted, iron shanties
lean against civic centres
and the Government buildings are getting so black
I can't tell where to apply for remission of rates
or a housing grant or a pension.

No doubt this explains why all my applications
seem to remain unanswered.
All I get from the man behind the grille
is the same old rhyme, "Your case isn't covered by our
    regulations,
but we'll consider your representations."
Nothing comes in the post.

So I keep on walking, but the streets are unfamiliar.
What a lot of them end in the river!
Do you know that the art-gallery's been burned down
and they're building some kind of temple?
(They must have relaxed the restrictions on immigration.)
All night long the side-streets
ring with the queerest noises, they call it music;
people wear blankets and leather.
Lately I saw a march of Service Veterans
mis-hearing an order, right-turn straight into a wall.
The sodden petal-faces
of drugged or love-mad children look through me
and pigeons lie dead in the parks.

Last week I applied to another counter
for a passport and airline ticket.
I was frightened. It's the pain I get just here
when I can't stop coughing.

It was a building of ancient grace,
with carvings of wreaths and a fountain playing,
but so terribly dark inside
I couldn't see who was behind the counter.

All I got was a burst of laughter,
a recording of birdsong, a smell of incense,
a strobe light turned in my eyes.
"You're really so anxious to leave?
Our representative will call tomorrow
with the documents to be signed."

He hasn't come. But I don't like to leave my room,
I've seen enough of this city.
And to think I used to have influence—influence—here!

FIRE SERMON

"Sinister powers," the ambassador said, "are moving
  into our ricefields. We are a little people
and all we want is to live."

But a chemical rain descending
has blackened the fields, and
we ate the buffalo because we were starving.

"Sinister powers," he said;
and I look at the newsreel child
crying, crying quite silently, here in my house.

I can't put out a hand to touch her,
that shadow printed on glass.
And if I could? I look at my hand.

This hand, this sinister power
and this one here on the right side
have blackened your ricefields,
my child, and killed your mother.

In the temple the great gold Buddha
smiles inward with half-closed eyes.
All is Maya, the dance, the veil,
Shiva's violent dream.

Let me out of this dream, I cry.
I belong to a simple people
and all we want is to live.

"It is not right that we slay our kinsmen,"
Arjuna cried. And the answer?
"What is action, what is inaction?
By me alone are they doomed and slain."

A hard answer
for those who are doomed and slain.

"All is fire," said the Buddha, "all—
sight, sense, all forms.
They burn with the fires of lust,
anger, illusion.

"Wherefore the wise man … "
"Be a lamp to yourself. Be an island."

Let me out of this dream, I cry,
but the great gold Buddha
smiles in the temple
under a napalm rain.

CHRISTMAS BALLAD

Then they retrieved the walking dead,
wiped his eyes clear of blood,
replaced his heart with a nylon one
and dry-cleaned his uniform.

Now, Son, we'll send you home.
With your hair brushed over the crack in your head
you look as good as ever you did.
You're the luckiest bloke was ever born.

Home he came and on the wharf
in her best bri-nylon stood his wife.
Darling you look well, she said;
only the children ran and hid.

He went out walking down the street.
Outside the pub his state-school mate
said, Christ, son, where you been?
Come and paint the old town red.

Things have changed since you been gone.
I turned my last-year's Holden in.
You wasn't here when the Cup was run.
You don't say much. Cat got your tongue?

Mercy, pity, peace and love,
shop in our department-store,
the Muzak angels sang above.
A long way off was the napalm war.

Love, mercy, pity, peace,
pluck us from the jungle mud.
Give a nylon heart and a metal head—
it's the newest gift for Christmas.

MASSACRE OF THE INNOCENTS

We speak with the voice
of your daughters, your sons,
We look through the eyes
of all innocent ones.
We are spring, which soon dies.

We are hope, and you kill us.
You will not forget.
We will haunt all your future
like regret—like regret.
We are love, which soon dies.

We are absence and loss.
All the years that you live
you may try to forget us—
no year will forgive.
We are man, who soon dies,

—as your children must die.
Let us live! Let us live!
No year will forgive you
that innocence dies.

JET FLIGHT OVER DERBY

Crossing this ravelled shore
fern-patterns of the tides
frayed like my branching nerves;
the last strung islands frayed.
And what is I? I said.

Rose-red a thousand miles
my country passed beneath.
Curved symmetry of dunes
echo my ribs and hands.
I am those worn red lands.

Stepped contours print my palms,
time's sandstorms wear me down,
wind labours in my breast.
I lost my foreign words
and spoke in tongues like birds.

Then past this ravelled shore
I meet the blues of sea.
Sky's nothing entered in,
erased and altered me
till I said, What is I?

A speck of moving flesh
I cross the bird-tracked air
and it's no place for me.
What's between sea and sky?
A travelling eye? A sigh?

This body knows its place,
and longs to stand on land
where bone, awhile upright,
walks on an earth it knows,
a droughty desert rose,

bearing the things it built;
difficult flower, tree, bird,
lizard and sandstone ridge.
I am what land has made
and land's myself, I said.

And therefore, when land dies?
opened by whips of greed
these plains lie torn and scarred.
Then I erode; my blood
reddens the stream in flood.

I cross this ravelled shore
and sigh: there's man no more.
Only a rage, a fear,
smokes up to darken air.
"Destroy the earth! Destroy.
There shall be no more joy."

THE DEAD ASTRONAUT

I circle still. You showed me love when time began;
and when this flesh had burned away, my bones
melted to nothing and eternity,
I cried to taste Time and your clay again.
I saw you veiled in air, impeccable Mary,
ageless Earth, clothed in old imagery.
There'd be no stone of you I would not kiss.

But I go blowing weightless in light's ways—
a hollow wingless seed, a seed of death—
and my eternity has no nights or days.
I circle you forever, visible Earth
who separate dark from light. You, you alone,
fabricate diamonds in your sightless stone
and make the universe into a truth.

Had I heart, eyes—as I am charred and blind—
I'd watch forever your altering light and dark—
your circling seasons, your renewing meaning.
Those words I used! Do you know you focus there
all of this space, the dream of the dumb sleeper
who is the axis of the galaxies?
Because of you, for you alone
this terrible sun began his endless shining.

Give me your night. I burn.

WEAPON

The will to power destroys the power to will.
The weapon made, we cannot help but use it;
it drags us with its own momentum still.

The power to kill compounds the need to kill.
Grown out of hand, the heart cannot refuse it;
the will to power undoes the power to will.

Though as we strike we cry "I did not choose it",
it drags us with its own momentum still.
In the one stroke we win the world and lose it.
The will to power destroys the power to will.

STILLBORN

Those who have once admitted
within their pulse and blood
the chill of that most loving
that most despairing child
known what is never told—
the arctic anti-god,
the secret of the cold.

Those who have once expected
the pains of that dark birth
which takes but without giving
and ends in double loss—
they still reach hands across
to grave from flowering earth,
to shroud from living dress.

Alive, they should be dead
who cheated their own death,
and I have heard them cry
when all else was lying still
"O that I stand above
while you lie down beneath!"
Such women weep for love
of one who drew no breath
and in the night they lie
giving the breast to death.

Rosina Alcona to
Julius Brenzaida

L iving long is containing
archaean levels,
buried yet living.
Greek urns, their lovely tranquillity
still and yet moving,
directing, surviving.

So driving homewards
full of my present
along the new freeway,
carved straight, rushing forward,
I see suddenly there still
that anachronism, the old wooden pub
stranded at the crossways.

Where you and I once
in an absolute present
drank laughing
in a day still living,
still laughing, still permanent.

Present crossed past
synchronized, at the junction.
The daylight of one day
was deepened, was darkened
by the light of another.

Three faces met.
Your vivid face in life,
your face of dead marble
touched mine simultaneously.

Holding the steering-wheel
my hands freeze. Out of my eyes
jump these undryable tears
from artesian pressures,
from the strata that cover you,
the silt-sift of time.

These gulping dry lines
are not my song for you.
That's made already.
Come in, dead Emily.

Have I forgot, my only Love, to love thee,
Severed at last by time's all-wearing wave?

A work of divinest anguish,
a Greek urn completed.
I grip the steering-wheel.
No other star has ever shone for me.

The pure poem rises
in lovely tranquillity,
as the Greek urn rises
from the soil of the past,
as the lost face rises
and the tears return.

I move through my present
gripping the steering-wheel,
repeating, repeating it.

The crossways fade; the freeway rushes forward.
"These days obscure but cannot do thee wrong."

WINGS

Between great coloured vanes the butterflies
drift to the sea with fixed bewildered eyes.

Once all their world was food; then sleep took over,
dressed them in cloaks and furs for some great lover—

some Juan, some Helen. Lifted by air and dream
they rose and circled into heaven's slipstream

to seek each other over fields of blue.
Impassioned unions waited—can't-come-true

images. Blown, a message or a kiss,
earth sent them to the sun's tremendous Yes.

Once met and joined, they sank; complete and brief
their sign was fastened back upon the leaf;

empty of future now, the wind turned cold,
their rich furs worn, they thin to membraned gold.

Poor Rimbauds never able to return
out of the searing rainbows they put on,

their wings have trapped them. Staring helplessly
they blow beyond the headland, to the sea.

LETTER

How write an honest letter
to you, my dearest?
We know each other well—
not well enough.

You, the dark baby hung
in a nurse's arms,
seen through a mist—your eyes
still vague, a stranger's eyes;

hung in a hospital world
of drugs and fevers.
You, too much wanted,
reared in betraying love.

Yes, love is dangerous.
The innocent beginner
can take for crystal-true
that rainbow surface;

surprise, surprise—
paddling the slime-dark bottom
the bull-rout's sting and spine
stuns your soft foot.

Why try to give
what never can be given—
safety, a green world?
It's mined, the trip-wire's waiting.

Perhaps we should have trained you
in using weapons,
bequeathed you a straight eye,
a sure-shot trigger-finger,

or that most commonplace
of self-defences,
an eye to Number One,
shop-lifting skills,

a fibrous heart, a head
sharp with arithmetic
to figure out the chances?
You'd not have that on.

What then? Drop-out, dry-rot?
Wipe all the questions
into an easy haze,
a fix for everything?

Or split the mind apart—
an old solution—
shouting to mental-nurses
your coded secrets?

I promised you unborn
something better than that—
the chance of love; clarity,
charity, caritas—dearest,

don't throw it in. Keep searching.
Dance even among these
poisoned swords; frightened only
of not being what you are—

of not expecting love
or hoping truth;
of sitting in lost corners
ill-willing time.

I promised what's not given,
and should repent of that,
but do not. You are you,
finding your own way;

nothing to do with me,
though all I care for.
I blow a kiss on paper.
I send your letter.

THE FLAME-TREE BLOOMS

It was you planted it;
and it grew high and put on crops of leaves,
extravagant fans; sheltered in it the spider weaves
and birds move through it.

For all it grew so well
it never bloomed, though we watched patiently,
having chosen its place where we could see
it from our window-sill.

Now, in its eighteenth spring,
suddenly, wholly, ceremoniously
it puts off every leaf and stands up nakedly,
calling and gathering,

every capacity in it, every power,
drawing up from the very roots of being
this pulse of total red that shocks my seeing
into an agony of flower.

It was you planted it;
and I lean on the sill to see it stand
in its dry shuffle of leaves, just as we planned,
these past years feeding it.

AUSTRALIA 1970

Die, wild country, like the eaglehawk,
dangerous till the last breath's gone,
clawing and striking. Die
cursing your captor through a raging eye.

Die like the tigersnake
that hisses such pure hatred from its pain
as fills the killer's dreams
with fear like suicide's invading stain.

Suffer, wild country, like the ironwood
that gaps the dozer-blade.
I see your living soil ebb with the tree
to naked poverty.

Die like the soldier-ant
mindless and faithful to your million years.
Though we corrupt you with our torturing mind,
stay obstinate; stay blind.

For we are conquerors and self-poisoners
more than scorpion or snake
and dying of the venoms that we make
even while you die of us.

I praise the scoring drought, the flying dust,
the drying creek, the furious animal,
that they oppose us still;
that we are ruined by the thing we kill.

REPORT OF A WORKING-PARTY

Ladies and gentlemen, we have returned
from our foray into the future.
Our report is appended.

The final peaks are impossibly steep.
It took us all our mathematics
to climb those exponential slopes.
We finally had to turn back
because we were starting too many avalanches.
We feared for your safety below.

Frankly we don't think you'll ever make the top.
Hidden by cloud (or smog) we were unable to see it;
there's vertigo in those verticals.
So we identified a certain ceiling
beyond which we consider settlement will be impossible.

Indeed, even at that height
our instruments detected certain warning-signals,
a lack of breathable air, a scarcity
of organisms other than ourselves;
so far above the tree-line
only certain insects appear to survive.

Apart from that, we were saddened
by the loss of some members of the working-party.
Our zoologist apparently was unable
to adapt to the height we reached.
We regret that he cut the rope.

About the Advance Party's fate we are uncertain.
It included, as you know, our economist,
the Chaplain, and the official representative
of the Government, Mr John Simple.
They were attempting to hack out a plateau
for the tents.
That incident started the avalanches.

Ladies and gentlemen, we are aware
our report must be a disappointment,
but we recommend you do not proceed.

Ladies and gentlemen ...

Ladies and gentlemen!

COMMUNICATION

My three-day friend met on the edge of dying,
I write these lines for you,
your line, they tell me, being disconnected.
I send this message though it won't get through.

Three days and nights we talked out to each other
our separate pains, deeper than strangers do.
Your number's disconnected now for ever,
but I talk on, though not to you.

Die as we must, we two were then related
in human honesty and suffering.
Only the buzz of silence meets me now,
I dial, but there's no one answering.

Yet I must go on talking to you dying.
I need to argue how we're held together,
how a connection brings a line alive
since we are all connected with each other.

"The heart is one" (sang Baez); it can get through.
Through the impersonal gabble of exchanges
lights suddenly flash on, the circuit pulses,
joins us together briefly, then estranges.

The line goes dead, but still the line is there,
for our reality is in relation.
The current bears the message, then stops flowing;
but it has proved there is communication.

HALFWAY

I saw a tadpole once in a sheet of ice
(a freakish joke played by my country's weather).
He hung at arrest, displayed as it were in glass,
an illustration of neither one thing nor the other.

His head was a frog's, and his hinder legs had grown
ready to climb and jump to his promised land;
but his bladed tail in the ice-pane weighed him down.
He seemed to accost my eye with his budding hand.

"I am neither one thing nor the other, not here nor there.
I saw great lights in the place where I would be,
but rose too soon, half made for water, half air,
and they have gripped and stilled and enchanted me.

"Is that world real, or a dream I cannot reach?
Beneath me the dark familiar waters flow
and my fellows huddle and nuzzle each to each,
while motionless here I stare where I cannot go."

The comic O of his mouth, his gold-rimmed eyes,
looked in that lustrous glaze as though they'd ask
my vague divinity, looming in stooped surprise,
for death or rescue. But neither was my task.

Waking halfway from a dream one winter night
I remembered him as a poem I had to write.

THE UNNECESSARY ANGEL

Yes, we still can sing
who reach this barren shore.
But no note will sound
as it did before.

In selfless innocence
first the song began.
Then it rose and swelled
into the song of man.

Every tone and key,
every shade it learned
that its limits held
and its powers discerned:

love and history,
joy in earth and sun,
its small chords embraced,
joining all in one.

But no note can come
from the flesh's pride
once the weapon's lodged
in the bleeding side;

once the truth is known:
Law surpasses Art.
Not the heart directs
what happens to the heart.

Yet we still can sing,
this proviso made:
Do not take for truth
any word we said.

Let the song be bare
that was richly dressed.
Sing with one reserve:
Silence might be best.

SHADOW

I stood to watch the sun
slip over the world's edge
its white-hot temples burning
where earth and vapour merge.
The shadow at my feet
rose upward silently;
announced that it was I;
entered to master me.

Yes, we exchange our dreams.
Possessed by day, intent
with haste and hammering time,
earth and her creatures went
imprisoned, separate
in isolating light.
Our enemy, our shadow,
is joined to us by night.

Joined by negating night
that counterpoints the day
and deepens into fear
of time that falls away,
of self that vanishes
till eyes stare outward blind
on one invading darkness
that brims from earth to mind.

Then came the after-image
burning behind the eye,
single and perilous
but more than memory.
When universe is lost
man on that centre stares
where from the abyss of power
world's image grows and flares.

World's image grows, and chaos
is mastered and lies still
in the resolving sentence
that's spoken once for all.
Now I accept you, shadow,
I change you; we are one.
I must enclose a darkness
since I contain the Sun.

HABITAT

I

Houses and bodies:
both limiting factors,
shelters, educators,
subject to alteration
by the inhabitants
under their own conditions.

This house is over fifty,
built to modest specifications
(a Worker's Dwelling).
It began as four rooms
(cook, eat, live, sleep).
They're still the main structure;
the rest hang on them.

Before we came here
it must have been real.
Old neighbours remember
the first-comers.
Cloudy outlines.

Digging the garden
I used to ponder their remnants:
crockery bits, smashed bottles,
iron bolts, shoesoles,
lost toys. Once we found
a small porcelain plaque
enamelled with chrysanthemums;
worth keeping.

Not much turns up now,
their time's silted under.

When we first came
the house seemed too big,
then too small,
now too big again.
When I'm alone
it creaks like footsteps.

Houses and bodies
have memories, but forget.
Things drop through cracks,
mice chew old letters.

You and I, house,
are in our fifties;
time now to pause
and look at each other.

II

Remember the three-day cyclone?
You rolled like a wooden ship
in waves of violence.
The front rooms flooded,
the doors jammed stuck,
but we rode it out.

Remember the long heat-wave?
Wood cracked and shrank,
tank-water ebbed to the bottom.
Air itself seemed flammable;
we were scared to scratch a match.

We trusted you as sailors
trust ships.
Assaulted by altering seasons
your weather-board walls
stayed tight, your galv-iron roof
shouldered them off.

But there are scars; wood-fibres
weaken, a little dust
sifts down, piles up.
Nails loosen.

III

An eight-foot carpet-snake
used to winter in the ceiling.
We heard him roll and stretch
when the evening fire was lighted.
He left each spring
on his own affairs.
Finally
some stick-happy farmer
took him for a trophy.
That winter the rats
came back.

The ceiling also sheltered
possums, mice, spiders.
A blossom-bat hung itself
neatly in my bedroom,
small fur umbrella
with live eyes.

Mud-wasps built cells
in hollows under books,
cicadas left horny ghosts,
split-backed, hooked to weatherboards.
The house was habitat
for things we never noticed.

Wood is hospitable,
even eatable,
subject to destruction;
the only stuff to live in
for destructible people.
Who'd live in steel and plastic
corseting their lives
with things not decently mortal?

We're perishable, house,
but nourishing.
I too am hostess
for numerous inhabitants—
a rich bacterial fauna.

Symbiosis—
that's our fate,
my wooden house.

IV

Furniture: humble, dependent,
asking for nothing
except to be there, to be used,
to be let stay around,
like an ageing aunt
waiting to hold the new baby.

Once in a street
I saw two old chairs
put out for the rubbish-collector.
They were shamed; their patches and stains
like age-spots and tear-tracks,
their bony legs
thin and bowed, their laps
suddenly empty.

Furniture likes its own place,
wears its way into carpets.
Move it around, even,
it looks dispossessed.
People are all it has left
of forests, of living and growing,
which is why furniture likes us,
can be betrayed.

Mirrors: cool ones.
Too quick on the uptake,
they've got all the snap answers before you.
They follow you round
and observe you.
They remember you instantly
like clever policemen,
and keep on reminding you
how you looked ten years ago.

Mirrors lie waiting in tombs.
Etruscan ladies
tried to take them along;
but glibly and faithlessly
they answer the tomb-robber.
They wait smooth and calm in the night
utterly certain
daylight will come back and find them
contemporary,
relevant,
quite up on the issues.

Mirrors repeat and repeat
that we're vain and ugly,
but will always need mirrors.
Only the final bomb
will melt the last mirror
with the last face.

What will the last face
look like?
Mirrors know.
It will contain all faces, all
human history
(which mirrors remember).

Shatter them: every knife-sharp bit
is a mirror, cursing you
seven years long.
Even their wooden frames
wince back, sensitive
as fingernails clipped too close,
from their ice-blink.

Mirrors reverse us.
Mirrors are mathematics,
reason, logic.
They stare at each other and demonstrate
Infinite Regress:
Reductio ad Absurdum:
Eternity: Zero:
the Cyclical Theory:
Vanitas Vanitatum.

Furniture wears out and dies.
Mirrors
never.

V

Bed
you are dressed
meekly in white
like a bride.

All day
you wait
silent
for night to undo you.

Atavist
warmth
forests
receive us and hide.

Patterns of ancient
movement;
stir in the limbs
sheltered
by covering leaves.

Dumb
sounds before words,
moist
breaths
uttered from unseen caves.

Brackish
Eocene heats:
plastic
subsiding sighs.

Rearing, rehearsing the animal
past in us,
prickling hair,
purr,
rhythmical sob.

Rising storm,
lightning,
rivers,
crash of the rains;

yielding at last
falling
away
under the waves.

Sea-smooth horizons
dumb under hanging
cloud
drown us in dream.

Dreams,
tongueless
images
licking the wounds,

soothe
like the brood of waters;
blood with the moon
moving
stilling heartbeat and vein;

healing the sore
with flesh
kind as eyelids
over
the stings of day;

loosening
disentwining
falling
away.

Bed
you are dressed
strangely
in white like a bride.

VI

The charity lotteries for Dream Houses
will always succeed.
They build on a deep base.
Women are always dreaming
about houses.

My own are always large,
faintly decaying,
with some rooms empty.
Their shadowy corridors
hide more than spiders.
Their front rooms are handsome,
but the action goes on at the back.

No one I know
lives in them.
They're occupied and guarded
by inner familiars:
the Two Black Villains,
the Handsome Man,
the Idiot Boy.
It's the women I know best:
the very old lady,
the child who follows me,
the Guide with Brown Hair
and the rest of the cast.

Heraldic animals
stand at the garden entrance.
My snakes are at home there.
We all play in difficult dramas
I can't quite interpret.

What's cooking in the kitchen?
Who's crying in the passage?
I wake and worry
but don't find the answers.

And outside—ah, outside!
The juggernaut machines,
the blue drifting gases,
the crashing aircraft!
Even a dream-house
can be a refuge.

But who wants them modern?
I'm happy with dust in the corners
and the old cast
to rehearse with.

VII

All
houses crumble or
fall
to the wrecker's tool:
scream of nail
torn from wood,
wall from wall;
or burn
one tall
rage of fire like a tree.
And I remember one,
stilted high,
white ant-riddled, unsound.
Winds knocked it to one knee,
then with a year-long
sigh
it settled to the ground.
One old man lived there
obstinately.
We saw the smoke rise still
from its wry chimney
till
he had to leave. Or die.
How will it be,
house, with you and me?

I had an aunt who lived
much of her life alone.
We are alike,
glad when guests have gone,
though often glad
also of company.
She died at eighty-three.
No one was there.
Do you need help to die?
Shall I?

Or finally
is what you know, enough?
When the roof's ripped off
to let in sky
and let out past to the air,
what need is there
for any to be by?
She was, maybe,
glad there was nobody
to notice how she died.
I like such lonely pride.

VIII

Lit up, within and upon
darkness of air and ground,
my house, you stand,
and darkness crowds around.

Guns level and bombs drop,
evil's come and to come,
eyes cock in the world's dark
for deeds yet to be done.

None of us innocent?
No; our light words hide
not one black dream
nor one imagined murder.

Guilt's our inhabitant
pacing all night inside
this well-lit frame.
Chaos incentres order.

Slow helices of smoke
signal up from the pit
our words contain,
twining within all reason.

We're bound for deeper dark.
I start up in my sleep
thinking it's dawn,
but that's another season.

Yet, dawns there were and are.
Hands, eyes, once interlaced
and can, and do, again.
Ride out the night, my house.

IX

We were fortunate, house; in a world of exiles
stateless, homeless wandering, spying, murdering,
wars, bewilderments, losses and betrayals,
we found each other.
In your spaces and awkward corners
we spread our lives out, fitted and grew together.

Your old trees dying warmed us with winter fires.
Your birdcalls, mice in cupboards, snakes in the garden,
made welcomes and nuisances for us, panics and symbols.
We ceased to be strangers.
Oiling your creaking hinges,
cursing your ill-hung doors, we changed in mute exchanges.

Storms beat in from the west, from eastward cyclones.
The traffic outside, the wars and rumours of wars,
the sad lost voices, the glow and rumble of cities,
you muted for us.
The radio plugged in your wiring,
let in, when we chose, enough of that surge and chorus.

Inside the books were read and the words were scribbled,
the talk went on, the friends and enemies came
and went; but we were content, coherent, employed
on our true affairs.
Our sicknesses, love and quarrels
continued in and around your beds and chairs.

What came in from outside was absorbed or wasted.
A pouring current of things and words and food
came channelled through doors and telephone, comings and
    goings.
People attract and direct
that current, are its transformers,
stations in space and time. We choose or reject

what passes us on the streams that circle the world.
Some things enter and leave, some become at home,
some are unanswered, irrelevant, turned away.
A kind of weaving
goes on all the time in houses, its pattern
determined by the years of taking and giving.

And we were fortunate, house, to have your shelter.
Your roof crouched among trees on the turning planet,
part of a surface receiving rain and sunlight,
kept off the shrieking
speed of space, the bad weather,
enclosed our portion of time, our pattern of making.

Thanks for our luck; against all accusations,
from the forlorn, the victims whirled in the wind,
I look back over our time here and affirm it,
having that right.
To live, to work together in intimate peace
is to prove in the dark the quality of light.

SOME WORDS

UNLESS

H ad a whole dream once
full of nothing else.

A bottomless pit,
eyes bulged out
across it,
neck stretched
over it.

A whole life I know of
fell into it
once;
and never came back.

Three white lines
joining exactly,
all the angles
equal.

Inside it—
symmetrical
cross-legged,
one finger up,
expounding a simple fact
sits Nobody.

A perfect confined space;
not one star
shines in.

ENOUGH

No use, we'll never catch it.
It's just ahead,
a puff
of flying light.

Want it! want it!
Wake up at night
crying for it,
walk round all day
needing it.

Till one day
it's there.
Not needed any more
not even wanted.

Look at it without a smile.
Turn away.

NEVER

Should never have done it, never.
Should never have left that country
where I was queen entirely.
Treacherous thaws betrayed me.

That land of I-will-never
gleaming with snow and silence
suited me with its iceblink,
it blue eyes fixed as mirrors.

Set on my peak, I queened it.
It was the spring that took me,
drowning in warmer waters
out to the lands of sometimes.

Here in the lands of sometimes
I stretched out hands lamenting,
but I'm a queen no longer,
melted my snows and glaciers.

They were so strong, so solid,
crystal as tears long frozen.
Here I'm at risk, half-drowning,
wanting my season, winter.

It will return and find me
caught in a depth of water,
freezing unseen in ice-depths,
never again to queen it,

to sit on my peak unmoving
the sceptre cold in my fingers,
my eyes on the blue-eyed glacier.
Should never have left it, never.

Ah, but I had to leave it.
No one can live there always,
the frost-bound queen of Never.
Once the blood moves, the flood moves,

the thaw begins, the ice-peaks
crumble, dissolve to river,
in which I swim or founder
through the warm lands of sometimes;

swim, drown, but now am human.
Change is my true condition,
to take and give and promise,
to fight and fail and alter.

I aim towards Forever,
but that is no one's country,
till in perhaps one moment,
dying, I'll recognise it;

those peaks not ice but sunlit
from sources past my knowing,
its beauty of completion
the end of being human.

AT A PUBLIC DINNER

No, I'm not eating. I'll watch the champing jaws,
solemnly eating and drinking my country's honour,
my country's flesh. The gravy's dripping red,
a nourishing stew for business. She's a goner—
crucified in fat speeches, toasted in wines
the colour of blood. And wounded past recall.
Let this occasion be her memorial.

It was all there in the first step onto land,
the flag raised, the guns fired.
No one but Harpur called her the land of equals,
the new Utopia ... Go away, we're tired;

we're tired of being asked about tomorrow.
Today the profit. Today the hideous old,
the rising price of uranium, beef and gold.
Today, for the dreamers, the totally useless sorrow.

DIALOGUE

All dialogue's a bargain:
while A supplies the words
B adds the silence.
Or here's the poem
set on a blank of paper.
The music's pattern
is eloquent only against its intervals.

So, sometimes,
half-lost in thought or reading,
I raise unfocused eyes.
Some luck of shadow
sets you in your own chair—
seen, not by will imagined,
simply because I need your silence there.

I half-start up, half speak;
even that half is made out of my knowledge
that you are gone. It comes
not from the time we spent together
but from the years without you:
the film's dark negative,
the silence after talk.

Your not-being's true
just as your being was.
It circles me, a lightless moon
seen by my light.
The years of unrelation
complete you for me.

All that I see says blandly,
"I'm Now, I'm three-dimensional";
yes, but what else?
Concave backs convex.
Turn Presence inside out
Absence is demonstrated.
Flick off the conscious switch,
there's Nothing, sprung
out of its secret place behind the world.

So here's our dialogue
made out of plus and minus,
zero and number.
I play with world's this-side—
but did we ever find that smooth magician
much more than half-convincing?

SPACE BETWEEN

S pace between lip and lip
and space between
living and long-dead flesh
can sometimes seem the same.

We strive across, we strain
to those who breathe the air,
to those in memory;
but Here is never There.

What is the space between,
enclosing us in one
united person, yet
dividing each alone?

Frail bridges cross from eye
to eye, from flesh to flesh,
from word to word; the net
is gapped at every mesh,

and this each human knows:
however close our touch
or intimate our speech,
silences, spaces reach
most deep, and will not close.

TWO DREAMTIMES
(*For Kath Walker*)

Kathy my sister with the torn heart,
I don't know how to thank you
for your dreamtime stories of joy and grief
written on paperbark.

You were one of the dark children
I wasn't allowed to play with—
riverbank campers, the wrong colour,
(I couldn't turn you white).

So it was late I met you,
late I began to know
they hadn't told me the land I loved
was taken out of your hands.

Sitting all night at my kitchen table
with a cry and a song in your voice,
your eyes were full of the dying children,
the blank-eyed taken women,

the sullen looks of the men who sold them
for rum to forget the selling,
the hard rational white faces
with eyes that forget the past.

With a knifeblade flash in your black eyes
that always long to be blacker,
your Spanish-Koori face
of a fighter and singer,

arms over your breast folding
your sorrow in to hold it,
you brought me to you some of the way
and came the rest to meet me,

over the desert of red sand
came from your lost country
to where I stand with all my fathers,
their guilt and righteousness.

Over the rum your voice sang
the tales of an old people,
their dreaming buried, the place forgotten ...
We too have lost our dreaming.

We the robbers robbed in turn,
selling this land on hire-purchase;
what's stolen once is stolen again
even before we know it.

If we are sisters, it's in this—
our grief for a lost country,
the place we dreamed in long ago,
poisoned now and crumbling.

Let us go back to that far time,
I riding the cleared hills,
plucking blue leaves for their eucalypt scent,
hearing the call of the plover,

in a land I thought was mine for life.
I mourn it as you mourn
the ripped length of the island beaches,
the drained paperbark swamps.

The easy Eden-dreamtime then
in a country of birds and trees
made me your shadow-sister, child,
dark girl I couldn't play with.

But we are grown to a changed world:
over the drinks at night
we can exchange our separate griefs,
but yours and mine are different.

A knife's between us. My righteous kin
still have cruel faces.
Neither you nor I can win them,
though we meet in secret kindness.

I am born of the conquerors,
you of the persecuted.
Raped by rum and an alien law,
progress and economics,

are you and I and a once-loved land
peopled by tribes and trees;
doomed by traders and stock exchanges,
bought by faceless strangers.

And you and I are bought and sold,
our songs and stories too
though quoted low in a falling market
(publishers shake their heads at poets).

Time that we shared for a little while,
telling sad tales of women
(black or white at a different price)
meant much and little to us.

My shadow-sister, I sing to you
from my place with my righteous kin,
to where you stand with the Koori dead,
"Trust none—not even poets."

The knife's between us. I turn it round,
the handle to your side,
the weapon made from your country's bones.
I have no right to take it.

But both of us die as our dreamtime dies.
I don't know what to give you
for your gay stories, your sad eyes,
but that, and a poem, sister.

ORIOLE, ORIOLE

Picking narcissus in the long grass
of the fenced acre by my house,
for twenty years long I stilled and heard
in the blackbean tree that greenvoiced bird,
Oriole is his singing name,
his wings a green stir in the green.
Oriole, oriole,
I whistle you up, I wait to hear.
No orioles sing to me this year.

Does poison creep through earth or air?
Did the last nest fall with a felled tree?
has every oriole gone away
and left my acre lonely?
Not a stirring heard or seen
of green wing, green melody.
Oriole, oriole,
I whistle you up, my green-in-green,
but day after silent day
you leave my acre lonely.

LAMENT FOR PASSENGER PIGEONS

("Don't ask for the meaning, ask for the use."
— Wittgenstein)

The voice of water as it flows and falls
 the noise air makes against earth-surfaces
have changed; are changing to the tunes we choose.

What wooed and echoed in the pigeon's voice?
We have not heard the bird. How reinvent
that passenger, its million wings and hues,

when we have lost the bird, the thing itself,
the sheen of life on flashing long migrations?
Might human musics hold it, could we hear?

Trapped in the fouling nests of time and space,
we turn the music on; but it is man,
and it is man who leans a deafening ear.

And it is man we eat and man we drink
and man who thickens round us like a stain.
Ice at the polar axis smells of me.

A word, a class, a formula, a use:
that is the rhythm, the cycle we impose.
The sirens sang us to the ends of sea,

and changed to us; their voices were our own,
jug jug to dirty ears in dirtied brine.
Pigeons and angels sang us to the sky

and turned to metal and a dirty need.
The height of sky, the depth of sea we are,
sick with a yellow stain, a fouling dye.

Whatever Being is, that formula,
it dies as we pursue it past the word.
We have not asked the meaning, but the use.

What is the use of water when it dims?
The use of air that whines of emptiness?
The use of glass-eyed pigeons caged in glass?

We listen to the sea, that old machine,
to air that hoarsens on earth-surfaces
and has no angel, no migrating cry.

What is the being and the end of man?
Blank surfaces reverb a human voice
whose echo tells us that we choose to die:

or else, against the blank of everything,
to reinvent that passenger, that bird-
siren-and-angel image we contain
essential in a constellating word.
To sing of Being, its escaping wing,
to utter absence in a human chord
and recreate the meaning as we sing.

ALIVE

L ight; and water. One drop.
Under the microscope
an outline. Slight
as a rim of glass;
barely and sparely there,
a scarcely-occupied shape.

What's more, the thing's alive.
How do I recognise
in a fleck so small
no human term applies—
no word's so minimal—
life's squirming throb and wave?

Locked in the focused stare
of the lens, my sight
flinches: a tiny kick.
The life in me replies
signalling back
"You there: I here."
What matters isn't size.

What matters is ... form. Form
concentrated, exact,
proof of a theorem
whose lines are lines of force
marking a limit. Trim,
somehow matter-of-fact,
even matter-of-course.
But alive. Like my eyes. Alive.

TO MARY GILMORE

Having arranged for the mail and stopped the papers,
tied loaves of bread Orlando-like to the tree,
love-messages for birds; suitcase in hand
I pause and regard the irony of me.

Supposed to be fifty-six, hair certainly grey,
stepping out much like sixteen on another journey
through a very late spring, the conference-papers packed
as a half-excuse for a double-tongued holiday;

as though I believed—well, then, as though I believed.
Remember Mary Gilmore, her little son
turned sixty-four, and bald? And Mary playing
her poet's game as though she'd never be done.

This is my place. It isn't far to my grave,
the waiting stone. But still there's life to do
and a taste of spring in the air. Should I sit and grieve,
Mary, or keep the ink running, like you?

Years have their truths, and each as true as another.
Salute, Mary. Not long now till we know
the blackened deathly world you once foresaw;
but now—let's live. I pick up my case and go.

"BID ME STRIKE A MATCH AND BLOW"

Set the match. Watch how the fire begins.
A wince, a flicker, blue,
the full gold at the core.
Spreading, it grips like teeth,
draws air like breath.
It has a work to do,
centuries of deadwood for raging through.
That's how the fire begins.

Air is its object and it thrives on air.
All that is burnable
waits for its change, inert.
Fuel and air commune within the fire,
a vanishing, a trance,
a final dance
alters their being. Stare
into its upward hastening for
some sign of visible God.
For nothing is more pure than fire in air.

Trees rise in it; whole dying forests rise,
whole peoples made of flame
storm upwards and are gone:
flights of death-ridden birds,
the fur and fear of blazing animals.
Earth's sap and emerald
die in a central gold;
drawn tall to dervishes of smoke they rise.

The speech of fire is all an upward prayer,
evangel to convert
to primal purity
all pasts that die,
all time's long error and black history
to be a speck of carbon in the sky.

GEOLOGY LECTURE

"We need some knowledge of the rocks beneath ... "
Oh yes indeed, oh yes, indeed we do.
The furnace of an old volcanic breath
survives and culminates in me and you.

"The Lower Paleozoic muds and sands
laid down five hundred million years ago
contain few fossils." Life's obscure commands
direct our blood, still salt from far below.

"Sea-lily stems, some radiolaria,
and vegetation unidentified ... "
We feel complacent. How evolved we are
who stare down knowingly at lens and slide!

"The horizontal layers gently fold;
the sediments consolidate to shale.
The last Ice Age ... " A reminiscent cold
shivers our spines as we absorb the tale.

"During the Cainozoic lava-flows
these ranges were built up." They wear away.
We perch upon them now in half a doze
sitting with gently folded hands today;

containing all prehistory in our bones
and all geology behind the brain
which in the Modern age could melt these stones
so fiercely, time might never start again.

WHITE NIGHT

The dream jumps me awake.
Earth's secretive dog, the moon,
grins sidelong through the pane.
Time's shallower than we thought.
Some meteorite's hot flake
rips blazing down, is gone—
or some sad manwrought metal?
We are tracked by our own evil.

The mind runs restless. Cast
back now, before time's done,
running head-down and thin
on the scent of the dying past.
Where does it all begin?
If evil has a beginning
it may disclose its meaning.

The hound sobs on the trail,
but the wolf's long dead—long dead
the unseen choice, the need
that led into this night.
Light-years of stars pour in
on to a sleepless bed;
the years fray, the threads weaken,
cloud crosses, corners darken.

"The boarhound and the boar
pursue their pattern ... "
but what stars reconcile
the two before they fail?
What long chase closes in
to wreck what helpless prey?

Lord, it cannot be I!

FINALE

The cruellest thing they did
was to send home his teeth from the hospital.
What could she do with those,
arriving as they did days after the funeral?

Wrapped them in one of his clean handkerchiefs
she'd laundered and taken down.
All she could do was cradle them in her hands;
they looked so strange, alone—

utterly jawless in a constant smile
not in the least like his. She could cry no more.
At midnight she took heart and aim and threw
them out of the kitchen-door.

It rocketed out, that finally-parted smile,
into the gully? the scrub? the neighbour's land?
And she went back and fell into stupid sleep,
knowing him dead at last, and by her hand.

TABLEAU

Bent over, staggering in panic or despair
from post to parking-meter in the hurried street,
he seemed to gesture at me,
as though we had met again; had met somewhere
forgotten, and now for the last time had to meet.

And I debated with myself; ought I to go
over the road—since no one stopped to ask
or even stand and look—
abandon my own life awhile and show
I was too proud to shirk that ant-like task?

And finally went. His almost vanished voice
accepted me; he gave himself to my hold,
(*pain, cancer—keep me still*).
We leaned on a drinking-fountain, fused in the vice
of a double pain; his sweat dropped on me cold.

Holding him up as he asked till the ambulance came,
among the sudden curious crowd, I knew
his plunging animal heart,
against my flesh the shapes of his too-young bone,
the heaving pattern of ribs. As still I do.

Warding the questioners, bearing his rack of weight,
I drank our strange ten minutes of embrace,
and watched him whiten there,
the drenched poverty of his slender face.
We could have been desperate lovers met too late.

WEDDING PHOTOGRAPH, 1913

I neloquent, side by side, this country couple
smiling confettied outside the family house—
he with his awkward faun-look, ears spread wide,
she with her downward conscious poise of beauty;
surrounded, wished-for, toasted by your clans
in the last threatening calm before the wars—
I look at you and wonder if I knew you.

Fathers and mothers enter an old pattern,
whoever they are; assume it for the children's
dependent and rebellious eyes. I see you
not through this amateur happy snapshot's sepias
but through the smell of a tweed shoulder sobbed-on,
through picnics, scoldings, moralities imparted
shyly, the sound of songs at a piano—

through all I had to learn and to unlearn,
absorb and fight against; through tears, then, better
remembered than through your love and kindnesses.
And she, pointing out birds or pansies' eyebrows,
gentle, fighting increasing pain—I know her
better from this averted girlish face
than in those memories death cut so short.

That was the most important thing she showed us—
that pain increases, death is final,
that people vanish. She never thought of that,
her second bridegroom, standing there invisible
on her right hand. Nor he of grief,
whose laughing easy look was furrowed later
by private and public matters. He lived long—

so long, I knew him well. Or so I thought;
But now I wonder. Here in this photograph
stand two whom I can ponder. Let me join
that happy crowd of cousins, sisters, parents,
brothers and friends. I lift a glass as well—
the greyhaired daughter whom you did not know.
The best of luck, young darlings.
Go on your honeymoon. Be happy always.

FALLS COUNTRY
(*for Peter Skrzynecki*)

I had an aunt and an uncle
brought up on the Eastern Fall.
They spoke the tongue of the falls-country,
sidelong, reluctant as leaves.
Trees were their thoughts:
peppermint-gum, black-sally,
white tea-tree hung over creeks,
rustle of bracken.
They spoke evasively,
listened to evident silence,
ran out on people.

She hid in her paintings,
clothed, clouded in leaves;
and her piano
scattered glittering notes
of leaves in sunlight,
drummed with winter rains,
opened green depths like gullies.

He took better to horses:
the galloping storms of hoofs
like eucalypts chattering,
or stones hopping on slopes.
Enclosed in the dust of mobs
or swinging and propping
among those ribbony boles
he was happy.
His eyes were as wary,
as soft as a kangaroo's.

Snow falling, the soft drizzle
of easterly weather
covers them, my old darlings.

What does the earth say?
Nothing sharp-edged.
Its gossip of lichen and leaf
its age-curved granites
its glitter of wetness
enclose them.

Is the spring coming?
Are there hooded orchids?
That's what their bones breed
under the talk of magpies.

Listen. Listen,
latecomer to my country,
sharer in what I know
eater of wild manna.
    There is
    there was
    a country
that spoke in the language of leaves.

REMINISCENCE

I was born into a coloured country;
spider-webs in dew on feathered grass,
mountains blue as wrens,
valleys cupping sky in like a cradle,
christmas-beetles winged with buzzing opal;
finches, robins, gang-gangs, pardalotes
tossed the blossom in its red-streaked trees.

My father had a tale of an old neighbour,
the kind of reminiscence one inherits.
Asked for difficult detail in his stories
at those bygone ample crowded teas,
(cup and saucer balanced on his knees):
"Madam, you might as well
ask me to enumerate the parrots."

Hundreds, thousands, birds uncountable
babbling, shrieking, swirling all around—
skiesful, treesful: lorikeets, rosellas,
lorilets and cockatiels and lowries,
Red-backed, Ring-necked, Orange-breasted,
    Turquoise,
Purple-crowned, Red-collared, Rainbow, Varied,
Scarlet-chested, Blue-browed, Scalybreasted,
Swift and Night and Paradise and Crimson,
Twenty-eight and Red-capped, Musk and Elegant—
I give up. But see him
sitting stiffly in a basket-chair
circled by their millions, formally
stirring three of sugar in his tea
in an afternoon I never knew
making conversation with the ladies.

Not a flock of parrots left to number.
Just a picture, fifty years behind,
left embroidered on my childish mind.
Parrots! They were something to remember.

PICTURE

S o eagerly lightly the man
  stroked his colours on—
the tawny sleepy slopes
the mood-dark mountains behind
and the fall and change of light
through clouds gentler than blue.
I stroke his hills too,
their bodies stretched in the mind.

Can only the young love
like this, with so tender a hand
and eye, see so
purely the earth's moment?
Past middle-age, I fidget,
pick at the years' callus
that cataracts my sight,
dulls my hand like a glove.

In what he paints I see
an earth I used to know,
light stroking slopes aglow,
earth various as flesh
and flesh its own delight;
and feel the young man stroking
his love, his earth, with a hand.
Time locks us up in the mind,
but leaves this window, art.

GRACE

Living is dailiness, a simple bread
that's worth the eating. But I have known a wine,
a drunkenness that can't be spoken or sung
without betraying it. Far past Yours or Mine,
even past Ours, it has nothing at all to say;
it slants a sudden laser through common day.

It seems to have nothing to do with things at all,
requires another element or dimension.
Not contemplation brings it; it merely happens,
past expectation and beyond intention;
takes over the depth of flesh, the inward eye,
is there, then vanishes. Does not live or die,

because it occurs beyond the here and now,
positives, negatives, what we hope and are.
Not even being in love, or making love,
brings it. It plunges a sword from a dark star.

Maybe there was once a word for it. Call it grace.
I have seen it, once or twice, through a human face.

THAT SEED

That seed I took from a low branch
of a rain-forest tree
wore a red fruit like an apple
that might have poisoned me;

but I set and watered it,
waited day by day.
Nothing seemed to come of it.
I threw the soil away.

Now in the garden where it fell,
quite against my plan,
springs up a thing as stray, as fierce,
as tall as a grown man.

Should I take an axe to it?
Should I let it grow?
It will shade my window-sill
and choke the flowers below.

It will beat its wild arms
in winds against my wall.
It may smash my roof down
if storm should make it fall.

Damn the unexpected!
I don't know.
Shall I take an axe to it
or shall I let it grow?

LAKE IN SPRING

The shallow reaches of the lake
on welcome-swallow days, lie still,
holding within a waveless blue
whatever comes, whatever goes
on path or hill.

So he and I not long ago
were there received and echoed back;
our living looks met eye to eye,
from calm and perfect surfaces
reflected to a perfect sky.

But now we move, we shift, we pass.
The images are overlaid.
The lake is driven by the wind
and stills again, and others cross
its mirror, and the world's remade.

Now when I bend to it again
another spring, another year
have changed and greyed the images,
and the face that lay beside
my own, no longer answers there.

There's little change in lake and sky,
they watch each other steadily;
but years took him and altered me.
Two look back in this calm weather,
but who is this, and who am I?

A ripple goes across the glass.
The faces break and blur and pass
as love and time are blurred together.

GOOD NEWS

Quite alone
   I walk in the streets;
grey fume of cars
grey foam of clouds
savage south wind
ears like cold oysters.
Rejoice, rejoice
I say to the lot of them,
the end's
been put off.
A tiny crack
shows in the wall
of the grey gaol
where maybe spring
has a seed waiting.

For a while longer
my friends
can sing and paint pictures
can love and quarrel
can fall into despair
and come up out of it.

And you
with sharks in your eyes
contracts in your hands
and balance sheets
that have to keep climbing;

you
masks with false smiles,
bribers, connivers,
smelling of facts
and factories
and underhand money
short-changing the world

and you saying I know
but you can't expect us
to do anything about it
we'll open a crack
in your grey brains
a fatal error
in your computers.

One crack in a grey wall
can spread
one seed can grow.
Don't you understand
that a minute gained
might mean
everything?

BLACK/WHITE

This time I shall recover
from my brief blowtorch fever.
The sweats of living
flood me; I wake again,
pondering the moves of anti and of pro.
Back into play I go.

Had it been pro-biotics that they gave me
would I still live?
Anti-biotics maybe snub the truth,
cheating the black king's move—
emptily save me,
a counter-ghost tricked from a rightful death.

But you can play on black squares or on white,
do without counters even; in theory
even the dead still influence what we do,
direct our strategy.
I'm none too sure exactly why I'm here,
which side I'm playing for—

But still, here's day, here's night,
the checkerboard of yes and no
and take and give.
Again I meet you face to face,
which in itself is unexpected grace.
To arms, my waiting opposite—
we live.

THE SLOPE

Dropping my head between my hands I said:
Black vortices in matter and the mind
draw all things to their end;
all tissue capable of joy and breath
whirls on that slope and disappears,
and man runs down destruction like a hound.
"That's your true trail,"
cries the great Analogue of us all,
"You are the instrument of this planet's death."

The core of suicidal Earth
plotted them, then? That politician,
his grey look sidling like a rat?
These profitmakers cheating for position?
These muddy men too numb to know they kill?
These, the consummate product of time's will?
If you can believe that,
cried my revolted spirit,
then die at once, you would be better dead.

Can you forget the ones you truly love—
poets and fighters with their eyes on truth,
swearing like Thomas Traherne, so perfectly
to hate the dull corruption of their greed
that you had rather suffer the flames of hell
than be like these? Will you deny
the burst of glory in the world and man?

I call you up, true men who lived and died;
my dead beloved, my guides, my living friends.
I say your names, I sing you to my side.
Keep far from me the sickness of despair.
Even on the last black slope
among mad images that rave or weep,
let all your voices call me back to air:
show me my true beginnings and their ends.

FROM

Fourth Quarter

1976

FOURTH QUARTER

You bitter sign,
last lemon-quarter grin,
tell me to throw it in?
I won't resign.

Tomorrow you'll be gone
into the black;
but you're just moving on
to make your comeback.

I won't be back again
or not this way.
But still there's gold to win
from the mullock's clay.

Old, terribly old
to the scornful young,
but still this rim of gold,
this last-light tongue

touches me till I shiver.
Grin in the sky,
I'm taker still and giver:
there's your reply.

EASTER MOON AND OWL

Keeping your old appointment,
spring's northern dawn,
you bring in autumn here.
The god's long done for in this hemisphere;
your full-tide flood of light
won't set him rising.

But the same owl, your ancient messenger,
crosses that light, his call
sounds here as there. Ruler of women
and singler-out of poets,
I greet him as your servant.

Men spy you out with eyes.
Their red brand's on your flank
and they plan colonies.
As for us, your true citizens,
we'll never make it
into those well-controlled
and solar-heated settlements.

Yet we still drag his tides.
His salt blood's subject
to the old spells of women
as to your own, Selene.
He fears the night, and still our music draws him.

To you, chill Domina,
I make the prayer of age. In my last quarter
let me be hag, but poet.
The lyric note may vanish from my verse,
but you have also found acceptable
the witch's spell—
even the witch's curse.

Muse, if they mock you,
you may yet grin last.
Man's signs are ominous.

TIGHTROPES

Lacking in one capacity, you need another,
fair balance at the end of the pole,
to walk the tightropes. Some people
are unable to see horizons, but compensate
by concentrating intensely
on the next two steps ahead.

I've cultivated stability
by keeping my horizons straight.
Now of a sudden we're crossing
very mountainous country. The peaks around
draw my attention to the gulfs below;
I'm suffering from nausea. Dangerous for acrobats,
this upness and downness, the landscape running crazy.

Concentrate, woman, concentrate.
Free verse is harder to bring off than rhyme,
liberty than slavery. Remember,
the pole-end weight, the accepted convention,
has dropped off.
Nor are you equipped with an inbuilt spirit-level.

Late in life, though, to acquire the habit
long unadmired in others
of seeing no further than the pace or two ahead
on a quaking rope.

INTERFACE (I)

Dreams: waves. Their wind-meandering changes
reach to the edge of shore, no further.
Their soft admonishing voices
sound from a sea where we can swim no longer.
Now we must wake. Whose heavy head
weighs down this shoulder?
whose hand this breast? My own. The mist disperses.

Feed in the new day's reel
of punched instructions.
Sit up, pull back the curtain,
stop the clock's hectoring.

Out of the far-below
sea's fading murmur
one voice: there's more to say.
Wait, child, stay with me.
I would, I would, but time won't have it so.
Beached by the old betraying sea
I drag my body further,
crawl to my unfinned feet and dress and go.

INTERFACE (II)

Nearly all those sea-smooth rocks
on the southern beach where only fishermen went
looked like small whales. One was a small whale.
We learned that from leeward.

Walking round the decaying monument
we learned other things too.
The bared bone of the eyesocket
hollowed deep in. Like the temples,
transparent, withering, of sad old people you love.

Whales tried the land early,
didn't like it. Easy to slip back
into the mothering upholding element,
be rocked again to half-sleep.

This is where they choose their suicides.
Dry harsh wind-battered beaches remind them
of an unaccepted challenge; their
old uneasy guilts
over that failure.

From the opposite direction, humans
come to their own extremes, remember
how they abandoned the faithful mother
to face a challenge they finally
couldn't meet,
and in a cross-traffic, take their own guilts
back to surrender.

INTERFACE (III)

Whales die of a sort of madness:
      They choose their own beaching.
Watch them come in like liners
under deranged captains.

Try to turn such whales aside
back to deep waters—
obstinately, blindly, certainly
they'll find another beach.

Death is inside the whale,
some diseased directive,
some inner treachery,
some worm lodged in the brain.

Afterwards, the whole air
of the coast's tainted
with an enormity,
corruption's total takeover.

You cannot bury the whale
in the beach it chose.
No sand is deep enough.
Some king-tide will uncover it.

Men must come, wearing masks
against decay's contagion,
chop it into small portions,
bulldoze it into trucks.

Far off, please. Very far off
where the smell of death can't reach us.
It's a huge task
to do away with a whale.

Whales are great mammals
but no wiser than men.
Take the head, you scientists,
investigate its workings.

You may find, deep in there,
the secret of destruction,
the tiny burrowing worm,
the virus in the brain.

You may expound its reason,
but the whale's past cure.
It has finally rejected
the whale-road, the free seas.

If you mourn its choice, remember,
not only whales have made it.
Whole peoples, countries, nations
have died in the same way.
Galaxies may be strewn
with staring burned-out planets
which took that path.

But this is to mourn a whale—
only a whale.

HALF DREAM

Half dreaming half awake
I felt the old boat rock at the lake shore
small pulse of waves in the moon-road
slop, lip, withdraw,
pull and slack of the rope
sigh in the trees.
Old boat
nibbles her rope, swings;
black swan stirs asleep.
Rise, fall of breath,
hesitant regular beat.
Tug on the wearing strand
all night long
sidling, slackening.

A peaceful dream. No sound
but leaf-talk, lip on sand
shift of swan-wing.
Half awake my heart
tested its moorings, turned
back to sleep.
Let the breath rise and fall,
the regular ripple and slack
fray at the strand.

DREAM

A degree or two of fever, a dose of aspirin,
and somewhere past midnight,
I think I wake from a dream.

So banal it was wholly convincing;
the clothes authentic, the set
three-dimensional, the cast and direction
faultless. The howling green hills of sea
storming the island and estuary
were quite familiar, attacking a country
whose map was clear in my mind. I remembered
everything as though I had lived there, though
I had never lived there.

A boring plot enough. First the Escape,
the door unlocked at dawn, the two,
trembling from hunger and torture,
waiting for the rescue-boat.
Then the Pursuit, the Capture, the Betrayal,
the roll of friends in the enemy's hands;
the Disaster; this time final. Nothing retrieved,
the known world lost, diced away
among the inhuman powers.

I had been so entirely convinced.
Waking was such a relief. I almost heard
the parent soothing: it's all right darling,
you are perfectly safe. This is the real world
and look, nobody's dying, nobody's being tortured,
the world is safe as houses.
Go back to sleep.

Obediently,
I lie back repeating
"No one is dying, nobody's being tortured,
this is the real world and perfectly safe."

THEY

They look like people
    that's the trouble.

Standing there at the door
leaning on the bar
shaking hands over the desk
they look like people.

Giving such a nice smile
a word about the weather
tickling the baby
shouting the drinks
even offering the isolated housewife
a quick pants-off behind the kitchen door
they look like people.

Only afterwards
when you're alone
you realize what you said
what the bargain was

you hear the click
as they say well thanks so much
and go off
to file the evidence

exactly like the click
in the telephone receiver.

PARTY WITH THE GODS
Hawaii 1974

It was the evening and the beer
gave us that dangerous dreaming-fit—
or else the symptoms of withdrawal.
Tyrants departing, could the gods
Come creeping back from forest hideouts?
And who came in but the old gods?

There was Vincent Eri from Niugini,
Albert the writer from Samoa,
Hone the shiningtoothed, the Maori
swinging a sharktooth on a chain,
Hussein, Professor of the Truth,
Fernando from Malaysia,
and I, white audience, represented
the humbled powers in defeat.

Round the Pacific's moaning shores,
dirty with gunboats, loud with planes,
the ancient countries stand and wait
longing to take their shape again,
shake off the years of Coca-Cola
and speak in voices of their own
the new-remembered poetry.

Toasting them all, from Maui on,
we watched Hone Tuwhare dancing,
his sharktooth bouncing on his chest.
Outside, the drift of different colours,
the shamed exploited in their T-shirts
advertising coke and dollars
stared through the plateglass in surprise.
The gods are seldom seen in pubs
dancing the haka in Hawaii.

It was the evening and the beer,
the moon on beaches made of money,
the palm-trees in the steamy night,
the animals hooting in the zoo,
the sound of waves from the Pacific,
gave us that dangerous dreaming-fit.
I sat and drank my beer and listened,
allowed to dream a part of it.

BRIEF NOTES ON CANBERRA

I   CITY AND MIRAGE

The tawny basin in the ring of hills
held nothing but the sunlight's glaze,
a blue-blank opaline mirage,
sheep cropping, flies, the magpies' warble.
Burley Griffin brimmed it with his gaze.

Cloud-architecture in reflected image:
arena, amphitheatre, gallery
on gallery of quivering marble,
rose from his mind—great circles, radials ...
Over the clear-strung air his fingers played
conjuring a rhetorical opera-city
for that bald eagle, King O'Malley.

Fantasies of power. The grey sheep nibble,
dogs snap at flies. Shoddy officials
argue his job away, confuse his plan.
Mirages, changed to lakes, lap sewage.
Cities are made of man.

II SCULPTURES

Canberra's sculptures are mostly
hollow
sharp-edged
with cold metal claws—
waiting for handouts?

The one I like
has curves and no edges.
One sweeping closed line
describes that naiad.

Between the Reserve Bank
the Law Courts
the Police
and the insurance offices
she's cleared a space for herself;

she has a small fountain
and never stops watching it.
Maybe she daren't
look up.

III MILITARY AIRCRAFT

This basin in the hills
holds a lens of clear air.
Day looks down through it
like a blue-eyed jeweller.

Tiny invisible midges
draw over it
snail-trails
of glistening snot.

Day
why don't you wipe your eye?

IV NOBODY LOOKS UP

Canberra
specializes in clouds—
great haughty ones
small frisky ones
marble acropolises
whiteheaded eagles
tableaux, processions,
galloping cavalry,
cottonwool snowscenes
with snowmen by Thurber.

They act so extravagantly
swirling their cloaks
and striking great poses—
Look at me. Look at me.

Canberra residents
don't seem to find them strange, but
maybe the newspapers
ought to review them.

V OAKS, ETC.

It isn't that I don't like
European trees.
Why, my great-grandfather came from …
Some of my best friends are …

But huddled together
in clumps and plantations
or lining the roads
like an official welcome
they look a bit lonely
slightly on guard, rather formal,
wishing the visit was over;

like the staff of an Embassy
at a party they don't really trust.

VI GOING OUTSIDE

I stepped out
into the day without thinking.

It rushed at me
took me by the throat
turned me back
and slammed the door after me.

—Blast you
can't you ever remember your coat and gloves?

VII ECOLOGICAL COMMENT

Considered as an ecosystem
Canberra is impossible.
No balance between input and output;
a monoculture community
whose energy goes entirely into organization.
Too little diversity
means instability
the scientists say.
No fooling.

Too many predators.
Too few producers.
Too little feedback
and very few refuges for prey species.

Somehow it continues to exist
as an ecological miracle.

THE DARK ONES

On the other side of the road
the dark ones stand.
Something leaks in our blood
like the ooze from a wound.

In the town on pension day
mute shadows glide.
The white talk dies away
the faces turn aside.
A shudder like breath caught
runs through the town.
Are *they* still here? We thought ...
Let us alone.

The night ghosts of a land
only by day possessed
come haunting into the mind
like a shadow cast.

Day has another side.
Night has its time to live,
a depth that rhymes our pride
with its alternative.

Go back. Leave us alone
the pale eyes say
from faces of pale stone.
They veer, drift away.

Those dark gutters of grief,
their eyes, are gone.
With a babble of shamed relief
the bargaining goes on.

REMEMBERING MICHAEL

When you were dying, we couldn't stop thinking of you,
counting what we had of you,
letters kisses poems.
They tasted chemical-strange. So did the world.

I sat in small-plane harness
bucking, dropping in wind over the coast-sea
Sydney to Newcastle.
Round me the nervous briefcases
sidled and shunted
from crophead to crophead
(Cromwell's men
going on missions
against the longhairs),
briefcases packed with our future in even black typing.
Over the tilting sea
streams of red sunlight poured.

Smelters, refineries, crouching among smoking phalluses
smoking six colours,
cylinders, blocks, cubes
swung at our left as we turned to the airfield.
Behind them a hell of a sunset
enraged their outlines,
a stumping circling dance of black geometrical dwarves
among black geometrical towers;
below them the chemical waters
attacked those leaking shores.

That wild copper mare of a sunset
reared right out of this world.
Flanks stabbed by chimneys,
acidic smoke in its veins,
kicking the sun's last arc
to death.

BY-PASS

There was just time
 to take the other way.
We saw it as we passed
but chose the highroad,
and what's around that curve
maybe we'll never know.

The highroad led,
widening, to this city
where violent boys
stare from street-corners
and factories blacken.

One-way. No U Turn.
The rules you keep here are the traffic rules.
You can't break those;
acres of plateglass ice
would shatter
blood glitter
on neon roads under the stop-and-go lights,
the ambulances come screaming.

If we turned now across the centreline,
escaped the cops somehow
and got away,
we'd find the roadblock set,
the red lamps strung across.

There's one chance only
to turn another way.

EVE SINGS

These human words, this apple-song,
I take from our green world that dies.
I give them into your human hands,
I look into your human eyes.

Can it be we who grow so old
or is it the world? Poor world—
the worms in your apple foul and waste
the apple and the apple-taste.

Your second-Eden promises
fail like the first, though still we love.
Strain for one more essential kiss—
such greed and joy it's been to live
to the end of earth and all it was.

The knowledge was of evil and good.
We learn it deeper, growing old,
but cannot change our human mould
or nay the word the serpent said.

The apple's bitter to the mouth,
our last windfall from green earth.
The sword turns all ways and the tree
drops one last fruit for you and me.
I gather it for your human hands
I look into your human eyes.

EVE SCOLDS

Still so entrepreneurial, vulgarly moreish,
plunging on and exploring where there's nothing
left to explore, exhausting the last of our flesh.
Poor Natura; poor Eve.
Sungods are parvenu. I never could believe
that old rib-story you told.
You, to come first? It was Night, Water,
Earth, Love, I.
You Adam, son of the Sun—
you thought his maleness chose
you out of the unshaped clay
(his huge masculine beard, his dictator-hand
giving you strength). But I—
I *was* the clay. Little boys
have to invent such tales.
It's insecurity—always your trouble. You say
I nag you, hag of the night
drawing attention to your weaknesses.

But my trouble was love—
wanting to share my apples. You
called that temptation, put us both in with Him.
Not fair; I should have run home to Mother.
Now, it's too late. I could never decide to leave.
Wholly bewizarded,
bullied, used as you use us, I rather liked it—
asked for it, no doubt.
But you and I, at heart, never got on.
Each of us wants to own—
you, to own me, but even more, the world;
I, to own you.

Lover, we've made, between us,
one hell of a world. And yet—
still at your touch I melt. How can there be
any way out of this?
As always, I go overboard for you,
here at the world's last edge.
Ravage us still; the very last green's our kiss.

ARCHITECTS

All buildings type the skeleton—
vertical structures braced and strong
with pelvic floor and shoulderbone,
the rooms within like organs strung
on muscle, rib and artery,
with corridors of nerve and vein,
threatened by time and gravity.
Buildings depict the shapes of work.

But when the architect must make
the shapes of Parliament and Crown,
of wisdom, art and government,
gallery, temple, library,
he takes the curve, the arch, the dome,
and chooses marble's clarity
to flesh the hard-pressed membrane out.
Skull's swell of thought and memory
houses time past and time to come ...

Your head lay heavy on my arm;
so massive, though so delicate,
that love could scarcely bear the weight.

BUILDERS

On great Ur-slabs of concrete terraces,
or rust-red bones of girder and cross-member,
they sit, eating their sandwiches
at noon. They look at home there
among the stylized trunks of metal forests,
the unfinished work.
Maybe the half-built is our proper habitat,
manhandling raw material
in basic contact, manipulation, direction
of various substances. Simple ...

Later, the place changes.
Dressed in plastic wallboards, fitted
with doors and windows, connected
by cables, wires and pipes to the feed-in world
it becomes part of a circuit.

Coming in later to consult officials,
sign papers, buy, sell, argue over contracts,
they observe the fake marble, the carpets
covering those bare encounters of concrete and steel,
the corridors scurrying with unfamiliar errands;
wondering. Wondering about building.
How whatever we construct gets complicated,
gets out of order and beyond control.

THE EUCALYPT AND THE
NATIONAL CHARACTER
(for Sir Otto Frankel)

*I believe it is the casual informality of form, so much in keeping with
what one has come to regard as the national character, which has given
the eucalypts their unrivalled place in the Australian landscape, and in
our perception and consciousness of Australia.*

O. H. Frankel, UNESCO Symposium on
Man and Landscape, Canberra 1974

Yes, we do perceive her as sprawling and informal;
even dishevelled, disorderly. That may be because
we are still of two minds about militarism and class-systems.
When we are informal, we're half afraid of bad form.
She, on the other hand, follows a delicate bent
of her own. Worn by such aeons, dried by such winds,
she has learned to be flexible, spare, flesh close to the bone.

Ready for any catastrophe, every extreme,
she leaves herself plenty of margin. Nothing is stiff,
symmetrical, indispensable. Everything bends
whip-supple, pivoting, loose, with a minimal mass.
She can wait grimly for months to break into flower
or willingly bloom in a day when the weather is right.
Meagre, careless, indifferent? With the toughest care,
the most economical tenderness, she provides for seed and
    egg.

Nor is she ever vulgar; she commits no excesses.
Her various gestures surround our pine plantations,
those fat green regiments that gobble our noble hills,
letting no light through, bearing no flowers. She is all light,
breathes in the noonday as lovers their lovers' breath.
We darken her sky with our cities.
She is artist enough to manage a graceful asymmetry;
but we are more apt to turn crooks.

FOR THE QUATERNARY AGE

When I looked down above the China Sea
         on archipelagos of sullen pearl
and gaps of ocean flicked by sunlight's fin,
it set me staring downwards into me.

Quaternary Age that made me in your dream,
fertile and violent, swung from ice to heat
to flood to famine—what you've grafted in!
Could I be calm when you are so extreme?

You tried to drown me in your melt of flood
and freeze me staring in your glacial step.
Burned by your intermitting fires I've known
splinters of crystal forming in my blood;

oppressed by shifts of rage and spells of calm
I felt your lightning spread my limited skull,
setting me tasks no wisdom would have done,
thrusting in probes, filling the wounds with balm.

You teach apocalypse and hymns of praise,
the use of fire, methods of stone and steel,
sacrifice, surgery, physics, the worship of sun.
Bound to your flying heels we wreck our days.

Your unpredictable dealings drive us wild.
We haruspicate, compute and pray your weather,
retreat to hive in cities, foul nests of men.
But here in this dragon-shell I'm still your child,

adoring this sudden light, the gaps between
terrors, the glow of cloud-tops, crevices
of green serenity. Whimpering, half in love,
I press on the armoured glass to watch you, lean
to your diverse passages, asking what you mean
by those mute and merciful designs of pearl.

You knock me back with a fang-flash and a snarl.

TERMITE QUEEN

In the absolute royal romance
this city-state began.
Clear rainbowed Psyche-wings
they rose on, He and She.

Pursued by Procne, Alcyone
and all winged dragons,
they reached their final rapture
and renounced flying.

Her blind obedient children
became her tools,
building a fort and prison
tunnelling darkness.

Now, gross and tended,
the clay-red temple's centre,
still she pours out
her milky stream of slaves.

She is nursery, granary, industry,
army and agriculture.
Her swollen motionless tissues
rule every tentacle.

Light is her danger.
She banishes love and joy
to the hostile air to run
their fearful cycle.

The whole great city trembles
with her pulse of terror,
when, outside, Echidna
claws at the skull-hard wall.

CASE-MOTH

Beak, claw, knifebright eye,
predator, antagonist,
winds that slash the naked flesh—
these try
all terms of possibility.
You invent your own reply;
but know:
traps are set wherever you go.

Homespun, homewoven pod,
case-moth wears a clever web.
Sloth-grey, slug-slow,
slung safe in a sad-coloured sack,
a twig-camouflaged bedsock,
shifts from leaf to next leaf;
lips life at a bag-mouth.

Quick now, play dead.
Pull the blanket over your head.
Stay still.
Watcher, waiter, eater, will
tire of waiting, soon go;
spring will warm
the snowstorm.
Eyes, varnished mask-face,
poke from the grey sheet,
clawed legs, hook-feet
find new holds; slow pace
edges sidewise but can move
to the place where food or love
wait.

Over the danger-depth of space
houdini-hung, she shuffles on.
Death's baffled. Wit's won.
Safe again, we're snug and smug.

Weaponless things
have some say.
Small prey
can yet escape.
Fear can grow swift wings
or like you, case-moth,
may weave against harsh weather
a warm house. But tough cloth
jails your shape.
Inside, your wings wither.

GROWING-POINT

A child in early spring, I stared
up at the sapling's growing-point;
a gathered strength, a total thrust
muscling itself, its swirl and sheaf
to one high clench of folded leaf.

My body answered tiptoe there,
a central need to rise as high
as limit, balance, let you go.
Around that axis spreads the weight
tree can afford by growing straight.

Breadth, form, completion—those depend
upon a proper symmetry.
The length of branch, the stance in space,
what leaf and fruit tree can sustain
dispose around a central strain.

I knew no word for growing-point,
but in myself the sapling rose,
an aim, a need, a leap to air;
where weighted, rounded, bough on bough
the tree fills out its limits now.

SWAMP PLANT

I have seen those very seldom-seen plants;
small earth-hugging rosette,
stem like a thread and downward-turning bell
of meditative blue. Half-size to a grasshopper,
what insect is small enough
to drink from you? *Mazus,*
Mazus pumila, somebody saw and named you.

Only science, then, has noticed you,
not poetry.
It's that way round in this country,
upside-down as ever.
Living on swamp-edges
turning your face to the ground, shyer than
    Wordsworth's violet,
no words but dog-Latin
have tagged you.

But for your colour—
such a colour as old sea-goddesses chose
(Mediterranean goddesses)
I would not have stooped to look.

But there are no flowers here
Persephone could have gathered;
nor do our people go
down on their knees at swamp-edges
or shorten their range of sight
to your less-than-a-finger's height.

Leaving you there, I take you home with me,
one tiny image
of still untouched unknown tranquillity.

ENCOUNTER

Knowing too much altogether about beetles:
Latin names, classifications, numbers—six legs, four
   wings,
thorax, antennae, eyes, segmented abdomen,
I stoop, cut off his light like a thunderstorm
or bird of prey. My interfering finger
chases this hurrying black-clad person,
turns him over. Earthquake. This beetle can scream!
Heaving and bellowing, world turned upside-down,
he begs and curses. Given a stick to fasten
on, he clasps it, click, like a pocket-knife,
a mechanical clown.

After that mutual surprise,
suddenly his whole shape turns to blur and buzz,
he's off, wholly at home in air, in life.

I've no idea what beetle is.
Beetle never recognized me. Nevertheless
it was a double event, a wild encounter.

PLATYPUS

At midnight and alone
there's a stir in my mind
from a summer afternoon
very long gone.
A girl leant on a fence
watching a pool;
an arrowhead of ripples
broke its clear silence.

Platypus, wary paradox,
ancient of beasts,
like a strange word rising
through the waterhole's rocks,
you're gone. That once bright water
won't hold you now.
No quicksilver bubble-trail
in that scummy fetor

under the bank's worn grass.
No warm summer day
would bring a girl to watch
that current pass
for your wild shy head.
The pool runs thick
with car-bodies, cans, oil.
The river's dead.

But at this late midnight
suddenly my mind
runs clear and you rise through.
I sit and write
a poem for your sake
that follows a word—
platypus, paradox—
like the ripples of your wake.

CREATION—ANNIHILATION

God in his element
pleased with his work and play
under the firmament
started the fifth great day.
Building the Elephant
from new-created mud,
whizzed round by fins and wings,
fishy and birdy things,
"Good," shouted God.

Slow Hippopotami
heaved from his clayey hand.
The golden Lion's eye
took light at his command.
Happy Hyena's cry,
roar of the Crocodile
answered his hearty voice:
"After your kind, rejoice
and be my Animal."

Mudscraps and sparks of light
he scattered everywhere.
Motes from his hand's delight
crowded earth, water, air,
too small, it seemed, for care;
too small for Adam's eye
when all the names began.
None of the words of man
reached lower than the Fly.

Anton van Leeuwenhoek
(seventeenth century)
—he was the first to look
into that squirming sea
under the Holy Book.
Ova and sperm he saw
under his single lens
down where the world begins—
animalcule and spore.

Minute, despised, the Fleas
sprang to appalling size.
Knee-joints of ants and bees;
wing-scales of butterflies;
weevils in granaries;
unseen rotifera
perfect as Elephant
waved all their cilia—
("Mere scraps and huslement"
of the Creation, as
Adam had thought they were.)

Already shaken by
crazy Galileo
whose telescopic eye
had set earth spinning so,
no one in bed could lie
safe, with those skies below,
man saw each water-drop
crowded with life and death.
How could he draw a breath?
Where would the worries stop?

Motion was everywhere,
all rules were running wild.
Man called to God in fear,
"Once I was Favourite Child!
Now I feel insecure,
creatures infest my blood,
I take no step that's sure,
even my food's impure.
Where are you, father, God?"

God, who had graduated
as any artist should,
beyond what he'd created
once he had seen it good,
was nowhere to be found,
by any man-made lens.
"He's died. He's gone to ground.
Theology's unsound.
He's become simply Ens!"

He left us in his will
(an ancient testament)
the whole Creation. Still,
insulted and bereft,
belittled by the sky,
besieged by the unseen,
we wonder angrily
how he could be so mean.

"His job was all Creation.
What is there left to do
but turn our talent to
what's always been its bent?
That must be what he meant.
Our job's Annihilation!"

FOR A BUTTERFLY FARMER

The rainbow's end was on your house
this evening when the rain was done,
violet blue green yellow red
elaborated cloud and sun.

One wing of light's great butterfly,
the vaporous colours brightened
to such a bow to bow to,
I was half frightened.

Is that a wing for time to hatch
from its grey cocoon?
You never knew it touched the ground
your house stood on.

If you'd known, would you have come
running with your net?
That's a brilliant specimen
nobody's gathered yet.

THE MARKS

Suddenly seeing my hand—
obedient bored pen-holder—
there on the field of paper,
I notice that oblong scar
at the base of the right forefinger.
That one's the first I remember.

A three-year-old, related
to me by memory only,
tripped and fell on a rock
(or was it a piece of glass?
I forget the agent enemy).
The world went scarlet with shock
and shook with appalling noise
like the yell of a branded calf.

Sting of rank iodine, scream
of linen ripped for a bandage,
and over the blood and grief
somebody's careless voice,
"The mark might stay till you die."

Die? Die? Die?
Like a fly or a sheep? A word
to strike you dumb on a sob.
If dying is what will happen
how shall I manage this trap
of a skin so ready to bleed,
and this hurtable bagful of red
in a world of sting and slap
and cut and knock and stab?

A long white line where the knife
slipped off a loaf of bread;
a nip from a blue mud-crab;
a scar from a barbed-wire jag;
a criss-cross pucker of burn;
a callus left by a pen;
a knuckle twisted by pain;
a random scribble of vein.

I have kept my skinful of red
on this hinged scaffold of bone
(with all due gratitude
to the help of medical science).
I have learned not to tumble down;
I can dodge and parry and hide;
I can handle kettle and knife.
It has been an enlightening life.

We have held off the enemy
and welcomed the friend and lover;
it has been a long alliance.
Director to employee
Hand: let's salute each other
though the mark of each failed encounter
will certainly stay till we die.

COLD NIGHT

Rain at the windows; in the house
a settled night of tearlessness.
That night a man came to my door
whom I had scarcely seen before.

Rain on his face and his hair wet
he looked a refugee from night,
hasty and trembling. One hard kiss
and he fled out to his own house.

I washed that kiss out of my mouth
cold as the rain that he ran through.
I'd my own troubles to hold in.
I never saw that man again—

dead. Dying then, the neighbours said,
and nothing to me, living or dead;

but walking sometimes on cold nights
the showers strike my naked face
hard, sudden, in a kind of kiss.

WOMAN IN ORCHARD

The woman in the orchard kneels
to love her body in the pool
and dream herself for ever young.
Look up, you fool,
the witch's eyes are watching you.
She is what you will be
hating what you are.

The peach-furred breast, the rufous hair,
the thigh's muscle, the heart's good—
that beauty's what the witch wants
and cannot have; and so she steals
not the flesh but the joy of it.
She has a quick wit,
knows what to get and how to get.
Look down, you fool;
the witch is watching from the pool
to make you what you will be
and poison what you are.

And who's outside the picture?
Look, look, you fool—
who but the man that painted it?
He sees the orchard-woman
and sees the witch behind her
casting the old and jealous spell.
Look how he brings the two together
in one reflection in the pool—
the ugly one you will be,
the lovely one you are.

PATTERNS

Too long away, too far,
now I come back to you;
the seven stones
the brown clay jar,
the carved seashell,
still in your former place,
familiar peace
persisting still.

You are confirmed again;
you link with the old pattern in my brain
and time rejoins.

My eyes ache. I've been halfway round the world,
telescoped days and stretched them out again.
New faces, voices, wants; ribbons of roads and air
wound in and then unwound,
drained
answers from blood, hand, mind.

Be my old silence. Be
the place and past and pattern that I know.
Be a loved verse re-read
before I pick my duties up and go.

TWENTY-FIVE YEARS

However intently sought, it comes back changed:
that clear blond evening on the pastoral hill,
grass gilt by the moon,
the swoop and song of the wires, the hare crouched still,
your hand on mine—
all comes clearly to mind, and all's estranged.

I said, I shall remember this. I do,
but not as it was. No wind, no scent, no sound;
all's out of reach,
a coloured slide on a screen. I see your hand
in mine and feel no touch,
only a will to grief. Yet it was true.

Confront it then with deliberate irony.
Can't you be glad that time takes off the edge
that used to cut so deep?
It's calm that wise men praise, not grief, not rage.
Turn over. Sleep.

But then the drowning wave—not memory—
that hurls me gasping down. Each vein, each artery
floods with a salt recall. Rescue. Throw me a rope.
It's not the past that dies. It's I who die.

AFTER THE VISITORS

All day I have lived in front of myself, my house
a hollow box of talk, of voices
crossing darting in mêlée, of crossing glances,
hands offering and taking food, cups, glasses,
crossing purposes flashing to air and diving.

I turn to myself again, now they are leaving,
about to go back to my proper house,
my private face.

Yes yes, of course I love you, I think I love you,
I think we agree, no we do not agree,
I do not believe you, yes darling I believe you—
we dip a moment and drink from eye to eye,
bodies slant and balance to and away
miming the flux of talk
or contradicting.

But now you are gone I shake you off and return
no longer needing to question or reply.

House settles. Walls calm. Air cools.
I put away glasses, adjust the house to my shape
and turn to my work. *Is it you again, alone?*
We are old companions, self. We can go on,
sometimes in love, sometimes lonely
with the old pang, the old delight,
the living balance between
waking and sleep.

AT CEDAR CREEK

How shall I remember the formula for poetry?
This morning I have abandoned the garden.
Too overgrown to recall the shapes we planned,
it flourishes with weeds not native to this country.

The thought of a calm wisdom, of manageable
    relationships,
of an old age with something to say
that any future will listen to
is scarcely reconcilable with the morning headlines.
Banking and Industry
welcome the big sell-out.
Report Urges New Approach:
Food or Famine?
Design for New Cities Condemned.
My desk is silted with papers.
Write to the Minister.
Protest torture of political prisoners.
Save the forests.
Protest the pollution of estuaries.
Demand no high-rise in this area.

Where to look for the formula?
Complex ritual connections
between Culture and Nature
are demonstrated by linguistic studies.
The myths of primitive people
can reveal codes
we may interpret.

Gifts of women cement early political systems,
assuring continuity.
Religions suppress the decays of time
and relate the Conscious
to the Unconscious (collective).
Metaphorical apprehensions
of the relations of deities, men and animals
can be set out in this schema.

Meanwhile keep lifting production for that is the answer
to inflation.
The rivers are silted already
here, and in Kyoto
I saw the sweet Kamo
choked with old plastic toys,
tyres and multiple rubbish.
The monks were singing
at the waterfall out of the mountain,
while shuffling in plastic slippers
we obeyed an ancient imperative
which serves to keep cleaner
the floors of the temple.

There was a formula
under the willows of Babylon.
But the children have never seen Zion.
They condemn alike
our action and our inaction.
They, however, also base their politics
on the exchange of women
and speak a language
clotted with ancient metaphor.

One can only connect
between things already distinguished,
but distinction has taken us
a very long way from base. Time
alters the shapes of the garden
and introduces new weeds;
while "even a tiny change on the natural scale
can bring disaster
to countless humans."

By the waterfalls of Cedar Creek
where there aren't any cedars
I try to remember the formula for poetry.
Plastic bags, broken beer bottles
effluent from the pig-farm
blur an old radiance.

FOR M.R.

All summer the leaves grow dense, the water-lilies
push up arrowhead after arrowhead,
burst into smoke-blue, hit the central gold,
and then retract themselves into bulb and mud.
Coming round the world, another season begins.

Martin, we have been writing to each other
for years, telling joys, griefs, happenings,
family gossip. Lives don't fit into letters
over one-half of the world. But talking over that space
we've been—what was it Plato said?—
happy companions in our pilgrimage.
You are English, Norman, Greek.
I battle that heritage
for room in another country, want to speak
some quite new dialect, never can;
it grows from my roots, it is my foliage.
Any time I flower, it's in the English language.

When all the living's done
it's poems that remain.
All that is personal, said Yeats,
soon rots
unless packed in ice and salt.
Poems can chill, shock,
stop you cold in your tracks,
functional as an axe.
But, too,
are a centring blaze in the field,
a sudden positive shape
sprung from the crowding leaves.

Reading your letters' news
I'd come on a poem. I felt
through the foliage of our lives
(and more than once is luck for any poet)
the arrow sprung to the target,
the shaft trembling in the central gold.

ENVY

Envy, the artist's inescapable sin,
takes no account of difference, distance, space,
time, tradition, medium, age or race.
I want to have been in every hand and skin,

held every painter's brush and writer's pen
and sculptor's chisel. What a greeneyed pain
caught me staring at tigers in the temple of Nanzen-
ji last year! They were my tigers, mine.

But most of all it's reading poetry
makes me storm my limits like a jaguar's cage.
My hair and fingers crisp with jealousy
wanting this poem and that in hopeless rage.

If we've a heaven or hell, art's daemon will announce
to my arriving soul in either one,
"You can be—you are—whatever you envied once.
What you longed to have done is waiting to be done

and all the boundaries are taken away.
You are Dante, Emily Bronte or Beethoven,
you can build the Taj Mahal, be Li Po or Manet.
Ask for a power and it shall be given."

Holding all skill and tradition, all times and eyes,
feeling the chill of the poles of art, the blaze
of its equator where the moment of making lies,
all lives and visions our own; past nights and days

my raging kin, we'd shape eternity
into earth's image, make the unseen seen
in forms of immutable jade. What hell or heaven could be
our proper justice, envy's retribution
or the reward of hopeless long devotion,
but reaching the highest power of what we've been?

LEARNING A WORD

I can remember you, Tom Snow,
boy stalk-high as a telegraph pole.
When I was nine, a rhyming girl
testing words in a world too tall,
I found a new one: Hero.

You had a coarse but quiet face,
handing change in the post-office store;
you had a toss of wavy hair.
I took my bullseyes and a stare
in that small sea-holiday place.

It was a wild grey autumn gale,
they said, that broke the small boat's back.
The waves ran higher than the wreck
hurling against the buried rock
a hull as suffering as a whale.

You swam alone to take a rope
out from the beach, like a long fish
towards the men who clung awash
watched by the anxious land. I wish
I could remember the tale's shape,

it was a year so long ago.
What I remember is that when
I came back, a girl of ten,
there was nobody called Tom Snow,
only a new word: Hero,

and somewhere a brass plate on a stone.
The small town watched the kingfisher sea
and the wind rattled the banksia tree.
Perhaps the thing was fantasy,
maybe I dreamed it, fitted on

a tale to a shouting hollow word
that sounded like the storm's black O—
a bubble of vowels rose and spread
round a dark and foundering head.
I rhymed the word with you, Tom Snow.

COUNTING IN SEVENS

Seven ones are seven.
I can't remember that year
or what presents I was given.

Seven twos are fourteen.
That year I found my mind,
swore not to be what I had been.

Seven threes are twenty-one.
I was sailing my own sea,
first in love, the knots undone.

Seven fours are twenty-eight;
three false starts had come and gone;
my true love came, and not too late.

Seven fives are thirty-five.
In her cot my daughter lay,
real, miraculous, alive.

Seven sixes are forty-two.
I packed her sandwiches for school,
I loved my love and time came true.

Seven sevens are forty-nine.
Fruit loaded down my apple-tree,
near fifty years of life were mine.

Seven eights are fifty-six.
My lips still cold from a last kiss,
my fire was ash and charcoal-sticks.

Seven nines are sixty-three, seven tens are
    seventy.
Who would that old woman be?
She will remember being me,
but what she is I cannot see.

Yet with every added seven,
some strange present I was given.

MOVING SOUTH

"It will be cold where you are going."
Yes.
Working today in this subtropical green
summer extravagance,
cutting back fleshy stems,
smelling steam-scented gardenias
I think of winter.

Last night a chained dog howled
in the heat of the full moon,
the old house rustled
like constantly turning pages.

But far off southward
a stony ridge lay waiting
for me to know it. I move
closer towards the pole.
Wind off the mountain snow,
small white-etched trees
leaning in leeward gestures.
I shall step carefully into the acid vapour
of morning frost. At night
I shall light fires.

Doesn't summer
half know itself a cheat, conjuring
all this green foliage
to hide the rocks, the earth
that waits to take it back?
Beauté de diable
its enchanting flesh
already beginning to droop like an old breast
on ribs of bone.

I'm tired now, summers,
of cutting you back to size.
Where I'm going you will be more succinct;
just time for a hurried embroidery
of bud, leaf, flower, seed
before the snow-winds snip you
to a root's endurance.

I may be more at home
observing your quick passages,
stacking up wood
against the length of winter.

BOUNDARIES

One leaf-scrap, photographed this way,
lies in a whole leaf-pattern—that's surprising?
the whole plant-history's coded in one seed
and not just plant: the whole planet, its changes,
its wobble and spin, air, water, stars,
the sun's force, the moon's pull, wax and wane.
You might find ways to photograph all that.
But there's no need.
I've seen even a hat
build under itself a person long since dead.
That lock of wild bronze hair
that Byron cut from a girl's head
sprang under my touch alive with the whole girl.

It's just that we think in limit, form and time.
Only language invents
future and past (now's gone before it's said).
What's I, what's here?
It's the whole flow that's real,
the whole change pouring through the lens of eyes
that first distinguish, then forget distinction;
record the many, then rejoin the all.

UNPACKING BOOKS
(*for Derek Walcott*)

On a dusty floor among piled rocking towers,
block-forts of prose, philosophy, history,
criticism, politics, sciences—word-cities
of civilization's greying geography—
I pick you up, poet of loves and pities,

and from green Caribbean nights again you sing,
This banjo-world have one string
and all men does dance to that tune.
Yes, yes and yes, my blood answers,
takes up the tune and dances.

You too know the greedy fever's aftermath,
legacies of dead empires, the bitter taste
of warring faction, the natal land's slow death,
all energy, fertility, fruit ripped out to waste.

The rot remains with us, the men are gone ...
Whatever we sang, dead politics denied;
the ruined rivers died, the forests died.
Yet poets keep an oath to hold and praise
what lives beyond the power-dreams of England,
    America, Spain.
Sweet naked Anadyomene drifts in to shore again
through oil-slicks, plastic discards, in our days.

Traherne said nothing had been loved as much
as it deserves. Though growing old I lament
too few answers to beauty's sight and touch,
too many words, I sit here now intent
on poetry's ancient vow to celebrate lovelong
life's wholeness, spring's return, the flesh's tune.

I twang that string again, rehearse the song
all ages sing, the dance I still remember,
taking a rhythm, a cue, a note from you,
player of violin and marimba.
There's an essential music still, a moon
where no man's landed, drawer of the heart
and muse of all our passion and our art.

FOUR POEMS FROM NEW ZEALAND

I   FROM THE WELLINGTON MUSEUM

Vine-spiralling Maori genealogies,
   carved paths through forests
inscribed with life-forms, coded histories
tangled my eyes
never quite able to meet that paua-stare.

Outside the museum
(built, like the city, on a fault-line,
they keep on telling you)
the city climbs and scrabbles,
arguing with contours, trying to keep square.

Having dropped out of the sky
to get here, I knew the double fetch of oceans
belting a narrow land. Ridged peaking crawls
of alps topped neat with sundae-snow.
Surge. Pressure. Cracks of farmland
scattered with wool-worms,
sheepyards, wooden houses.

The city's only joke, winds tweak
hair into watering eyes.
Rain-blows whip up the bay.

A grizzled man, scotch-eyed, grey-overcoated
stares from the terrace. A straggle of Maori boys
come swinging curls and tangles. Packs
cling like children on their backs.
Around his donegal-granite stance
their laughter parts, loops out
like water spiralling around a stone.

This sky flies clouds, gulls, ghosts.
Deep down, the world-plates struggle
in strangling quiet on each other.
Offshore, deliberate breakers hit the coasts.

Gashes of wind on green-scummed water.
Gnawed terraces shelve the scoria hills,
the sea a hidden theme
beyond the dunes. Gorse, bracken, blackberries
scab over wounded ground.

Suddenly here an ancient crack of valley
left to itself, its cloak of darkgreen feathers
trembling with wind, drops down beside the rails.

Over the forest names
the Maoris left, they have imposed
another country's history
(Palmerston North, New Plymouth).
Over the bared and crumbling hills
sheep eat, eat, eat and trot dementedly.

In small towns, tea-rooms
are called White Heather, Dewdrop Inn.
On rainy stations, pinkfaced countrywomen
drag children wrapped in wool.
Sometimes the softeyed longhaired young
run hand in hand carrying hikers' packs.
COME ALIVE, the poster tells them.

Most birds in these square farmlands
are sparrows, skylarks, starlings.
Just once I see, hawking a narrow river,
one flash, kingfisher-blue.

III ENTERTAINMENT

Such kind uncertain ladies in their best
gather to entertain the visitor.
The local talent stands by the piano
fingering music-pages
criss-crossed with sticky-tape.
They sing "I Love You Truly"
to an audience in neat and nervous rows.
This district
"is essentially one of clean sentiment",
declared the Tourist Bureau publication.

The town, however, was christened
in honour of an Elizabethan playwright
whose sentiments were often questionable.
Much farther south,
another questionable poet, Burns,
broods on another town.

Politely introduced, I lose my terror.
I read them Alec Hope:
age. Passion. Loss, and death.

They lean a little forward. Faces answer,
"We too have not much time
to find the one in whose lost folds of hair
we long to sleep. Here too the early snows
have already fallen."

The single terrible white peak
rears in the window-frame.
It is for tourists. Just a tourist-mountain.
"But sometimes, we too pause
and look, and look away."
So white, it casts a shadow on the day.

A narrow shelf below the southern alps,
a slate-grey beach scattered with drifted wood
darkens the sullen jade
of Tasman's breakers. Blackbacked gulls
hunt the green turn of waves.

One girl with Maori eyes
gathers up driftwood for a winter fire.
But for her smile, the beach is bare.
I am a one-day stranger here,

not knowing even the gulls' language.
I hawk their beach too, looking for momentos
(as the souvenir shops wisely spell it).
A coppery log, a Maori twine of roots—
can't carry that.

Behind me, the sky's paled
by a swoop of mountains, scope of snow
northward and southward. Jags, saw-teeth, blades of
    light
nobody could inhabit. Not my country.
I go back to my loves, my proper winter.

Here in the chant of sea-edge, grind of shingle,
I choose one stone,
a slate-grey oval scrawled with quartz
like a foam-edge, an edge of mountains
white as my hair.

I take you this for love, for being alone;
for being, itself. Being that's ground by glaciers,
seas and time. Out of the sea's teeth
I chose it for you, for another country,
loving you, loving another country.

Poems 1978–1980

BACKYARD

Knifed with green-glowing blades
and scissor-striped with shade
this square of grass and pioneering weed
frequented by blue moth, white butterfly
is forest level with my eye
where travellers toil and hurry. I
focus in closer, trying to live there too,
or switchback up from birdshadow to sky.

Blake's ancient men
blow-bearded spheres of feather-grey
rear on their dying stem,
loosening parachutes of dangling seed
and set them flying spiderwise.
Swung in parabolas they sink and rise,
halting on dock and thistle, burr, plantain;
glider-observers of terrain
where beetles blunder through a sorrel maze.

Autumn swings earth round sun
at the invisible lasso's end,
turning this latitude south and winterward.
This scrap of surface knows what's going on
and has its orders memorised.
Feed, pack and swaddle seed; store in the root
food to see the winter out;
prepare your planned retreat.
Ants hurry harvests underground.
Earth-dwellers scout

and burrow cells exactly larva-sized.

In last alchemic leaves held to the light,
in soundless bursts of seed,
in the tough satin of the spider's case
and the foam-plastic comb the mantis lays,
in branched green-copper-scaly spires of dock
the season's shorthand coils its final code;
This treeless trampled scrap of earth
fibrous with rot and weed
repeats its ancient orders. Use all death
to feed all life. The lockup of the frost
will melt, the codes translate with nothing lost.

SMALLTOWN DANCE

Two women find the square-root of a sheet.
    That is an ancient dance:
arms wide: together: again: two forward steps: hands meet
your partner's once and twice.
That white expanse
reduces to a neat
compression fitting in the smallest space
a sheet can pack in on a cupboard shelf.

High scented walls there were of flapping white
when I was small, myself.
I walked between them, playing Out of Sight.
Simpler than arms, they wrapped and comforted—
clean corridors of hiding, roofed with blue—
saying, Your sins too are made Monday-new;
and see, ahead
that glimpse of unobstructed waiting green.
Run, run before you're seen.

But women know the scale of possibility,
the limit of opportunity,
the fence,
how little chance
there is of getting out. The sheets that tug
sometimes struggle from the peg,
don't travel far. Might symbolise
something. Knowing where danger lies
you have to keep things orderly.
The household budget will not stretch to more.

And they can demonstrate it in a dance.
First pull those wallowing white dreamers down,
spread arms: then close them. Fold
those beckoning roads to some impossible world,
put them away and close the cupboard door.

LATE MEETING

The last, the very last
flower of the autumn
lifts its too-pale
head in the wind from the snows.

The last, the very last
journey from the hive
tempts out the wind-worn bee.

They meet, they mingle,
tossed by the chilly air
in the old ecstasy,

as though
nothing existed past
the moment's joining,

as though
from this late take-and-give
some seed might set.

His dimming faceted eyes
reflect a thin
near-winter sunlight,

the gusts of wind
tremble her petals round him,
a failing shelter.

END OF A MONARCHY

The sunset's classical crater
erupts. Billows and skeins
of cirrus, cirrostratus,
altocumulus, cumulus
dispose above the plains
their various shapes and altitudes
for the great Irradiator.
Wornout soils from the west
haze upwards in pinkening dust;
clouds take up welcoming attitudes
for the old Big Show to begin.

Reaching edges, cliffs, finality,
it's right to dramatise,
bring in tragedy, comedy, irony,
wear masks for emphasis.
Stamping his life's last stage
the original King, earth's ruler
meets his dark tanist twin
with a crossing of swords, a rage
of purple, scarlet, crimson,
for the death of a day or an age.

We know the end of our play
as a common human ill.
What we get of pomp and ritual
leaks to a final funeral.
No higher court of appeal
will save us, prole and underling,
whatever counsel may say;
but the King is never undone.
A little expedient conjuring
and here he is again ...

Today, in a different guise,
in a supersonic jet
keeping up with the nuclear set
and the exponential leap.
In a sonic boom of surprise
his multinational vectors
shatter the anxious sleep
of his subjects. Now he is met
at dawn by prime ministers, guards,
and chairmen of directors—
never by priests and bards.

Sun-king, Irradiator,
what does your briefcase hide?
What are the contract's terms?
And supposing the dollars are real
what do we get on the deal?
If we crash, we're broke to the wide.
And you? At the end of the day
when your jet goes west to the Twin
will the last Big Show begin,
the closing night of the play?

VICTIMS

They are ageing now, some dead.
In the third-class suburbs of exile
their foreign accents
continue to condemn them. They should
not have expected more.

They had their time
of blazing across headlines,
welcomes, interviews, placings
in jobs that could not fit,
of being walked around carefully.
One averts the eyes
from horror or miracle equally.

Their faces, common to humankind,
had eyes, lips, noses.
That in itself was grave
seen through such a flame.

The Czech boy, talking,
posturing, desperate to please,
restless as a spastic trying
to confine his twitches
into the normal straitjacket—
what could we do with him?

The neighbours asked him
to children's parties,
being at sixteen a child;
gave him small jobs
having no niche to hold him
whether as icon, inhabitant
or memento mori.

He could not be a person
having once been forced to carry
other children's corpses
to the place of burning.

But when we saw him walk
beside our own children
darkness rose from that pit.
Quickly but carefully
(he must not notice)
we put our bodies
between our children and the Victim.

Absit omen, you gods—
avert the doom,
the future's beckoning flame.

Perhaps he did notice. At last
he went away.

In what backstreet of what city
does he keep silence, unreadable
fading graffito of half-
forgotten obscenity?

Think: such are not to be pitied.
They wear already
a coat of ash seared in.
But our children and their children
have put on, over the years
a delicate cloak of fat.

BRENNAN

Self-proclaimed companion
of prophets, priests and poets,
walker on earth's last fringes,
haunted lover
of the beckoning darkness,
last Symbolist, poor hero
lost looking for yourself,
your journey was our journey.
This is for you.

History's burning garbage
of myths and searches
sends up its smoke-wreath
from the city dump.
It stings in our eyes too.

Seeking in the flesh of youth
for Eve's spring meadows
of blue and golden flowers,
deep in their centres
you saw the empty question—
the question of the sphinx
half-nature and half-woman.
It mocked, No answer?

Walking the streets of your poem
you told dead Mallarmé
Here's your great book,
finished at the ends of earth.
It's the story of Man. Above you
in the black of Crown Street
the Cross's pointers
directed you in silence
to the pit of darkness
the South Celestial Pole.

In this continent, last-invaded
landfall of the Navigator,
full of survivals; Chimera's
final landing-ground;
you saw the Wanderer's
emptiest, loneliest desert.
On that stage, always pretentious,
you wore the solemn cloak
of old philosopher-kings.
Your ruined hawk-face
shone under your wide hat
reddened with drink.
Your home was the black of Crown Street
the kings being gone.

Lost dog of the end of a story,
black leaf blowing
in a wind of the wrong hemisphere
you died before your death.
Smallest of stars, perhaps,
you cling in the pit of darkness
to the depth of Lilith's hair.

SEASONAL FLOCKING

Last week outside my window
the tree grew red rosellas,
berry-bright fruits, the young ones
brocaded with juvenile green.
I said, the autumn's ending.
They have come out of the mountains
and the snowcloud shadows.

This week on the road to town
in the red-hung hawthorn,
eleven of the Twelve Apostles;
eight black cockatoos, their tails
fanned to show yellow panes,
uncounted magpies and currawongs
greasily fat from the dump and the butcher's throwouts—
that breeding-ground of maggots.

All of them flocked together,
crying aloud, knowing
the end of autumn.
Sharp-edged welcome-swallows
gathered and circled upwards.

Frost soon, and the last warmth passes.
Seed-stems rot on wet grasses.

At the end of autumn
I too—I want you near me,
all you who've gone, who scatter
into far places or are hidden under
summer-forgotten gravestones.

FOR A PASTORAL FAMILY

I   TO MY BROTHERS

Over the years, horses have changed to land-rovers.
Grown old, you travel your thousands of acres
deploring change and the wickedness of cities
and the cities' politics; hoping to pass to your sons
a kind of life you inherited in your generation.
Some actions of those you vote for stick in your throats.
There are corruptions one cannot quite endorse;
but if they are in our interests, then of course ...

Well, there are luxuries still,
including pastoral silence, miles of slope and hill,
the cautious politeness of bankers. These are owed
to the forerunners, men and women
who took over as if by right a century and a half
in an ancient difficult bush. And after all
the previous owners put up little fight,
did not believe in ownership, and so were scarcely human.

Our people who gnawed at the fringe
of the edible leaf of this country
left you a margin of action, a rural security,
and left to me
what serves as a base for poetry,
a doubtful song that has a dying fall.

II   To my generation

A certain consensus of echo, a sanctioning sound,
supported our childhood lives. We stepped
on sure and conceded ground.
A whole society
extended a comforting cover of legality.
The really deplorable deeds
had happened out of our sight, allowing us innocence.
We were not born, or there was silence kept.

If now there are landslides, if our field of reference
is much eroded, our hands show little blood.
We enter a plea: Not Guilty.
For the good of the Old Country,
the land was taken; the Empire had loyal service.
Would any convict us?
Our plea has been endorsed by every appropriate jury.

If my poetic style, your pastoral produce,
are challenged by shifts in the market
or a change of taste, at least we can go down smiling
with enough left in our pockets
to be noted in literary or local histories.

III   For today

We were always part of a process. It has expanded.
What swells over us now is a logical spread
from the small horizons we made—
the heave of the great corporations
whose bellies are never full.
What sort of takeover bid
could you knock back now if the miners,
the junk-food firms or their processors want your land?
Or worse, leave you alone to hoe
small beans in a dwindling row?

The fears of our great-grandfathers—
apart from a fall in the English market—
were of spearwood, stone axes. Sleeping
they sprang awake at the crack
of frost on the roof, the yawn and stretching
of a slab wall. We turn on the radio
for news from the U.S.A. and U.S.S.R.
against which no comfort or hope
might come from the cattle prizes at the Show.

IV   PASTORAL LIVES

Yet a marginal sort of grace
as I remember it, softened our arrogant clan.
We were fairly kind to horses
and to people not too different from ourselves.
Kipling and A. A. Milne were our favourite authors
but Shelley, Tennyson, Shakespeare stood on our shelves—
suitable reading for women,
to whom, after all, the amenities had to be left.

An undiscursive lot (discourse is for the city)
one of us helped to found a university.
We respected wit in others,
though we kept our own for weddings,
unsure of the bona fides of the witty.

In England, we called on relatives,
assuming welcome for the sake of a shared bloodline,
but kept our independence.
We would entertain them equally, if they came
and with equal hospitality—
blood being thicker than thousands of miles of waters—
for the sake of Great-aunt Charlotte and old letters.

At church, the truncate, inarticulate
Anglican half-confession
"there is no health in us"
made us gag a little. We knew we had no betters
though too many were worse.
We passed on the collection-plate
adding a reasonable donation.

That God approved us was obvious.
Most of our ventures were prosperous.
As for the *Dies Irae*
we would deal with that when we came to it.

V CHANGE

At best, the men of our clan
have been, or might have been,
like Yeats' fisherman.
A small stream, narrow but clean,

running apart from the world.
Those hills might keep them so,
granite, gentle and cold.
But hills erode, streams go

through settlement and town
darkened by chemical silt.
Dams hold and slow them down,
trade thickens them like guilt.

All men grow evil with trade
as all roads lead to the city.
Willie Yeats would have said,
perhaps, the more the pity.

But how can we be sure?
Wasn't his chosen man
as ignorant as pure?
Keep out? Stay clean? Who can?

Blue early mist in the valley. Apricots
bowing the orchard trees, flushed red with summer,
loading bronze-plaqued branches;
our teeth in those sweet buttock-curves. Remember
the horses swinging to the yards, the smell
of cattle, sweat and saddle-leather?
Blue ranges underlined the sky. In any weather
it was well, being young and simple,
letting the horses canter home together.

All those sights, smells and sounds we shared
trailing behind grey sheep, red cattle,
from Two-rail or Ponds Creek
through tawny pastures breathing pennyroyal.
In winter, sleety winds bit hands and locked
fingers round reins. In spring, the wattle.

With so much past in common,
on the whole we forgive each other
for the ways in which we differ—
two old men, one older woman.
When one of us falls ill,
the others may think less
of today's person, the lined and guarding face,

than of a barefoot child running careless through
long grass where snakes lie, or forgetting
to watch in the paddocks for the black Jersey bull.
Divisions and gulfs deepen
daily, the world over
more dangerously than now between us three.
Which is why, while there is time (though not our
    form at all)
I put the memories into poetry.

WORDS, ROSES, STARS
(*for John Béchervaise, answering a Christmas poem*)

A rose, my friend, a rose—
and what's a rose?
A swirl of atoms bodied in a word.
And words are human; language comes and goes
with us, and lives among us. Not absurd
to think the human spans the Milky Way.

Baiame bends beside his crystal stream
shaded beneath his darker cypress-tree
and gives the gift of life, the endless dream,
to Koori people, and to you and me.
Astronomers and physicists compute
a mathematic glory in the sky.
But all those calculations, let's admit,
are filtered through a human brain and eye.

If I could give a rose to you, and you,
it would be language; sight and touch and scent
join in that symbol. Yet the word is true,
plucked by a path where human vision went.

HUNTING SNAKE

Sun-warmed in this late season's grace
under the autumn's gentlest sky
we walked, and froze half-through a pace.
The great black snake went reeling by.

Head-down, tongue flickering on the trail
he quested through the parting grass;
sun glazed his curves of diamond scale,
and we lost breath to watch him pass.

What track he followed, what small food
fled living from his fierce intent,
we scarcely thought; still as we stood
our eyes went with him as he went.

Cold, dark and splendid he was gone
into the grass that hid his prey.
We took a deeper breath of day,
looked at each other, and went on.

RAINFOREST

The forest drips and glows with green.
The tree-frog croaks his far-off song.
His voice is stillness, moss and rain
drunk from the forest ages long.

We cannot understand that call
unless we move into his dream,
where all is one and one is all
and frog and python are the same.

We with our quick dividing eyes
measure, distinguish and are gone.
The forest burns, the tree-frog dies,
yet one is all and all are one.

Notes at Edge

BREVITY

Old Rhythm, old Metre
these days I don't draw
very deep breaths. There isn't
much left to say.

Rhyme, my old cymbal,
I don't clash you as often,
or trust your old promises
of music and unison.

I used to love Keats, Blake.
Now I try haiku
for its honed brevities,
its inclusive silences.

Issa. Shiki. Buson. Bashō.
Few words and with no rhetoric.
Enclosed by silence
as is the thrush's call.

MOUNTAIN

Eastward, Mount Budawang
deliberately releases
stars, moon and sun
upward by night or day, one following one;

or rolls out nightly
and daily back again
a scroll and screen of cloud.

By dawn or twilight
it cuts a fine dark figure on the sky—
a lengthened strip of black calligraphy.

SUN-ORCHID

Sun-orchid, Thelymitra,
what a blue of blues you've chosen
to remind this sullen season
that still the sky is there.

Its tender cherishing colour
is like the hills in summer
when a eucalyptine vapour
dreams up in windless air.

Another poet, staring,
saw the sun in your centre, burning
core of fire, and, dazzled,
closed eyes upon that secret.

Wrapped in your Mary-blue,
veined with a flush like roses,
you stand in contemplation
of a spring as cold as winter,

but, blessed from your creation,
the calm of your robe encloses
a gold like revelation.

ROCK

I dug from this shallow soil
a rock-lump square as a book,
split into leaves of clay.

A long curved wash of ripple
left there its fingerprint
one long-before-time lost day.

I turn a dead sea's leaves
stand on a shore of waves
and touch that day, and look.

FOX

That rufous canterer
    through my eye's corner
crossing an empty space of frost-red grass
goes running like a flame.

Against storm-black Budawang
a bushfire bristle of brush.
Under the candlebark trees
a rustle in dry litter.

Fox, fox!
Behind him follows the crackle of his name.

EPACRIS

Grey-green, as high as a hand
    beside that lichened stone,
it has clenched pale buds
no bigger than river-sand
while spring and summer passed.

Now as the summer ends,
slowly, day by day,
it opens those ant-sized bells;
their honey harvest, the last
for small black hastening ants
whose nest waits under the stone.

VIOLET STICK-INSECTS

A landscape of leaves, oblique,
curved to the tension of light;
and among them he and she,
one a leaning twig
one a gnawed thin-bellied leaf.

Eating, they hang
still, or rock with the wind,
one with the branch that moves.

Any shadow might be a beak,
but as twig or leaf they are safe.
Yet he planes on a downward swing
unfolding a brilliant wing—
a fearless violet flash
to centre that grey and green.

RIVER BEND

What killed that kangaroo-doe, slender skeleton
tumbled above the water with her long shanks
cleaned white as moonlight?
Pad-tracks in sand where something drank fresh blood.

Last night a dog howled somewhere,
a hungry ghost in need of sacrifice.

Down by that bend, they say, the last old woman,
thin, black and muttering grief,
foraged for mussels, all her people gone.

The swollen winter river
curves over stone, a wild perpetual voice.

Lichen, Moss, Fungus

Autumn and early winter
wet this clay soil with rains.
Slow primitive plantforms
push up their curious flowers.

Lichens, mosses and fungi—
these flourish on this rock ridge,
a delicate crushable tundra:
bracket, star, cup, parasol,
gilled, pored, spored, membraned,
white, chestnut, violet, red.

I stoke the fire with wood
laced with mycelia, tread
a crust of moss and lichen.
Over the wet decay
of log and fallen branch
there spreads an embroidery, ancient
source of the forests.

Caddis-fly

Small twilight helicopter,
four petals, four skins of crystal
veined taut with chitinous fibre
carry you into my wineglass.
Why such a dying fall?

I sat under leaves, toasting
a simple moon, a river,
the respite of an evening
warm as the hand of a lover.
Did you have to cry Alas?

I lift you out on a finger
dripping red with wine
to dry beside the campfire,
but you won't fly again.

All of a sudden
you gather four wings together,
still drooping, sodden,
and dive to the fire's centre.

Why should I mourn, little buddha,
small drunkard of the flame?
I finish my wine and dream
on your fire-sermon.

GLASS CORRIDOR

Down the glass passageway
three of us walk. Left. Right.
and who's in the middle?

That's the lying inventor,
the self-contemplator,
with moonrise on one hand
sunset on the other.

We three walk through
a forest of tree-branches,
a swaying maze of gestures
eastways, westways.

Who knows which I am,
this criss-cross evening—
or how many?

The Shadow of Fire (Ghazals)

ROCKPOOL

My generation is dying, after long lives
swung from war to depression to war to fatness.

I watch the claws in the rockpool, the scuttle, the crouch—
green humps, the biggest barnacled, eaten by seaworms.

In comes the biggest wave, the irresistible
clean wash and backswirl. Where have the dead gone?

At night on the beach the galaxy looks like a grin.
Entropy has unbraided Berenice's hair.

We've brought on our own cancers, one with the world.
I hang on the rockpool's edge, its wild embroideries:

admire it, pore on it, this, the devouring and mating,
ridges of coloured tracery, occupants, all the living,

the stretching of toothed claws to food, the breeding
on the ocean's edge. "Accept it? Gad, madam, you had
    better."

EYES

At the end of winter my self-sown vine sends up
sprays of purple flowers, each with two green eyes.

Driving home in the night I startled a fox.
The headlights fixed him staring and snarling back.

There's altogether too much I know nothing about:
my eyes slide over signals clear to the fox.

But what I do see I can fix meanings to.
There are connections, things leave tracks of causation.

The fox-trot marks in the hardened silt of the road
led to those chicken-feathers caught in the fence.

The fox's two green eyes echo his universe;
he can track rabbits better than I can foxes.

But I saw the chicken-feathers caught in the fence;
and fox, I know who's looking for you with a rifle.

You know no better than the two green eyes on the pea-
flower
the link between the feathers and the sound of the shot.

ROCKFACE

Of the age-long heave of a cliff-face, all's come down
except this split upstanding stone, like a gravestone.

Sun-orchids bloomed here, out and gone in a month.
For drought-stricken years, I haven't seen those flowers.

In the days of the hunters with spears, this rock had a
name.
Rightly they knew the ancestral powers of stone.

Jung found in his corner-stone the spark Telesphorus.
Earth gives out fireflies, glow-worms, fungal lights.

Walking here in the dark my torch lights up
something massive, motionless, that confronts me.

I've no wish to chisel things into new shapes.
The remnant of a mountain has its own meaning.

SUMMER

This place's quality is not its former nature
but a struggle to heal itself after many wounds.

Upheaved ironstone, mudstone, quartz and clay
drank dark blood once, heard cries and the running of feet.

Now that the miners' huts are a tumble of chimney-stones
shafts near the river shelter a city of wombats.

Scabs of growth form slowly over the rocks.
Lichens, algae, wind-bent saplings grow.

I'll never know its inhabitants. Evening torchlight
catches the moonstone eyes of big wolf-spiders.

All day the jenny-lizard dug hard ground
watching for shadows of hawk or kookaburra.

At evening, her pearl-eggs hidden, she raked back earth
over the tunnel, wearing a wide grey smile.

In a burned-out summer, I try to see without words
as they do. But I live through a web of language.

CONNECTIONS

The tiny clusters of whitebeard heath are in flower.
Their scent has drawn to them moths from how far
away?

When I look up at the stars I don't try counting,
but I know that the lights I see can pass right through me.

What mind could weave such a complicated web?
Systems analysis might make angels giggle.

A child, I buried the key of a sardine tin.
Resurrected, I thought, it might unlock the universe.

Picking up shells on the beach, said Isaac Newton.
Catch a modern physicist using such a comparison.

I can smell the whitebeard heath when it's under my nose,
and that should be enough for someone who isn't a moth;

but who wants to be a mere onlooker? Every cell of me
has been pierced through by plunging intergalactic
     messages,

and the cream-coloured moths vibrate their woollen wings
wholly at home in the clusters of whitebeard heath.

OPPOSITIONS

Today I was caught alone in a summer storm
counting heartbeats from flash to crash of thunder.

From a small plane once I looked down a cliff of cloud.
Like God to Moses, it exploded into instructions.

Home, a yellow frog on the shower-pipe
startled my hand and watched me as I watch lightning.

Frog, my towel is wet, my hair dripping,
but you don't for such reasons take me to be a refuge.

Small damp peaceful sage with a loony grin,
("one minute of sitting, one inch of Buddha")*

a long time back we clambered up the shore
and learned to play with fire. Now there's no stopping us.

Back to the drainpipe, frog, don't follow me.
I'm off to dry my hair by the radiator.

I can't believe that wine's warm solaces
don't help the searcher: the poet on the wineshop floor

was given his revelations. The hermit of Cold Mountain
laughs as loudly perhaps—I choose fire, not snow.

* Manzan (1635–1714)

MEMORY

Yesterday wrapped me in wool; today drought's
    changeable weather
sends me down the path to swim in the river.

Three Decembers back, you camped here; your stone hearth
fills with twigs and strips peeled from the candlebark.

Where you left your tent, the foursquare patch is unhealed.
The roots of the kangaroo-grass have never sprouted again.

On the riverbank, dead cassinias crackle.
Wombat-holes are deserted in the dry beds of the creeks.

Even in mid-summer, the frogs aren't speaking.
Their swamps are dry. In the eggs a memory lasts.

They will talk again in a wet year, a year of mosquitoes.
The grass will seed on that naked patch of earth.

Now only two dragonflies dance on the narrowed water.
The river's noise in the stones is a sunken song.

SKINS

This pair of skin gloves is sixty-six years old,
    mended in places, worn thin across the knuckles.

Snakes get rid of their coverings all at once.
Even those empty cuticles trouble the passer-by.

Counting in seven-year rhythms I've lost nine skins
though their gradual flaking isn't so spectacular.

Holding a book or a pen I can't help seeing
how age crazes surfaces. Well, and interiors?

You ask me to read those poems I wrote in my thirties?
They dropped off several incarnations back.

DUST

In my sixty-eighth year drought stopped the song of the
    river,
sent ghosts of wheatfields blowing over the sky.

In the swimming-hole the water's dropped so low
I bruise my knees on rocks which are new acquaintances.

The daybreak moon is blurred in a gauze of dust.
Long ago my mother's face looked through a grey motor-
    veil.

Fallen leaves on the current scarcely move.
But the azure kingfisher flashes upriver still.

Poems written in age confuse the years.
We all live, said Bashō, in a phantom dwelling.

PRESSURES

Winter gales, spring gales, summer—under such
    pressures
the contours of things crouch, their angles alter.

The sapling that yesterday cut this view with a vertical
today is very slightly leaning eastward.

Brown butterflies strike my window-pane—
when I get up to look they have always become dead leaves.

Gravity's drag, time's wear, keep pressing downwards,
moving loose stones downslope, sinking hills like wet
    meringue.

I move more slowly this year, neck falling in folds,
pulses more visible; yet there's a thrust in the arteries.

Blood slows, thickens, silts—yet when I saw you
once again, what a joy set this pulse jumping.

WINTER

Today's white fog won't lift above the tree-tops.
Yesterday's diamond frost has melted to ice-water.

Old age and winter are said to have much in common.
Let's pile more wood on the fire and drink red wine.

These hundreds of books on the shelves have all been read
but I can't force my mind to recall their wisdom.

Let's drink while we can. The sum of it all is Energy,
and that went into the wood, the wine, the poems.

Logs on the fire burn into smoke and ash.
Let's talk today, though words die out on the air.

Out of the past and the books we must have learned
    something.
What do we know, what path does the red wine take?

I cleared white hair from my brush on the dressingtable
and dropped it into the fire. Some protein-chains the less.

How long would my hair be now if all the clippings
from the salon-floors returned to join their links?

The paths that energy takes on its way to exhaustion
are not to be forecast. These pathways, you and me,

followed unguessable routes. But all of us end
at the same point, like the wood on the fire,

the wine in the belly. Let's drink to that point—like Hafiz.

PATTERNS

"Brighter than a thousand suns"—that blinding glare
circled the world and settled in our bones.

Human eyes impose a human pattern,
decipher constellations against featureless dark.

All's fire, said Heraclitus; measures of it
kindle as others fade. All changes yet all's one.

We are born of ethereal fire and we return there.
Understand the Logos; reconcile opposing principles.

Perhaps the dark itself is the source of meaning,
the fires of the galaxy its visible destruction.

Round earth's circumference and atmosphere
bombs and warheads crouch waiting their time.

Strontium in the bones (the mass-number of 90)
is said to be "a good conductor of electricity".

Well, Greek, we have not found the road to virtue.
I shiver by the fire this winter day.

The play of opposites, their interpenetration—
there's the reality, the fission and the fusion.

Impossible to choose between absolutes, ultimates.
Pure light, pure lightlessness cannot be perceived.

"Twisted are the hearts of men—dark powers possess them.
Burn the distant evildoer, the unseen sinner."

That prayer to Agni, fire-god, cannot be prayed.
We are all of us born of fire, possessed by darkness.

INDEX OF FIRST LINES